THE DEVIL TO PAY

THE DEVIL TO PAY

The Mutiny of the Connaught Rangers,
India, July, 1920

BY

ANTHONY BABINGTON

LEO COOPER

LONDON

First published in Great Britain in 1991 by
Leo Cooper
190 Shaftesbury Avenue, London WC2H 8JL
an imprint of
Pen & Sword Books Ltd
47 Church Street, Barnsley, S. Yorks S70 2AS

Copyright © Anthony Babington, 1991

A CIP catalogue record for this book is available
from the British Library

ISBN 0 85052 327 3

Photoset and printed in Great Britain by
Redwood Press Limited, Melksham, Wiltshire

Contents

1	THE START OF THE MUTINY	1
2	THE DEVELOPMENT OF THE MUTINY	14
3	BLOODSHED	25
4	THE AFTERMATH	39
5	THE DAYS OF RECKONING	49
6	PRELUDE TO MARTYRDOM	59
7	SINN FEIN	70
8	THE MOTIVES FOR THE MUTINY	79
9	THE BIRTH OF A LEGEND	90
10	THE TREATY	102
11	'A GRACIOUS ACT'	114
12	THE HOMECOMING	125
13	JOHN FLANNERY'S CAMPAIGN	137
14	THE REWARD	150
15	THE ULTIMATE ACCLAIM	166
	Source Notes	179
	Bibliography	192
	Index	197

Acknowledgements

There are a number of individuals and organizations without whose generous advice and assistance this book could not have been written. They include (in alphabetical order):

Mr J. C. Andrews, Chief Librarian and the Staff of the Ministry of Defence Library, Whitehall; Professor Stuart Barr, Worcester; Mr Patrick Buckley, Department of the Taoiseach, Dublin; Dr Phil Connolly and the Staff of the National Archives of Ireland, Dublin; Mr Cook and the Staff of the India Office Library and Records, Blackfriars; Ms Celia Coram, Hackney; Mr Bob Cotton, *The Christchurch Star*, New Zealand; Mrs Alice Fornara, Sussex; Dr C. M. Francis, St. Martha's Hospital, Bangalore, India; Corporal Ray Duke, Athlone; Mrs Mona Garvey, Galway; Mr Douglas Gill, Islington; Captain R. A. Hinchy, Dublin; Dr Keith Jeffrey, University of Ulster, Jordanstown; Mr Charles Kerrigan and family, Sligo; Mr Stephen Lally and family, Bolton; Ms Jane Leonard, King's College, London; Mr Chris Maguire, Hackney; Mr Bernard McGee, Information Officer, Commonwealth War Graves Commission, Maidenhead; Mr Hugh Massy, Woodbridge; Mr Kevin Myers, *The Irish Times*, Dublin; the Department of Irish Folklore, University College, Dublin and specially Mrs Bairbre O'Floinn; Dr Eunan O'Halpin, Dublin City University; Mrs Rosemary O'Halpin, Dublin; Mr Peter Power-Hynes, Barnet; Mr Noel Shiels and the Staff of the Sound Department, Radio Telefis Eireann, Dublin; Messrs Kevin and Martin Staunton, Dublin.

Thanks are also due to staff of the following secular and religious institutions for their unstinting aid:

The British Library, Bloomsbury and Newspaper Reference Library, Colindale; Imperial War Museum, Lambeth; Irish Bureau of Military History, Dublin; National Army Museum, Chelsea; Public Record Office, Kew; National Library of Ireland, Dublin; Post Office Archives, Blackfriars; Veterans Allowances Section, Department of Defence, Galway; Order of Franciscans Minor, Capuchins (England, Ireland, India and Curia Generale); Redemptorist Fathers (England and India).

Valuable contributions have also been made by some individuals who, for various reasons, have requested anonymity. To them and correspondents too numerous to list, who kindly replied to hundreds of enquiries, sincere gratitude is also extended.

Extracts from Crown Copyright material held in the Public Record Office; Oriental and India Office Collections, British Library appear by permission of the Controller of Her Majesty's Stationery Office. Quotations from RTE interviews and 'Mutiny At Solon' are by permission of RTE, Dublin. Documents from the National Archives, Dublin are reproduced by permission of the Director. Permission to quote extracts from Mrs Bairbre O'Floinn's interview with Charles Kerrigan has been granted by the Head of the Department of Irish Folklore, University College, Dublin. Quotations from the Papers of Major-General L. A. E. Price-Davies VC, Col. F. W. S. Jourdain and Mr A. Y. McPeake held at the Documents Department of the Imperial War Museum appear with the permission of the Executors of Col. F. W. S. Jourdain and the family of Major-General Price-Davies. Passages from 'The Connaught Rangers Mutiny by One Who Knows' are reproduced with permission from the copyright holders, Independent Newspapers Ltd. Anvil Books Ltd. gave permission to quote from their publication, 'The Connaught Rangers' by T. P. Kilfeather. The BBC have kindly given permission to use extracts from 'In Search of a Mutiny'.

The author has made every effort to trace individuals for permission to reproduce copyright material quoted in this publication but some remain elusive. To anyone whose copyright this work unintentionally infringes, I extend apologies.

Preface

This book is intended to be a full, accurate and unbiased account of the mutiny of the 1st Battalion of the Connaught Rangers in the Punjab in 1920.

Although, over the years, the mutiny has been the subject of two books, a play, several radio features and numerous articles, it has never been properly researched and its political repercussions in both England and Ireland have been virtually ignored. Furthermore, the presentation of the facts has seldom been either unemotive or impartial.

Every available source has been examined in preparing the book, including the official British Government records relating to the mutiny and its aftermath which were originally 'closed' for a period of seventy-five years but which, very recently, have been made available for public inspection.

I am very grateful to Julian Putkowski for the invaluable guidance and help he has given me in carrying out the necessary research.

ANTHONY BABINGTON

Chapter 1

THE START OF THE MUTINY

THE CONNAUGHT RANGERS, the 88th of Foot and popularly known as 'The Devil's Own', was one of the proudest and most trustworthy regiments in the British Army. Originally formed in 1793, it had taken part in numerous campaigns and both its officers and men had achieved a considerable reputation for their courage and tenacity. During the First World War the regiment had been expanded into six battalions which, between them, had fought in most of the principal theatres of operations. The 1st Connaught Rangers, one of the pre-war regular battalions, had served on the Western Front, in Mesopotamia and in Egypt.[1]

After the signing of the Armistice in November, 1918, the process of demobilization had begun as the Army was re-formed with a peacetime establishment. In May, 1919, the 1st Battalion of the Connaught Rangers was posted to Dover to train, equip and build up its numerical strength for a tour of duty in India. Many of the men who enlisted in the next few months were veterans who had served with the regiment during the recent war; others were young recruits coming mostly from Connaught, the western province of Ireland. As a prelude, they would all have been required, without exception, to take an oath, swearing to bear 'true allegiance' to King George V and to 'observe and obey' the orders of their officers.

The Battalion was still understrength when it sailed for India towards the end of October, 1919. It arrived at Bombay on 24 November and travelled by train a few days later to join the British garrison at Jullundur, a town and cantonment in the Punjab, which was to be its final destination. The Punjab, the most northerly province of what was then British India, is bounded on one side by the lower Himalaya hills and is adjacent to the North-West Frontier, the mountainous region near the border with Afghanistan, where the tribesmen were waging continuous warfare against the garrison troops in the area. In all probability Jullundur was not a particularly popular military station at that time. An important road and railway junction, it is situated in an immense, fertile plain where the climate is oppressively hot during the summer months although it becomes cool, and even frosty, in winter. The Connaught Rangers were accommodated at Wellington Barracks within the cantonment. The town, approximately four miles away, was permanently out-of-bounds to other ranks who were, however, allowed to use a local bazaar for their personal shopping.[2]

At Jullundur the battalion continued its training. When the hot weather started, A Company went to Jutogh, 200 miles away in the hills, and most of C Company were posted to Solon, another hill-station approximately the same distance from Jullundur. B and D Companies remained at Wellington Barracks, together with a detachment of about fifty NCOs and men from C Company.[3] The official regimental history records that a large draft of recruits from the United Kingdom arrived at Jullundur in May, and goes on to say:

> but for some unknown reason, possibly in consequence of the precarious internal situation in India at the time, permission to distribute them to the companies to which they had been posted was refused. Instead, the newcomers were kept assembled on the hot plains – a regrettable decision, and especially so in the case of young and recently arrived soldiers.[4]

A number of the men from this draft took part in the mutiny, which started at the end of June.

The accredited story of the Connaught Rangers mutiny has always been based upon the accounts given by two of the ringleaders. Lance-Corporal John Flannery wrote a series of articles under the pseudonym 'One Who Knows', which were published by the *Sunday Independent* in the early part of 1925. Private Joseph Hawes set down his portrayal, under his own name, years later in 1949, and admitted that there might be lapses in his memory as he had neither made any notes at the time nor had he kept a diary. The versions of the events given by Hawes and Flannery have been accepted as the truth, despite their rival claims to primacy in the mutiny, in books, plays and documentaries. If their 'recollections' had been checked with more reliable sources it would have been apparent that both of them were ready to exaggerate and to falsify the facts in order to eulogize the mutiny and to magnify the parts they played in it themselves.

The mutineers were tried at three separate courts martial, two of which related to offences committed at Jullundur and the third concerned the happenings at Solon. The transcripts of these trials would, of course, provide an invaluable description of the occurrences at both places. The Rules of Procedure in the Manual of Military Law laid down that the record of the evidence given at a General Court Martial must be preserved in the office of the Judge Advocate General for not less than seven years.[5] In practice they were seldom retained for longer than the specified period except in cases where a sentence of death had been passed and had actually been carried out. As a consequence, all the documents appertaining to the Jullundur trials were probably thrown away many years ago, and those connected with the Solon trial, although still extant, are closed to public inspection until 1998 on grounds of sensitivity. However, two Irish local newspapers in the early 1920s published between them what appear to be the full, unedited Summaries of Evidence for all three of the courts martial, a fact which has either been overlooked or else ignored by the writers and commentators on the mutiny in the past.

The Summary of Evidence would have been taken at a preliminary hearing in accordance with the Rules of Procedure, and every mutineer would have been supplied with a copy to enable him to prepare his defence. All the witnesses for the prosecution were required to make statements on oath, which would be taken down in writing in the presence of the accused men who had the right to cross-examine if they wished to do so.[6] The Summaries for both the Jullundur and the Solon trials were recorded between 6 and 13 August, 1920, so that the witnesses were testifying about events which had occurred only six or seven weeks previously. The statements relating to the Jullundur cases were published in the *Roscommon Herald* during February and March, 1922,[7] and those in respect of the Solon trial appeared in the *Longford Leader* in January and February, 1923.[8] Both papers admitted that they had obtained the Summaries from convicted mutineers, the *Roscommon Herald* describing their copy as having been 'smuggled out of Dartmoor Convict Prison'.

According to the history of the mutiny written by Joseph Hawes it began on the evening of Sunday 27 June, 1920, as a result of discussions he had held with four of his friends in the canteen at Wellington Barracks, Jullundur.

I tell them [he says] about the hurling match I had seen proclaimed by the British forces at the point of the bayonet, all assemblies being proclaimed in Clare at the time. Some of the others spoke about what they saw in the Irish papers and letters from home. During the discussions I put up the point that we were doing in India what the British forces were doing in Ireland, and the next question was 'What are we going to do about it?' We agreed to proceed to the guardroom in the morning and declare that we would no longer serve the King as a protest against the atrocities of the British forces in Ireland.[9]

Hawes came from Kilrush, a market town in County Clare on the estuary of the River Shannon. He had volunteered for the army at the end of 1914 and had served on the Western Front and in Gallipoli. In 1919 he had re-enlisted in the Connaught Rangers as a regular soldier. In the same year his brother had become an active member of the Irish Republican Army which was then conducting an armed revolution against British rule throughout Ireland.[10] The others present in the group were Christopher Sweeney, who had joined the regiment in 1917 after serving for seven years in the Royal Navy; two privates from Westmeath, Patrick Gogarty and William Daly, whose younger brother was to lead the mutiny at Solon; and Stephen Lally, another veteran of the recent war, who had been brought up in Workington where his parents had settled after emigrating from Ireland.

Hawes omitted one important detail from his initial reference to the breaking up of the hurling match in Clare. He dealt with the matter more candidly in a radio interview in 1963 when he said:

I was home on holidays after the war had all been over [sic], and I went to a hurley match in County Clare, in which I was going to participate as one of the contestants, and this match was to raise funds for the Volunteers, and British forces entered the field and drove us out of it at the point of bayonets.[11]

By November, 1919, when this had occurred, the Irish Volunteers had been declared an illegal organization,[12] and any meeting held to raise money for them would have constituted an unlawful assembly. Even so, Hawes declared in the interview, he was outraged by what he considered to be the oppressive behaviour of the authorities. He went on:

It rankled in my mind all the time while I was in India from 1919 until 1920. I had a brother who was on the run at that particular time, with the I.R.A. in Ireland.[13]

After the discussion in the canteen on the Sunday evening, Hawes says that he and his four friends went to a small disused room in the barracks with the intention of remaining there until reveille the following morning. Whether the start of the mutiny was quite so spontaneous as Hawes makes out, and whether it emanated solely from his own personal initiative, must be open to doubt in view of the sworn contemporary statements in the Summaries of Evidence. A private soldier at Wellington Barracks testified that on the Sunday morning a poster had been exhibited in the Regimental Library. This was taken down and later produced at the trials. It read:

Shall Erin forget? – No! Well Irishmen, just think of the way our dear country is today, suffering from the horrors of Prussianism in our Irish homes, and the way our people are treated. Could any Irishman look at that being done? Look at what they done in 1916. They would do the same to us if they were able. Well, men, I hope you will take this into your mind and revenge. If you were to be shot, stick up for your Irish home which is ruined by the troops in our dear country. It is our duty to fight now and try to make her free once more. So ground arms and be an Irishman.

> Oh, Father, dear, the day will come
> When for vengeance we will call.
> The Irishmen to Field and Stern,
> Shall rally one and all will be the man
> To lead the van and wave the flag of green,
> For it is loud and high we'll raise the cry –
> Revenge for Skibbereen!
> Start at once, Boys![14]

The verse, with the exception of the last line, comes from the traditional Irish ballad 'Skibbereen'. The singer is relating how, during the Great Famine in the 1840s, he was evicted from his home at Skibbereen by a ruthless landlord – not an uncommon experience at that time when tenants had no money to pay their rents. He then takes part in the Young Ireland rebellion of 1848, and, eager for revenge, he is 'hunted through the mountains as a traitor to the Queen'.

It seems a strange coincidence that Hawes and his friends should have made a decision to ground their arms in protest against British military action in Ireland quite independently of a poster displayed at Wellington Barracks on the same day, which urged all Irish soldiers to take such a course.

5

Soon after reveille on the morning of Monday, 28 June the five potential mutineers went to see their friend Lance-Corporal John Flannery, the NCO in charge of the Royal Army Temperance Association recreation rooms at the barracks, to give him their names and addresses and to tell him what they were intending to do. They took this step, Hawes has said, so that if they were 'shot out of hand' he could inform their relations exactly what had happened to them.[15] According to Hawes, Flannery, who had served with the Connaught Rangers since 1908, did his best to dissuade them from their plan and to convince them of its futility.[16] As a result of this advice William Daly decided to abandon the protest and return to his company lines, but the other four remained adamant.[17] In after years John Flannery gave a somewhat different version of the conversation, claiming that as soon as he heard of their proposal he had taken charge of the mutiny himself.[18]

At about 8 o'clock that morning Joseph Hawes and his three remaining companions made their way to the regimental Guard Room. They found that Sergeant Shaw, the sergeant of the guard, was away at breakfast, so they reported to the NCO in charge, Lance-Corporal O'Brien. They told him that 'they wished to hand themselves over as they were in sympathy with Ireland'.[19] O'Brien observed the unkempt appearance of the group, who had slept in their uniforms, and he formed the opinion that they had probably been out of barracks all night drinking and were now looking for a place in which to sleep for a while before reporting back to their companies to face the inevitable charges for their absence. On this basis he placed all four of them under close arrest and confined them with his other prisoners.[20] He said later that he had been unimpressed with the reasons they gave for seeking to be confined as he had considered that as regular soldiers they should not become involved in political issues. 'Not that I didn't sympathize with my country in a vague sort of way,' he added, 'but I'd no love for the Sinn Feiners.'[21] As soon as Sergeant Shaw returned from breakfast he asked the four men why they had volunteered for the Guard Room and they asserted once again that they were taking their action because they were 'in sympathy with their country'.[22]

There are differing accounts of the subsequent events of that day. It is clear that the whole of B Company had paraded at an early hour to march off to some nearby rifle range, and that the remainder of the troops at Wellington Barracks, those belonging to D Company and the C Company detachment, were due to parade at 9 o'clock. John Flannery says that before that time he addressed a meeting of around fifty C Company men, urging them to return to their rooms and to inform all their comrades about the action taken by the four privates in the Guard Room. He asked them to emphasize that the protest would not be effective unless it was supported by every Irishman in the battalion.[23] This incident is not mentioned in any of the other descriptions of the day's events and it is possible that it was invented by Flannery in order to establish his early participation in the mutiny. It is true, however, that about thirty members of C Company refused to parade at 9 o'clock, and when ordered to do so by the orderly sergeant responded by shouting 'Up the Rebels'.[24] The matter was reported to Company Sergeant-Major Tame, the acting Regimental Sergeant-Major, who immediately went to the company lines to speak to the men. They told him that 'they were all of one mind, and were going to do no more work or parades of any description'. In view of their obduracy, the only thing he could achieve was to persuade them to see their Company Commander about their grievances.[25]

Major Robert Payne, DSO, one of the senior majors in the Battalion and the officer in command of C Company, decided to speak to each of the recalcitrant soldiers separately in his company office. He had with him there Lieutenant Walter Robertson and Company Sergeant-Major Cahill. Robertson said later in his testimony:

> The first man interviewed was Private Moran. Major Payne asked him to state his case and he stated that he would not soldier any more on account of the way the English Government were dealing with the Irish question, or words to that effect. Major Payne ordered him to the Guard Room, which he did [sic]. The remainder of the men ran round on the other side of the bungalow. Major Payne fell them in and ordered them off to the Guard Room. After slight hesitation they complied with the order.[26]

A similar account of the incident was given by Major Payne who said that he had placed Private Moran under arrest because of the insolence of his manner.[27]

At half-past nine that morning Sergeant-Major Cahill marched the twenty-four newly arrested men from C Company to the Guard Room and handed them over to Sergeant Shaw, who then had twenty-eight protesters in his charge. Hawes had described the layout of the regimental Guard Room at Wellington Barracks. The sides were composed of bars, he wrote, 'like a cage'. Sliding doors could be drawn across them, but because of the intense heat the doors were only used during sand-storms or monsoons.[28] He does not indicate the size of the 'cage', but he says that after the arrival of the C Company contingent the prisoners were all confined together and passed the time singing rebel songs, interspersed with shouts of 'Up the Republic'.[29]

Lieutenant-Colonel H. R. G. Deacon, the Commanding Officer of the Battalion, was still hoping that if he made a personal appeal to the mutineers they would abandon their protest and the whole affair could be hushed up. The Colonel was a 51-year-old Irishman who had been in the Regiment since the 1890s. He was a very experienced soldier who had taken part in various campaigns and had been decorated several times for gallantry, but his handling of the mutiny is generally adjudged to have been both irresolute and incompetent. Later that morning he arranged for the men to be released from custody so that he could address them. They formed up in a single line outside the Guard Room and he stood in front of them with several of his officers and his acting Regimental Sergeant-Major. Hawes has described what happened:

> He referred to his service with the Connaughts, 33 years, and to the great history of the Connaughts as fighting soldiers and to their proud flag. He went on to advise us, he was actually crying, to return to our bungalows and the whole matter would be forgotten. He made a very eloquent appeal. I was afraid he might convince the men.[30]

Directly the Colonel had finished speaking, Hawes wrote, he himself stepped forward and declared that all the battle-honours gained by the Connaught Rangers in the past had been won for England and not for Ireland. But what they were doing at that moment would be counted as the greatest honour of them all. In the event, only two men were influenced by the Commanding Officer's plea and returned to their company; the rest went back to the Guard Room, where they were joined by a member of the guard who removed his belt and bayonet and asked to be confined with his comrades, making a total of twenty-seven imprisoned mutineers.[31]

Soon afterwards, D Company were halted in the vicinity to be dismissed at the end of their morning parade. The prisoners in the Guard Room started a demonstration for their benefit, some of them cheering and some shouting 'Up Sinn Fein!' or 'Up the Rebels!' Despite the efforts of the officers to prevent them from doing so, a number of D Company men came up to the bars of the Guard Room, where they were heard urging the mutineers to break out.[32] In his account of this occurrence Joseph Hawes, who has mistaken the designation of the company involved, says:

The B Company men suggested that we leave the Guard Room and organize outside. The Sergeant of the Guard was afraid to disobey the B Company men, who still had their arms and opened the gate when asked. We left the Guard Room and held a discussion outside with B Company.[33]

If this had really happened, it is surprising to find that so serious an incident as the Guard Sergeant being compelled by intimidation to release his prisoners was altogether omitted from the first official report on the mutiny, which was enclosed with a General Despatch to the War Office on 9 December, 1920.[34] Nor was it mentioned by Sergeant Shaw in his statement for the Summary of Evidence.

The official report says that at about eleven o'clock on the first morning of the mutiny Lance-Corporal Flannery asked for, and obtained, permission to try to persuade the men in the Guard Room to abandon their protest.[35] John Flannery seems to have commanded a measure of respect in C Company, possibly because he was an older soldier and was reputed to be better educated than most of the others. A contemporary photograph shows him as a man of unprepossessing appearance, with a narrow face, a receding hair-line and a drooping moustache. His expression is truculent, almost scowling. Sergeant Shaw recalled that Flannery went into the Guard Room and said to the mutineers, 'I know you are good Irishmen, but come out of here and don't be foolish'.[36] His words had no effect.

It is apparent that at some time during the morning the mutineers did leave the Guard Room, but the circumstances of their doing so are obscure. Lieutenant-Colonel Deacon merely referred to them being 'persuaded' to come out by other men in the battalion.[37] It is incredible that the Battalion officers should have remained completely inactive at this stage; they were probably waiting for a lead, which did not come, from their Commanding Officer. In contrast, the mutineers were lacking neither in purpose nor determination. Flannery, who by then had switched sides, speaks of a meeting being held in the Recreation Room at the barracks for all the NCOs and privates 'in sympathy with the movement'. It was reported, he says, that practically all the Irishmen in the battalion were in favour of a mutiny, and they proceeded to draw up a programme 'stating what the men were prepared to do and also what they were resolved not to do in the matter of parades, duties and routine work'.[38] Joseph Hawes, who thinks that the meeting was held in the Regimental Theatre, describes it in more detail.

A committee of seven was duly elected, he wrote, including Lance-Corporal Flannery and himself, and Flannery was also appointed to be the mutineers' spokesman. The members of the committee then held a short meeting in private after which they outlined their plan of action to the others. Mutineers were to retain their arms and ammunition, and the regimental guard was to be replaced with a guard of their own. The Union Jack would be lowered from the flagstaff at Wellington Barracks and the tricolour of the Irish Nationalists would be hoisted in its place. Roving sentries and night patrols would be mounted during the hours of darkness. The soldiers who had chosen to remain loyal to the King would be granted protection, but would be segregated from the rest. Finally, it was emphasized that from then on the only orders the mutineers would obey would be those issued by their own committee.[39]

At two o'clock in the afternoon Corporal Murphy, one of the soldiers who had chosen to remain loyal, was resting in his bungalow when an NCO had entered shouting 'Fall in all Sinn Feiners!' Murphy ignored the order, in spite of being warned of a beating if he did not obey.[40] Outside the bungalow about 200 men from C and D Companies were paraded under Lance-Corporal McGowan, a member of the mutineers' committee, and were marched to the Officers' Mess where a message had been sent that they wished to see the Commanding Officer. On the way they were met by Major Nolan-Ferrall, the D Company Commander, and Lieutenant Leader, the Adjutant, who tried unsuccessfully to turn them back. A furious argument ensued and the two officers only withdrew from the scene after the Adjutant had been threatened with violence.[41] Lieutenant-Colonel Deacon agreed to see the mutineers outside the Officers' Mess. Lance-Corporal Flannery and Private Hawes, acting as their spokesmen, told the Commanding Officer that they were taking their action as a protest against the way in which their fellow-countrymen were being treated and that they would not soldier any more until all the British troops had been removed from Ireland. Meanwhile, they said, they wanted the regimental guard to be dismissed and replaced by a guard of their own. Lieutenant Kelly, who was present at the time, described Hawes' manner as being 'downright insolent',[42] and Hawes himself did not deny that while he was addressing the Colonel he was smoking a cigarette.[43] When they had finished speaking, Deacon warned the men of the seriousness of their conduct, but he undertook to pass on their grievances to higher authority and to issue immediate orders for the dismounting of the guard. Having extracted these undertakings, the mutineers marched off in triumph while

Deacon, aware that the situation was now beyond his control, went back to the Battalion Orderly Room to prepare an urgent report for his Divisional Commander.

Within a short space of time the mutineers had exerted an effective authority over Wellington Barracks. They took over the Guard Room and posted their own sentries, who received instructions that nobody was to enter the gates without the permission of the mutineers' committee. A tricolour, made out of strips of material purchased from the bazaar, was soon substituted for the Union Jack on the flagstaff, and a number of men pinned green, white and orange rosettes on their tunics to demonstrate their adherence to the Irish Nationalist cause.[44] Major Nolan-Ferrall made a last effort to show that he was still in command of D Company by ordering them to parade early in the afternoon. About forty of his men obeyed and he directed that every soldier who did intend to remain loyal must hand in his rifle and bayonet to the company storeroom. At this moment Private Hawes came running up shouting that they were to disregard the Major's orders. Standing in front of the parade, he said, 'Be Irishmen! I have got a rifle to protect myself and I will not hand it in for anyone'. He then dismissed the Company, telling them to return to their bunga-lows taking their arms with them.[45]

During Monday morning Lieutenant-Colonel Deacon was relieved of his command of the Battalion by his superiors and Major Payne was temporarily appointed in his place. Divisional Headquarters must have been aware of the gravity of the situation both from a disciplinary point of view, and also because the conduct of the mutineers might seriously endanger the security of all the British troops in the area.

After the Armistice in 1918, wartime inflation in India had been followed by a period of severe depression, during which millions of Indians were united by a common hatred of British rule and a fervent desire for national independence. It had seemed for a while as though the perpetual and deep-seated communal antagonisms between the Hindus and the Muslims might be laid aside in the urgency of this common purpose. After the war the Khilafat, a pan-Islamic move-ment, had made rapid progress among Indian Muslims. It had bred among its adherents an awareness of identity, and in its more extrem-ist forms a nationalistic militancy. The upsurge of Khilafatism was welcomed by Mohandas Gandhi, the acknowledged leader of India's national aspirations, who, though himself a Hindu, had placed the creation of a Muslim–Hindu alliance in the forefront of his political programme.

Serious disorders had occurred in the Punjab during the spring of 1919 after the Government of India had introduced the ill-conceived Rowlatt Acts, generally known as the 'Black Acts'. These measures provided a peacetime extension of the wartime emergency legislation passed by the Supreme Legislative Council in 1915. Gandhi immediately launched a nationwide campaign for the repeal of the Acts, and he called upon all Indians to disobey them. The strongest response had come from the Punjab where demonstrations, marches and massive meetings had later taken place throughout the province. An ugly scene occurred at Amritsar, the sacred capital of the Sikhs, on 10 April, 1919, after two religious leaders were arrested and expelled from the district. When a group of their followers went to the bungalow of the Deputy Commissioner to demand their release, they were fired on by British troops, several of them being killed or wounded. Soon afterwards an inflamed mob rampaged through the city burning British banks and attacking English men and women. General R. E. D. Dyer was sent with a military force from Jullundur to restore order, and the riots soon subsided. On 13 April, the day of the infamous Amritsar Massacre, Dyer had ordered a party of troops to open fire on a crowd of about 10,000 unarmed men, women and children attending an open-air meeting in the city. The carnage continued for ten minutes after which the troops withdrew, leaving some 400 people dead and around 1,200 wounded. Sir Michael O'Dwyer, the despotic Lieutenant-Governor of the Punjab, had announced his approval of General Dyer's action, and had placed his whole province under martial law.

In June, 1920, India, especially the Punjab was seething with discontent, and the latent turbulence might have erupted at any moment.

Flannery has related how, during the afternoon of 28 June, 'it was noticed that the natives appeared to be getting excited and there were groups of them hanging around the barracks'. He was told that the merchants in the bazaar believed that the mutineers were about to plunder their shops and that:

the lower class of the natives were preparing to take advantage of the fact that the Rangers had refused to perform any duty; and were under the impression that they could revolt and loot to their hearts' content.

As soon as he heard this, says Flannery, he went down to the bazaar and assured the people that there was going to be no looting of any description.[46]

On the Monday afternoon Lieutenant-Colonel Thomas Leeds, the Commanding Officer of the 56th Punjabi Rifles, one of the Indian battalions in the Jullundur garrison, went to Wellington Barracks to address the mutineers who paraded for him under the orders of Lance-Corporal Flannery. The Colonel reminded them of the serious military offence they were committing and suggested that they were over-reacting to their emotions. If they resumed their normal duties immediately, he said, no disciplinary action would be taken against them. They could set out their grievances in writing and these would be referred to the proper authorities. Flannery turned to the men and enquired whether anybody was willing to accept the Colonel's proposition, but none of them indicated that they wished to do so. Seeing that they were determined to continue the mutiny, Leeds proceeded to warn them about the danger of allowing any weapons to fall into Indian hands, and he asked them to surrender their rifles and ammunition to the Battalion officers. The official report on the mutiny says that they agreed to do this, but later went back on their word.[47] Company Sergeant-Major Tame said in his statement that after Lieutenant-Colonel Leeds had left the barracks the mutineers paraded to hand in their arms, but when Hawes and two other men announced that they were not going to comply with the undertaking the remainder of the men followed their example.[48]

Nothing of consequence occurred during the first night of the mutiny, said Hawes, 'except rumours of all kinds about the forces coming to attack us, and all precautions were taken to meet any attack that might eventuate'.[49]

John Flannery has elaborated on two of the rumours. The first, in the early evening, was that the Indians were going to attack the battalion's married quarters, and the second, towards midnight, was that British troops were marching on Jullundur to arrest the mutineers. It was decided that any attack on the barracks should be resisted, wrote Flannery:

The guard was immediately reinforced, and men armed with rifles and machine-guns were placed in commanding positions in the barracks. These men had instructions to allow no armed men to enter the barracks. Patrols sent out to ascertain the movements of the troops returned with the information that they had camped about three miles away from the barracks. It was then evident that they did not intend to march to the barracks that night.[50]

Chapter 2

THE DEVELOPMENT OF THE MUTINY

THERE CAN BE LITTLE DOUBT that if the British or Indian troops in the vicinity of Jullundur had launched an attack on Wellington Barracks during the early stages of the mutiny they would have met with armed resistance. However, the authorities were determined to keep the affair in a low key and to avoid the possibility of bloodshed if it was possible to do so. It would seem that both Lord Chelmsford, the Viceroy, and General Sir Charles Munro, the Commander-in-Chief, believed they could prevent any serious developments from taking place, as the first official report on what had occurred was not sent to London until 2 July.

On the morning of Tuesday, 29 June, Lieutenant-Colonel Deacon received a letter through the post addressed 'C. O., Connaught Rangers'. It read:

> Sir, I bring to your notice the recent trouble committed by British troops in Ireland. The Connaught Rangers are determined to stand by Sinn Fein; our indignation will be shown by action and not by words. We cannot, as Irishmen, stand by and see our relations murdered. We demand the withdrawal of the military in Ireland. Until our orders are complied with, you are not personally safe.
>
> Sinn Feiners of the Connaught Rangers
> The late Adjutant, Mr Leader, may prepare for death.[1]

The mutineers suspected that at some time during the day the officers, assisted by the men who had remained loyal, would attempt to impound their rifles, leaving them powerless to defend themselves against the approaching troops. To prevent this from happening all personal arms and ammunition were put into a guarded bungalow in the middle of the barracks.[2] At nine o'clock that morning Lance-

Corporal Flannery ordered all the men to assemble in the regimental theatre. In his own account of the meeting, Flannery says he began by asking any soldier not in sympathy with the mutiny to leave immediately. He appealed to those who remained 'to keep the name of the Connaught Rangers free from stain and to have no recourse to violence of any kind'.[3] Whilst a general discussion was taking place on what they should do next, they received a message that Colonel Jackson, a staff officer from the headquarters of the 16th Indian Division, to which they were attached, had arrived at the barracks and was anxious to speak to them.

The Colonel was invited to enter and was allowed to address the men from the stage. He told them that he had been appointed by Major-General Sir George Barrow, the Officer Commanding Northern Command (India), to investigate their grievances. He added that he was an Irishman himself with experience of Irish troops, and it was intended that he should act as an intermediary between the mutineers and the military authorities. He asked them to nominate seven representatives to speak on their behalf, and directly they had done so, he said, he would start discussions with the seven in the Battalion Orderly Room. Colonel Jackson then left the theatre and the mutineers elected their representatives by ballot. The seven who were chosen included Lance-Corporal Flannery and Private Hawes.[4]

Major-General Sir George Barrow, who had been entrusted by the Commander-in-Chief with the handling of the mutiny, had his headquarters at Murree, a hill-station in the Punjab. By coincidence he had been in the Connaught Rangers when he was first commissioned at the age of 19, but he had later transferred into an Indian cavalry regiment. Although General Sir Charles Munro, the Commander-in-Chief, was a Scotsman, he too had an Irish connection as his mother had come from Co. Cork.

Both Hawes and Flannery have described the discussions which took place in the Battalion Orderly Room between Colonel Jackson and the representatives of the mutineers. Their accounts are very different, but the one given by Flannery appears to be the more authentic. He says that Jackson invited them to express their grievances 'without reserve'. They then told him that their purpose was to protest against the 'reign of terror' the British Government was conducting in Ireland, and they gave him examples of recent incidents they had read about in letters from home. The Colonel made notes of what they were saying, and promised to refer their statements to the Divisional Commander. Meanwhile, he told them, the mutineers would be relieved during the next two days by men from other

15

regiments, and they would be sent to a camp which was being prepared for them nearby. In order to avoid any possibility of a hostile confrontation while the change-over was taking place the relieving troops would march in at one side of the barracks at the same time as the Connaughts were leaving from the other. He asked them to go back and tell the rest of the mutineers what he had said. Before the representatives left the Battalion Orderly Room they asked Colonel Jackson if the mutineers could all be paid as usual that week 'as this would act as a preventative to any tendency the men might have to commence looting when they found their pay had been stopped'. Jackson undertook that the necessary arrangements would be made.[5]

The representatives then went back to the theatre to tell the rest of the mutineers what had transpired at the discussion. Flannery has written,

> The general agreement at this meeting was that they would submit to all the arrangements which had been made, and they would offer no violent resistance to the authorities unless they tried to separate them. They resolved to adopt the policy of passive resistance on all other occasions.[6]

A number of men raised the question as to what would happen to the Sinn Fein flags which the mutineers had suspended over the barracks. They said that if they saw them being torn down by the incoming troops a fight would be certain to develop. In order to prevent this from happening, it was agreed that the mutineers would lower the flags themselves before they left the barracks, and that they would carry them to their new camp. As an additional mark of defiance, they would march out wearing Sinn Fein rosettes, made out of material which they had bought at the bazaar.[7]

Joseph Hawes has refuted any suggestions that the mutineers capitulated to Colonel Jackson's terms, but it must be remembered that he was writing at a time when the mutiny had been enshrined in Ireland as a patriotic legend and the mutineers were extolled as a band of intrepid freedom-fighters. In consequence, his account is persistently marred by inaccuracies and exaggerations. According to Hawes, Jackson opened the discussion that day by telling them that Jullundur was already encircled by loyal troops and the mutiny would be suppressed, 'even if it took every soldier from all over the British Empire' to overcome their resistance. The Colonel went on to assure them of the hopelessness of their position and of the inevitable bloodshed that would result if they chose to fight it out. His proposal was that a party of British soldiers should disarm them, and they would then be escorted to a camp on the plains where they would remain while their protest was being considered by the authorities. The representatives put forward a counter-proposal, Hawes says,

> that a party of mutineers would collect the arms and stack them in a bungalow over which a mutineer guard would be put; also, that we would march out to this prepared camp under our own mutineer committees, and unescorted by British troops.[8]

Hawes maintained that the negotiations between Colonel Jackson and the mutineers' representatives lasted for the whole day, with the Colonel making frequent telephone calls to his superiors. The representatives refused to yield, he says, and they made it quite clear that if they were unable to reach an agreement they were prepared 'to fight to the bitter end'. Eventually, in the evening, Jackson gave way and accepted the mutineers' terms unconditionally.[9]

Lieutenant Leader, the Adjutant of the Battalion, was the only prosecution witness who mentioned Colonel Jackson's visit to Wellington Barracks in his statement for the Summary of Evidence. He said that the Colonel had seen the mutineers in the morning and that they had agreed to hand in their arms by four o'clock in the afternoon. 'This was only partially done,' he continued, 'and the arms of the mutineers were never completely handed in.'[10]

Hawes has rounded off his description of the day's events by asserting that the mutineers' patrols reported that 'there was a large body of troops in the vicinity, including artillery units'.[11] In point of fact, the official records show that the force which was ordered to Jullundur to suppress the mutiny consisted of a company of South Wales Borderers, a company of Seaforth Highlanders and a company from the Machine-Gun Corps reinforced by an additional section.[12] These units between them would have mounted an appreciable firepower on account of their heavy and light machine guns. There was no artillery with the force, but a battery of Field Artillery, with six field-guns, was in a barracks at Jullundur throughout the mutiny. There were, in addition, seven Indian infantry battalions and a cavalry squadron stationed in the cantonment, so there was no shortage of troops in the area.

It is quite impossible to establish how many of the troops at Wellington Barracks were actively participating in the mutiny. The official estimate is that there were 200 mutineers on 28 June, and that figure had risen to 390 by 30 June, whereas 100 men had declared themselves to be loyal and had been accommodated with another unit in the cantonment.[13] One cannot assume, however, that all those who were classified as 'mutineers' were genuinely committed to what was taking place. Sam Pollock, author of *Mutiny for the Cause*, who was an enthusiastic laudator of the mutiny, and who had had the opportunity of discussing the sequence of events with Joseph Hawes, has commented that for all the show of solidarity at the start, 'It later transpired that only a tiny minority of the men involved were whole-heartedly behind the ring-leaders'.[14] It must have required considerable courage for any soldier at the barracks to dissociate himself from the activists after the mutiny had started. An Englishman, Frank Rye, who had been serving with the 1st Connaught Rangers at the time, said years later that his principal reason for joining in the mutiny had been fear of his comrades. 'You had to be very careful what you said with these people,' he told a newspaper reporter; 'I certainly didn't dare to say anything about Ireland.'[15] His apprehensions were not unjustified, for instances of vengeance and intimidation are known to have occurred. Pollock has admitted that some of the loyal NCOs were 'fairly roughly handled' while they were collecting their kit from their bungalows prior to leaving the barracks.[16] On the first evening of the mutiny two C Company men, Privates McCormack and Salmon, both of whom had remained loyal, were sitting together in the canteen when they received a message that they were going to be tied up and dragged to the Guard Room.[17] Just before midnight McCormack was handed a letter headed 'In the Name of Erin'. It went on:

> McCormack, Traitor – One advice to you: make your peace with God. You are a traitor to your land. Therefore, in the name of Ireland you will suffer the penalty – Death – in a few days' time. One advice, prepare yourself with God, because you are finished. Your country has no use for you. Death is near.
> By the true Irishmen in the name of the Irish Republic.[18]

In the early hours of the Tuesday morning Sergeant Sheehan and Corporal Murphy had been woken up by a Private Regan who gave them the alternative of leaving the barracks within ten minutes or being killed by the mutineers. When Sheehan was running from the bungalow Regan hurled a table-lamp at him. Arrangements were made for both these NCOs to be temporarily billeted with another unit.[19] During the afternoon all the professed loyalists who had remained in barracks were paraded and their rifles were taken away from them.[20] The rancour of the mutineers was particularly directed against the NCOs remaining loyal. A Lance-Corporal Hughes was so frightened by the threats he had received that he applied for official protection.[21]

If the mutineers at Jullundur, having submitted to Colonel Jackson's proposals, had quietly awaited the arrival of the relieving troops without taking any further action, it is possible that the whole incident might have been treated by the military authorities as a transient and fairly inconsequential outburst of ill-discipline in an Irish regiment in extremely emotive circumstances. As it was, at some time on Tuesday, 29 June the mutineers' committee made the fateful decision that emissaries should be sent to the detachments of the Battalion at the hill-stations of Solon and Jutogh requesting them to join in the mutiny. Lance-Corporal Keenan and Private Kelly volunteered to travel to Solon together. In collecting material for his book on the mutiny Sam Pollock appears to have relied almost completely on information given to him by Joseph Hawes and several other ex-mutineers. Knowing that the road and the railway would be watched, Pollock wrote, Keenan and Kelly chose to make the journey of over 200 miles across country on foot. Pollock described how, with dogged determination, they set out from Jullundur during the Tuesday morning, toiled across the scorching plains to the base of the Simla Hills, and climbed up to a place not far from Solon by dawn on the Wednesday.[22] He apparently overlooked the fact that in order to have achieved this they must have covered the distance at an average speed of over eight miles an hour. Other far more reliable accounts relate that the two men left Jullundur railway station on the Tuesday evening on a northbound train.[23]

It seems that no emissaries ever travelled to Jutogh, but an Indian might have been sent there with a message. It is known, however, that soon after the start of the mutiny Major Truell, the Company Commander of A Company, which formed the Jutogh detachment, paraded all his men and told them about the occurrences at Jullundur. He then appealed to them to remember the great traditions of the Connaught Rangers, and to be loyal to them. After the Company was dismissed, only one private had declared himself to be in sympathy with the mutineers, but he had changed his mind later and had sought permission to return to duty.[24]

Among the men in the C Company detachment at Solon was a 20-year-old private, James Daly, who was generally known to be a supporter of the Irish republican movement. He came from Tyrrellspass, near the town of Mullingar in Co. Westmeath, and had been in the Army a little over a year, having enlisted on 4 April, 1919. His elder brother had been one of the originators of the protest at Jullundur but had ceased to take part on the advice of Lance-Corporal Flannery. James Daly was remembered in his village as being 'a sturdy, dark-haired, red-faced lad'.[25] He was described by a fellow-private in C Company as a 'hot-head' and a person who liked to keep to himself.[26] It is not surprising that the emissaries from Wellington Barracks should have decided that Daly was the first person they should approach when they reached the camp at Solon.

Lance-Corporal Keenan and Private Kelly travelled all night in the train from Jullundur and reached Kalka, the northern terminus of the Great Indian Peninsular Railway, early in the morning of Wednesday, 30 June. During the journey they were questioned several times by military policemen, but their explanation that they were on their way to join C Company at Solon had been accepted without further enquiries being made. Having reached Kalka, they decided to walk the last twenty-five miles to the camp as they thought it would be too risky to finish their journey on the narrow-gauge railway which wound up the mountains to Simla, calling at Solon en route.

A number of loyal NCOs had stayed on in Wellington Barracks and one of them, Sergeant Edwards, had discovered around nine o'clock on the Tuesday evening that Keenan and Kelly had left Jullundur with the intention of spreading the mutiny to Solon. After searching the barracks without success to find an officer or a warrant-officer to whom he could pass on this information, Edwards determined to act on his own initiative. He managed to obtain a van from the battalion transport section and pursued the northbound train on the roadway which ran roughly parallel to the rail-tracks. He stopped several times at police posts to ask for assistance, but they showed no interest in his mission. Finally, he reached Kalka and from there he walked for three and a half miles to Kasauli, where the 2nd Battalion of the Royal Fusiliers had their headquarters. He was taken before the Adjutant who treated his statement with disbelief and had him arrested for being absent from his barracks without a pass. The unfortunate Edwards was then confined in the Royal Fusiliers Guard Room for three days before being returned to Jullundur under escort.[27]

The Tuesday night passed comparatively peacefully at Wellington Barracks. The mutineers' committee had posted sentries outside the officers' bungalows to protect them from being attacked by the more unruly elements among the mutineers. For the most part, however, a reasonable standard of discipline was maintained. Two men were caught in the process of breaking into the 'wet' canteen after it had been closed for the night, and were brought before the committee, who punished them with extra guard duties. A more serious incident almost occurred when a crowd of Indians from the bazaar district planned to raid the totally disorganized barracks. At the last minute they decided to abandon their plan.[28] They were probably influenced by Lance-Corporal Flannery's warning that the mutineers would not tolerate any looting by civilians, and also by the fact that the Indian troops within the cantonment were available to deal with an attack.

The Connaught Rangers detachment at Solon consisted of most of C Company together with the Regimental Band. Major Alexander, DSO, the Second-in-Command of the Battalion, was in charge of the camp, assisted by Lieutenant O'Brien, his acting Adjutant, who looked after all matters of administration. C Company had four officers there, Captain Badham MC, the Company Commander, and four lieutenants. Leslie Badham, the son of a Co. Westmeath clergyman, was then 32 years old and was one of the senior captains in the regiment. He had been commissioned before the outbreak of the First World War and was a lieutenant in the 1st Connaught Rangers when they had joined the British Expeditionary Force in 1914. During his early months on the Western Front he was awarded the Military Cross and was Mentioned in Despatches for gallantry in the field. His service in the front line had been cut short when he was severely wounded in April, 1915, and had lost the sight of his right eye.

As soon as news had reached them of the occurrences at Wellington Barracks, the officers of the Solon detachment suspected that trouble-makers might be sent to their camp to spread the mutiny. Lieutenant O'Brien gave instructions to Sergeant McNamara, his Provost Sergeant, that he should be particularly vigilant to detect intruders into the area, and told him to post some regimental police at Solon railway station with orders to arrest any Connaught Rangers arriving there who did not belong to the detachment. Just after five o'clock on the afternoon of Wednesday, 30 June Lance-Corporal Murphy, one of the junior NCOs in C Company, discovered that Keenan and Kelly had managed to slip into the camp undetected and were then in Bungalow 27, which was on the very edge of the camp beside the railway track, with Private James Daly. Murphy reported this to his section commander, Corporal Kelly, who did nothing about it and who was subsequently court-martialled with the rest of the mutineers for his neglect of duty.

Murphy waited for half-an-hour and then, realizing that Corporal Kelly did not intend to take any action, he reported his information direct to Sergeant McNamara, who hurried to Bungalow 27 and placed Kelly and Keenan under close arrest. Lieutenant O'Brien interviewed the two emissaries from Jullundur in the Guard Room and they told him a garbled story about having been detailed by the mutineers' committee to accompany a sergeant who was visiting his wife in Dagshai, a military cantonment nearby. They said that they had fulfilled their mission and had decided to walk to Solon in order to visit some of their friends at the camp. Not surprisingly, this explanation for their presence was rejected by the Adjutant who directed Sergeant McNamara to take them to the station and to return them to Jullundur by train with an escort. The damage had been done, however, as Keenan and Kelly had already sown the seeds of mutiny at the camp and their removal from Solon had little effect on the consequences. Early in the evening when the detachment Orderly Sergeant was warning men for guard duty, Private Moorehouse, a 19-year-old soldier with less than one year's service, refused to leave his bungalow and made the somewhat sinister remark, 'If anything turns up, I will be one of the first men to ground arms'.[29]

About half-an-hour after Moorehouse's flagrant disobedience, Private James Daly ordered C Company to parade outside the camp Coffee Shop. According to the official report between seventy and eighty men obeyed his command.[30] Daly then marched them to the Officers' Mess, a long low hut, where all the C Company officers and the Adjutant were having their dinner. Lieutenant McWeeney, MC, has described what took place. In the middle of the meal, he said, he heard the sound of a body of marching troops, who appeared to halt directly outside the entrance to the Mess. A moment later a waiter told Captain Badham that some men wished to speak to him. Badham went out, followed by the rest of the officers. By the light of the moon and the illumination from the windows of the hut they saw what appeared to be the majority of C Company drawn up in two ranks, with Private Daly standing in front of them. Daly told Captain Badham that none of the men were going to soldier any more until all the British troops – some witnesses reported that he had used the term 'British dogs' – had been withdrawn from Ireland. Further, he said, they were demanding the immediate release from custody of Lance-Corporal Keenan and Private Kelly. When he had finished speaking Badham informed him that the two emissaries were already on their return journey to Jullundur, accompanied by an escort. Badham then addressed the men, warning them of the serious consequences that would follow if they persisted in their action and urging them to resume their military duties. He told them that the company would parade at nine o'clock the following morning, and he would expect to see every man present. Daly interrupted with the comment that none of them had any intention of parading at all until their demands were met.[31]

The officers present must have realized how effectively the spirit of insubordination had been implanted in the camp when Captain Badham attempted to call the men to attention and they blatantly ignored his words of command. Thereupon, James Daly stepped forward and took over, asserting that he was now in charge of the detachment. His orders were readily obeyed and he marched off the troops in the direction of the railway station. Their purpose in going there is unknown; it might possibly have been to rescue Keenan and Kelly from their guards if they had not yet left for Jullundur.

As soon as he heard what was happening, Major Alexander had hurried to the Officers' Mess, arriving just after the mutineers had left. He called an immediate emergency meeting of the detachment officers to decide what they ought to do next. Most of the subalterns were of the opinion that, provided the protest was carried no further, the whole occurrence should be hushed up, but Major Alexander took the view that the breach of discipline had been so grave he was under a duty to make a full report to the Commander of the Ambala Brigade, who was the senior officer in the area.[32]

After their visit to the railway station, the mutineers marched back to the camp and crowded into the canteen, where they drank and sang Irish Rebel songs until after midnight. Before they dispersed to their bungalows James Daly issued an order that they must fall in the next morning to march to Jutogh, presumably with the intention of persuading A Company to join the mutiny.

Years later Charles Kerrigan, who had been a Private in the camp at Solon, recounted his memories of the outbreak of the mutiny there. Kerrigan, who had then been 19, was the son of a farmer in Co. Leitrim. He had enlisted in the Connaught Rangers in May, 1919, and had embarked for India with a draft of reinforcements during the following December. Their life at the hill station, he said, was reasonably pleasant with training taking place early in the day and often finishing by 11 am. His own letters from home had not contained accounts of British outrages and he did not recall having heard about them from his companions. The first he had known of the arrival of the emissaries from Jullundur was when James Kelly came round the bungalows urging the men to join the revolt. In Kerrigan's opinion the outbreak at Solon had been a gesture of solidarity by the detachment with the actions of their friends at Wellington Barracks. He thinks it was largely influenced by the resolute and assertive personality of Private James Daly.

When they went to bed on the first night after the arrival of the emissaries, said Charles Kerrigan, the men of the Solon detachment were uncertain how the situation was going to develop, but they were determined to continue the mutiny.[33]

Chapter 3

BLOODSHED

ON TUESDAY, 30 JUNE, while Lance-Corporal Keenan and Private Kelly were completing their journey to Solon, the day was passing fairly uneventfully at Jullundur, although the atmosphere remained extremely tense as the Indians in the locality were known to be following the progress of the mutiny with close attention.[1] It has often been alleged that the military authorities were trying to draw a veil over what was happening, but according to John Flannery, local journalists were allowed to visit the barracks without hindrance.[2] The Official Despatch reported that at this stage the mutineers were continuing to hold their own meetings and parades. It went on:

> Except in one isolated instance, the act of a single drunken man, no acts of violence occurred. Numerous threatening letters were, however, received by Officers, Warrant Officers and Non-Commissioned Officers.[3]

At seven o'clock in the morning on Thursday, 1 July Keenan and Kelly arrived back at Wellington Barracks with an escort from C Company. The Adjutant, Lieutenant Leader, placed both men under arrest and arranged for their detention at the Royal Artillery Guard Room in the cantonment.[4] As soon as he heard about the apprehension of the Solon emissaries, Lance-Corporal Flannery summoned a meeting of the mutineers in the Regimental Theatre to decide whether or not it would affect their intentions to hand over peaceably to the relieving force, which was due to reach Jullundur that evening. A resolution was passed insisting that Keenan and Kelly should be released forthwith. Flannery conveyed the demand to Lieutenant Leader, who treated it in the supine manner which, presumably, had been authorized by Lieutenant-Colonel Deacon, the Commanding

Officer. 'I undertook to ask whether the G.O.C. Division would release the two men,' said Leader in his statement of evidence. 'An answer was received later in the day that he would not allow these men to be released.'[5]

John Flannery, who, like Joseph Hawes, was never reluctant to sacrifice truth in favour of self-adulation, claimed that he exacted from the authorities an undertaking that all the mutineers in custody, including Keenan and Kelly, would be released directly the mutineers were installed in their new camp. As a result of this assurance, he says, the mutineers returned to their bungalows to collect their equipment, their arms and their ammunition so that the relief might be transacted in an orderly and efficient manner. According to Flannery, when everything was ready he paraded the men again and invited anyone to fall out if he would prefer to remain in barracks with the loyal troops rather than to march out with the rebels; several of them availed themselves of this opportunity and took no further part in the mutiny.[6]

Both Hawes and Flannery have estimated the size of the relieving force to be considerably larger than the numbers given in the Official Report, although there is no doubt that it far outmatched the mutineers in fire-power. Hawes also exaggerates when he says that 450 Connaught Rangers elected to leave Wellington Barracks and to march to the new camp.[7] The Official Report puts the number at 'about 250'.[8]

The relieving troops had not been reinforced and still consisted of detachments from the Seaforth Highlanders, the South Wales Borderers and the Machine-Gun Corps. They entered Wellington Barracks at six o'clock on the Thursday evening and, working under the orders of Lieutenant Leader, they arrested all the men who had not specifically undertaken to remain loyal.[9] They met with no resistance and the take-over was accomplished without the slightest trouble. As soon as he was satisfied that the relief force was fully in control Lieutenant-Colonel Deacon directed the Company Sergeant-Majors to go round telling all the newly arrested soldiers they could, even then, elect to join the loyalists. A number of men declared that they were anxious to do so. Deacon said in his statement of evidence that four men had already come to him complaining they were being forced to remain with the mutineers, and he said that several others, frightened to declare themselves, had gone into hiding in the barracks.[10]

The mutineers then formed up and marched off under the orders of Lance-Corporal Flannery. As they went out through the barrack-gates they were watched by Mrs Carney, the wife of the Battalion

Medical Officer, who was herself an avowed Irish Nationalist. Years later in a broadcast interview she recalled the scene. A lot of the men looked very young, she said, and although they seemed to be cheerful, she found it the most pathetic sight she had ever seen. Some of them were travelling in the backs of bullock carts; some were on foot. They were taking all their possessions with them in boxes, and many of them were also carrying their pets – monkeys, parrots, cockatoos or mynah birds.[11] Several ex-mutineers have given a somewhat different account of the exodus from Wellington Barracks, claiming that the men marched out triumphantly, singing nationalist songs, and with a Sinn Fein flag at their head.

The mutiny at Jullundur was disturbing enough for both the civil and the military authorities in India, but the situation which had arisen at Solon was even more serious on account of its locality. In those days Simla, a small town situated on a ridge of the Himalayan foothills, was the summer capital of India. It was the resort, during the hot weather, of the Viceroy, together with his secretariat and all of his headquarters establishments. Solon happened to be athwart the railway and only proper road which linked Simla with Kalka and Delhi. G. N. Molesworth, who at the time was the officer in charge of the Discipline section in the Adjutant-General's Branch at Army Headquarters in India, has written:

> The Government of India, with the Viceroy in residence, was cut off from any aid from India and it was feared that the mutineers might march on Simla. In the Capital there was only a weak detachment of Indian infantry providing Viceregal Guards and a small detachment of Gunners at Jutogh nearby. The detachment of the Auxiliary Force in India was called out and arrangements made to bar the way should the necessity arise.[12]

Thursday, 1 July was destined to be a fateful day at Solon. Major Alexander still believed that if he addressed the whole company he would be able to bring the mutiny to an end without further trouble, so he ordered a Detachment Commander's parade to take place at nine o'clock that morning. Before the time of the parade a number of men had gathered in Bungalow 27, where James Daly was accommodated, and which was now flying a tricolour flag. At nine o'clock Company Sergeant-Major White entered the bungalow and told the occupants to fall in outside. 'This is our headquarters,' Daly replied. 'If Major Alexander wants to talk to us, he'll have to come here to do it.' On being informed of this, Alexander would have been fully justified in having Daly arrested for insubordination; instead, surprisingly enough, he agreed that he would speak to the mutineers in Bungalow 27 instead of addressing them on the company parade ground. The explanation may have been that he was extremely worried as to how the situation might develop. He certainly was not regarded as a weak officer. One of the lieutenants who was serving in C Company at the time described him as being 'an impressive figure of a man – but very cold and dry'.[13]

Major Alexander's meeting with the mutineers took place on the verandah of Bungalow 27. He began by telling them that their decision to refuse to parade as a protest against the employment of British troops in Ireland would have no effect on the policy of the Government and would entail serious consequences for themselves. Directly he had finished speaking, Private Daly came forward to assure the men that what they were doing would be reported in every newspaper in the United Kingdom and that all the other Irish regiments in the army would follow their example. Alexander admitted subsequently that any influence he might have exerted on the men was wholly nullified by Daly's words. In the middle of the morning Colonel Wooldridge, the Officer in Command of the Ambala Brigade to which the Solon garrison was attached, visited the camp to deliver a message to the mutineers, who agreed to parade for him, but declined to stand at attention when listening to what he had to say. The Colonel asked them to put their protest into writing and promised that, when they had done so, he would send it to the proper authorities. Meanwhile, he said, they must continue to work normally. He invited anyone who wanted to abandon the mutiny to stand to one side, but nobody moved. Finally, he gave them another hour, during which he would expect them all to confirm to the Commanding Officer that they were ready to return to duty. At this point Daly once again intervened, urging the men to ignore what the Brigade Commander had said to them and to stand firm. After the hour had elapsed, the mutineers sent a joint reply to Major Alexander informing him that none of them would parade again until every British soldier had been withdrawn from Ireland.[14]

The officers at Solon were desperately anxious to deprive the mutineers of their personal weapons but they had no idea of how this could be achieved. The men's rifles were kept in their bungalows locked in racks, the keys of which were held in the Company Office. There were also a few boxes of cartridges in some of the bungalows, though the main supplies of ammunition were in the camp magazine. The mutineers were determined to obtain control of their rifles. Early on the Thursday afternoon Company-Quartermaster-Sergeant Glenn was working in the Company Office when Daly and another private soldier walked in and demanded to be given the keys to the racks. They told Glenn they had heard that troops from other units were approaching the camp and they must have weapons with which to defend themselves. After Glenn had adamantly refused to hand over the keys, Daly went back to Bungalow 27, where the rest of his followers were waiting, and issued an order that the racks were to be broken open and the rifles removed from them.[15] Lieutenant O'Brien, the Adjutant, heard what was going on and sent Lieutenant Mac-Weeney and a sergeant to investigate. They found that a number of the rifle-racks and ammunition boxes were already open and empty. MacWeeney found Private Daly and asked him if he knew who had been responsible for this. Daly replied defiantly that he had helped to do it himself.[16]

A key figure in the events at Solon was the Roman Catholic Chaplain to the camp, Father Benjamin Thomas Edwin Baker, a Londoner who served with the (English Province) Franciscan Mission. Father Baker was in the unique position of being trusted by both the officers and the mutineers. Apart from his strong personality, he was apparently a very humorous man, as one of his close friends in India said that he was always 'full of fun and mischief'.[17] Baker shared in the general apprehension as to what might happen now that the mutineers had armed themselves, and he offered to try to persuade them to surrender their rifles forthwith. Major Alexander, who had lost all control of the situation, welcomed his assistance. The priest had no easy task. However, after three hours of admonition and exhortation in Bungalow 27, the mutineers agreed to deliver up their rifles that same evening. Father Baker also received a promise from James Daly that, whatever action they took from then on, 'there would be no violence of any sort'.[18]

The mutineers kept their word and at about six o'clock in the evening they handed in their rifles and ammunition to the Company Office. All the weapons were then placed in the camp magazine over which a 24-hour guard was mounted, consisting of an officer, two sergeants, two corporals and fourteen men from the regimental band. Major Alexander gave strict orders that the sentries were to be armed with loaded rifles and they were 'to shoot to kill, if necessary, to prevent any arms being removed from the magazine'. Lieutenant Walsh, an officer with war experience, was the first guard commander. He was told by the Adjutant that the guard must be instructed to fire at anyone approaching the magazine who did not halt when challenged.[19] These directions might have seemed slightly fanciful when they were first issued, but they assumed a new urgency a short while later when the Adjutant received information that an attempt was going to be made to attack the magazine that night and to recover the rifles. Lieutenant O'Brien had the reputation of being a resolute disciplinarian and was hardly the sort of officer with whom the mutineers could have afforded to trifle. Then 33 years old, he had enlisted in the Connaught Rangers as a private in 1907 and had risen to the rank of Company Sergeant-Major before being commissioned in November, 1914. As a Lieutenant, and later as an acting Captain, he was continuously in the front line and he had been awarded the Military Cross and Mentioned in Despatches for gallantry. After the war he had stayed on as a regular officer.[20]

A curious and perhaps a significant incident occurred in the camp that evening. Lance-Corporal Franklin, an NCO who had remained loyal, visited the canteen and saw what at first he took to be a meeting of the mutineers taking place there. On looking more closely, he realized that Lance-Corporal Nolan, another loyal NCO, was being tried by a 'court' presided over by Private Daly. Franklin was just in time to hear Daly pronouncing Nolan guilty and sentencing him to death. Later on Daly maintained that the trial was connected with 'a family affair'; one of his supporters was more explicit and said the Lance-Corporal had been charged with calling a woman by an improper name.[21] It is hard to believe, however, that at this stage of the mutiny the ringleader would have concerned himself with anything entirely unrelated to the matter in hand. It is interesting to note that one of the Solon mutineers, Corporal Kelly, was to plead in his defence that he acted under duress after being warned that any NCO who refused to join in the mutiny would be dealt with severely. But whatever offence had been alleged against Nolan, the episode demonstrates the extent to which James Daly was exerting his authority over the group which was gathered around him.

There can be no question that Daly was responsible for instigating the foolhardy attack on the magazine that night, or that he was answerable, indirectly, for the deaths of two of the men who were shot when it took place. Several of the mutineers have given their accounts of what happened. Private John Moorehouse said that the purpose of the attack was to 'strike a blow' in support of their comrades at Jullundur. 'The mutineers had no arms except a few bayonets,' he explained, 'so that unless they could capture the magazine, their chances of success would be nil.'[22] On the other hand, Private Patrick Hynes believed that their purpose was to obtain weapons so that they could resist the troops who were coming to take over the camp.[23] Most of the mutineers spent the evening in the canteen; Private James Gorman described what they were doing there as 'having their bit of enjoyment, as is the case in every crowd . . . having their wee drink'.[24] The mutineers left the canteen between half-past nine and ten o'clock to return to their bungalows. While they were doing so Daly and three others went off to conduct a reconnaissance of the positions of the sentries around the magazine. They were challenged by Lieutenant Walsh who covered them with his revolver and asked them what they wanted. Daly made a lame reply that they were on their way to the canteen but Walsh, knowing that it had just closed, ordered the men to turn around and clear off. At that, they disappeared into the darkness. Walsh immediately alerted the guard and sent a message to Lieutenant O'Brien in the Officers' Mess to say that he expected that a raid on the magazine was imminent.[25]

Private Kerrigan had not gone to the canteen that evening. He was in bed in his bungalow when the reconnaissance party returned. He said that Daly was 'raging' and he ordered every man to parade outside for an attack on the magazine.[26] According to Gorman they were told to take bayonets with them. He says that he and a few others tried to persuade Daly against carrying out the raid, pointing out to him the impossibility of getting past a heavily armed guard, but Daly refused to accept their advice. Another man who was there recalls that Daly and his henchmen were shouting, 'Fall in all Irishmen. Fall in all Irishmen to attack the magazine'.[27]

The camp at Solon was roughly rectangular in shape. In a level clearing at one end were the Orderly Room, the Officers' Mess and the magazine, all in separate huts. They were divided from the rest of the camp by a steep hill, covered by low scrub and bushes, which descended to another level space containing the men's bungalows and the canteen. As soon as he received Walsh's message Lieutenant O'Brien rushed to the Guard Room, where the sergeant in charge had already received a warning and had turned out the members of the guard in readiness. The Adjutant now took control and posted the men to form a cordon in front of the magazine, with their rifles loaded. Lieutenants MacWeeney and Sarsfield, who had been in the Officers' Mess, seized their revolvers and ran out to join Lieutenant Walsh. They found him at the top of the hill, waiting with a few men from the guard. At that moment Captain Badham and Father Baker were also hurrying to the vicinity of the magazine; it is not clear where they had been or how they had heard of the impending attack.[28]

James Daly formed up his raiding party, which numbered about fifty, outside the canteen, and ordered them to advance up the hill in three parallel columns. Each man was armed either with an un-sheathed bayonet or a heavy iron bar. It was close to midnight when they began their climb, with Daly out in front setting the pace. The guard on top of the hill saw them approaching, shadowy figures in the moonlight, and called on them to halt. As a further warning, Lieuten-ant Walsh fired a couple of shots from his revolver over their heads. The effect was immediate. A number of the mutineers turned and ran back; the remainder faltered. Then a voice was heard shouting, 'Come on, boys. They're only firing blank,' and Daly gave the command to charge. About a dozen men obeyed his order and rushed forward after him.[29] Realizing that nothing else was going to stop them, Walsh fired at the group three times.[30] In the confusion which followed Father Baker ran up imploring the mutineers to retreat and the guard not to open fire on them. Baker has told in his journal how he grabbed hold of Daly and asked what he was doing after his promise that there would be no violence. Daly replied with an assertion that both Father Baker and the officers had also broken their word.[31] None of the accounts given by people who were at Solon at the time have thrown any light on the reasons why Daly made this accusation. There is a possibility that he was merely speaking wildly in an effort to mitigate his betrayal of the solemn undertaking he had given to his priest.

Even after he had been admonished by Father Baker, James Daly continued to act in an irrational manner. He remained where he was for a while and shouted, 'If you want to know who is the leader, it is me, Private James Daly of the 1st Battalion the Connaught Rangers, from the town of Mullingar in County Westmeath.' Then, confront-ing the members of the guard with his bayonet in his hand, he challenged any of them to come forward and fight him in single combat with naked bayonets. It is natural to wonder whether Daly was under the influence of alcohol. Captain Badham, who was near him when this took place, said later that in his opinion Daly had been perfectly sober. On the other hand, Charles Kerrigan, in an interview in 1987, said there had been 'a lot of drink involved' in the events of that evening at Solon,[32] and Lieutenant Walsh reported that one of the mutineers who took part in the final charge appeared to be drunk.

As soon as Lieutenant Walsh had fired at the advancing mutineers, they broke off the attack and fled back down the hill. Private Sears, who was close to Daly, was struck in the head by a bullet and was killed instantly. Private Egan, who had also been at the front of the charging party, was wounded in the shoulder. The body of a second dead man, Private Smyth, was found on the top of the hill a little distance from the other casualties. It has been suggested that Smyth was not taking part in the attack on the magazine but was just interested to see what was happening. The point has never been clarified. Charles Kerrigan has described Smyth as being a drunkard who was habitually brought back to camp by the Indians.[33]

While Egan was lying on a stretcher waiting to be taken to hospital, Father Baker came up, not knowing whether or not he had been severely, even mortally wounded. The priest has written in his journal:

> I then knelt at his side and began to prepare him for a short form of confession and absolution. Daly, falling on the ground, exclaimed: 'My God, I did not think there would be bloodshed'. The eyes of the wounded man were quite bright, and I saw he was not going to die, so I pulled Daly up and scolded him a little.[34]

In 1971 Lieutenant MacWeeney set down his recollections of the attack on the magazine for the nephew of the last Colonel of the Connaught Rangers. Although the passage of fifty-one years might have blurred his memories of exact details, nevertheless it must have been an experience the substance of which would not have been easily forgotten. He wrote:

> A number of men, probably about 20, led by Daly, who was very visible as he was wearing a white shirt, and all carrying bayonets or heavy sticks, crossed from right to left where Walsh and I were standing. Encouraged by Daly, they moved along the path and turned up the main track leading upwards to where O'Brien and his bandsmen were standing across the top of the track. It seemed obvious that a serious confrontation was about to take place within a few seconds, especially as Daly & Co. had quickened their pace. It seemed essential that something had to be done quickly to try and avert the worst happening, so about 6 or 8 revolver shots were fired over the heads of the group of men on the path . . . There was a fair amount of confused shouting, O'Brien warning them to halt, and at that moment when it appeared to hang in the balance whether they would advance again the shots halted them. Father Baker erupted on to the scene running from behind O'Brien's position (he had been coming from the direction of the bazaar when he heard the shots). He rushed between the two parties with his arms widespread and asked O'Brien not to fire. O'Brien said he wouldn't if they went back. So Father Baker urged Daly to retire which I think they were glad to do. At this stage Private Smith [sic] was discovered lying

dead beside the main path. I don't think he was with Daly's party as he was a quiet man but probably came along to see what would happen as he was rather apart and seemed to have been hit in the head by a descending bullet.

A .45, as you know, has a pretty limited range. Also a Private Egan discovered he had been slightly wounded in the chest probably by a ricochet. Whilst this was happening, Private Sears with a bayonet in his hand rushed up the small path towards where we were standing. He was called on to halt several times, paid no attention and a shot had to be fired. He was unlucky, but for all practical purposes he committed suicide. The assistant surgeon, or George Wood the R.A.M.C. doctor (an Irishman), was quickly on the scene and examined and dealt with the casualties. Daly and his supporters retired to their barrack huts, and C.S.M. White and the NCOs got things quietened down.[35]

Three of the participants in the episode were to give their judgements in retrospect on the conduct of Private James Daly. Charles Kerrigan, who had taken part in the raid on the magazine, doubted whether there would have been a mutiny at Solon at all if it had not been for Daly. 'He was in charge of the whole thing,' said Kerrigan, 'and he kind of lost his head.'[36] Eugene Egan, the mutineer who had been wounded during the raid, commented that, although Daly was undoubtedly the leader of the mutiny, there had been two others closely involved with him. Egan thought Daly 'a good lad', although he talked too much.[37] Lieutenant Desmond MacWeeney did not consider that Daly's actions could properly be described as 'brave' on the night of the raid. He went on:

I don't think that that's the right adjective to use. It was a reckless thing to do, if you like. It was more reckless than anything else. I don't think for a moment he counted the consequences ... If O'Brien hadn't been a very strong character, he could have easily told [the guard] to open fire and killed a dozen men without argument and nobody could have blamed him.[38]

After the attack on the magazine had been abandoned the bodies of the two dead men were removed to the mortuary, and Egan, after treatment from the Medical Officer, was removed to the local hospital. His wound was not serious as the bullet had passed through his chest without touching his ribs or his lungs.[39] No one was certain whether or not Daly and his followers would attempt another raid, and Captain Badham issued orders that the subalterns should take it in turn to stay on duty with the guard for the rest of the night. Father Baker,

34

determined to be on the spot if a further act of violence should occur, had his bed made up on the verandah of one of the bungalows occupied by men who were known to be mutineers. The camp then settled into silence with the atmosphere of tension in no way diminished. Just after dawn next morning Father Baker considered that the immediate danger had passed and he went to his chapel to celebrate Mass, before paying an early visit to Private Egan at the hospital.[40]

At about half-past six that morning, before the mutineers had left their beds, a force of 100 men from the South Wales Borderers arrived at Solon railway station and marched to the camp.[41] Without wasting any time, most of the party who had been identified in the raid were arrested in their bungalows. None of them put up any resistance. Captain Badham himself, accompanied by Company Sergeant-Major White and Sergeant McNamara, carried out the arrest of Private Daly; probably to their surprise, and undoubtedly to their relief, he submitted quietly and fell in with the other mutineers outside his bungalow. A total of thirty-two men were put under close arrest. According to James Gorman, they had scarcely been given time to get dressed and some of them were still in their bare feet.[42] They were marched with an armed escort to the camp school-hut and locked inside. Another thirty men, who had not been implicated in the mutiny to the same extent, had their bayonets taken from them but were allowed to return to duty.[43]

During the afternoon all the prisoners from the school-hut were marched to the railway station and taken by train to Lucknow. Immediately upon their arrival they were put into the Military Detention Barracks, where they were to remain for the next two weeks. Gorman has said that for the first few nights they were issued with two blankets each and were left to sleep on the bare floor.[44] There were no reports of any further protests or acts of insubordination on the part of the Solon mutineers during their confinement at Lucknow. It would appear that they had resigned themselves to their captivity and were prepared to wait patiently for the courts martial which they must have realized would inevitably follow.

★   ★   ★   ★   ★

The camp which had been specially prepared for the Jullundur mutineers was described by Joseph Hawes as being an unshaded tract of land approximately three miles from Wellington Barracks. It consisted, he said, of a square-shaped enclosure surrounded by a six-foot-high barbed wire fence, with machine-gun posts covering all four sides of the perimeter. He alleged that the prisoners had to spend their nights and their days in ordinary military bell-tents, which made life in the camp 'almost unbearable'. He wrote:

> The canvas of the tents seemed to attract the heat; you could not stick inside and there was no protection from the sun outside, so that each day saw its quota of men overpowered with the heat and taken away to hospital.[45]

Thomas Tierney, another inmate of the camp, said that the prisoners not only suffered from the heat, but were plagued by insects coming up through the sand on which they slept.[46]

If Joseph Hawes is telling the truth about the special camp, it was very wrong and very callous to keep the Jullundur mutineers under canvas on the Indian plains during the hottest months of the year. Not only was excessive discomfort involved, but also a grave risk to health and life. During the period of mobilization in 1914 several Connaught Rangers died from heatstroke on a train journey to Karachi. An even more serious incident had occurred in 1916 when 154 British soldiers had been overcome by heat while travelling in a troop train to Lahore and nineteen of them had died.[47] Mrs Carney told years later of her husband's anger, as Battalion Medical Officer, when he first saw the conditions in which the prisoners were living. He expressed his views on the matter in two strongly worded reports to Higher Command, and when they were both ignored he had submitted a third report stating that the treatment to which the men were being subjected was 'inhuman'. Lieutenant-Colonel Deacon, who had seen this before it was despatched, had requested Captain Carney to delete the word 'inhuman', but the Medical Officer had declined to do so.[48]

It must be said that Lance-Corporal Flannery, in his detailed account of the mutiny, makes no complaint about the living conditions in the special camp and does not refer to the prisoners being under canvas. Further, Brigadier-General C. I. Jerrard, who had been a subaltern in another regiment stationed in Jullundur at the time of the mutiny, said later that he never saw a bell-tent used in that part of India during the whole of his service there.[49] However, there is no doubt that the British Army in India was equipped with bell-tents at the time.

The mutineers were told by the officer in charge of the special camp that they would be treated as military prisoners, and that any of them who approached the boundary wire after dusk would risk being shot by the sentries.[50] In accordance with the undertaking given by

Colonel Jackson on the previous Tuesday a pay-parade was held in the camp the day after the mutineers had arrived there. As each man received his money he was given another opportunity to declare his loyalty and to return to Wellington Barracks. 'These persuasions,' said John Flannery, 'met with a fair amount of success.'[51]

An official telegram from the Viceroy to the Secretary of State for India alluded to an episode which occurred at the camp on Saturday, 3 July, when twenty prisoners refused to fall in for morning fatigues. 'A scuffle ensued,' the telegram stated, 'but this was settled without damage on either side. These men were warned of the consequences in the event of their refusing a second time, and they paraded in the evening without incident.'[52] Five prosecution witnesses dealt with the matter in their evidence at the courts martial. The mutineers were paraded at six o'clock that morning and Major Payne, who was acting as Second-in-Command of the Battalion during the absence of Major Alexander at Solon, told them that they were going to be employed that day in building a road through the camp. As the necessary tools had not yet arrived, he said, he was going to dismiss them for the time being, but a fatigue-party would be detailed to take down a marquee which at present was standing on the route the road would follow. Major Payne said in his statement:

> They went off to strike the tent, but they did not do so. This was chiefly due to the fact that the remainder prevented them. I then got a guard of the South Wales Borderers to arrest these men. I tried to get the men whose names were called out to come and do their fatigue. They did not do so and when we tried to get them out, the others prevented them from doing so. I decided I should not fire on these men without referring to higher authority. I reported the matter and Colonel Jackson, G.S.O. 1 16 Division came down and spoke to the men. They asked him, if they went back to do their fatigue, would they come back? He replied, of course they would. They were ordered to do the fatigue that evening, and they did it.[53]

Both Hawes and Flannery have blamed Major Payne for what occurred. They say that included among the twenty men he detailed for the fatigue were most of the recognized leaders of the mutiny, and thinking that this was simply a stratagem to separate them from the others, they refused to fall in as a party. This angered Payne, according to them, and he went off to fetch a squad of armed guards from the South Wales Borderers. Then he marched the mutineers out of the camp to a compound a few hundred yards away, where he drew them up with their backs to a wall and he formed the guard into a single line facing them. Again he ordered the fatigue party to step forward, and when no one moved he sent in some of the guard to drag them out forcibly. A scrimmage ensued with the guards getting the worst of it, and Payne ordered the South Wales Borderers to load their rifles and take aim. Hawes and Flannery go on to say that at that moment an elderly Roman Catholic chaplain, Father Corelli, came running up and stood in front of the mutineers, imploring the guard not to fire. At that moment Colonel Jackson appeared on the scene and stopped Payne from giving the order to fire.[54]

The priest who intervened to save the mutineers was, in fact, the 69-year-old Father Lievin, the Roman Catholic Chaplain at Jullundur. Father Antonio Correya (his name was not Corelli) was a chaplain at Dagshai, some distance away.

After Church Parade the following morning the special camp was evacuated and all the prisoners were moved into a separate part of Wellington Barracks which had been set aside for use as a temporary prison-block.[55]

Chapter 4

THE AFTERMATH

ALTHOUGH THE MUTINY HAD STARTED at Jullundur on Monday, 28 June, it was officially reported to London for the first time on Friday, 2 July in two telegrams sent to the India Office by the Army Department of the Government of India. The first telegram dealt with the events at Wellington Barracks and stated that a temporary censorship was being imposed on all Irish regiments,

> in order to ascertain the character of the correspondence that may be proceeding from Ireland and in order to determine whether the Irish regiments are in communication with each other in India for the purpose of combining against authority.[1]

The second of the telegrams covered the raid of the magazine at Solon and ended with the words 'All is now reported quiet and the detachment has been disarmed'.[2]

The Secretary of State for India at this time was the Hon. Edwin Montagu, second son of Lord Swaythling, who had held the office since June, 1917 and even prior to that had had a close association with Indian political affairs. When he heard of the mutiny, Montagu came to the conclusion that it would be better to issue a frank communiqué about it forthwith, rather than allowing the first accounts to leak out through false or exaggerated rumours. Accordingly, the India Office prepared a communiqué disclosing that some of the Connaught Rangers stationed at Jullundur had refused to work 'as a protest against what they regard as the oppression of their friends in Ireland', and that they had deposited their arms and ammunition in safe custody until detachments of other regiments had arrived at the barracks. The statement also described, briefly but accurately, what had taken place at Solon.

The India Office had informed the War Office about the mutiny immediately they had received the telegrams. As this was a disciplinary matter, it was referred to the Adjutant-General's department where it was handled by Brigadier-General Childs, the Director of Personal Services. There is a minute in the India Office files, written personally by Edwin Montagu and dated 3 July, in which he recorded that he had read his proposed communiqué to a Colonel Fitzpatrick, an officer on Childs's staff. 'After some hesitation,' the minute continues, 'he said he did not think the W.O. would object,' but he considered that the communiqué should not be issued 'unless something first appeared in the newspapers about the outbreak.'[3] During the following day the India Office received another telegram from the Viceroy stating that the press in India had already been told about the mutiny and he had no objection to his earlier telegrams being published. 'There was reason to hope,' he added, '(especially when it is realized that indiscipline will not be tolerated) that the loyal element will predominate amongst the Irish troops in India.'[4] In consequence, the Press communiqué was issued by the India Office on 4 July.

On the morning of 5 July *The Times* published a report on the mutiny from their correspondent in Simla, under the headlines 'Tampering With The Army' and 'Sinn Fein in India'. In his account of the protest at Jullundur, the correspondent commented cynically, 'The men involved represented to the commanding officer that they were no longer able to serve, but they were quite prepared to draw their pay'. He ended by saying:

Although the affair is unpleasant the military authorities are confident and have adopted suitable measures to deal with the situation.[5]

On the same day another newspaper, the name of which cannot be identified, outlined the events which had occurred at Jullundur and went on to say:

The whole affair is regarded as being entirely due to political causes and the Sinn Fein agitation, and it is hoped that the prompt measures already taken by the authorities will prove successful in causing the men to settle down.[6]

It might have been expected that the India Office communiqué would receive a considerable amount of coverage in the Irish newspapers, but this was not so. Only two papers dealt with the matter in any detail, *The Freeman's Journal* and *The Cork Examiner*. *The Freeman's Journal*, under the headline 'Irish Troops Revolt. Connaught Rangers Lay Down Arms', referred to it as 'One of the most sensational events of Irish interest'. The report continued:

> The incidents are the more sensational because of their occurrence in the Punjab, where Amritsar is still unforgotten. No similar incident is recorded in the more recent annals of the British Army.[7]

Nor did the mutiny evoke a great deal of interest in England, despite the fact that it had caused two fatal casualties. At Question Time in the House of Commons on 7 July Edwin Montagu was asked whether he could give any details 'regarding recent occurrences in the Connaught Rangers'. He replied that since the communiqué had been issued the only information he had received from the Government of India was to the effect that 'down to the 4th July nothing further of any importance had occurred'.[8] Another telegram from the Army Department of the Indian Government was, in fact, received by the India Office on 9 July. It contained a more comprehensive account of the mutiny and confirmed that the company stationed at Jutogh had not taken part in it, but had remained 'unquestionably loyal' throughout. The present situation, the telegram stated, was that the Jullundur mutineers, whose numbers were steadily decreasing owing to defections, were being held in custody at Wellington Barracks until accommodation could be provided for them in the military detention barracks at Lucknow, and the necessary steps were being taken to convene a Court of Enquiry into the mutiny before the courts martial took place. There was no sign of trouble in any other Irish regiment in India. The telegram concluded:

> We have every reason to believe that the whole affair was engineered by Sinn Fein. Large Sinn Fein flags were hoisted in barracks when the mutiny first broke out at Jullundur. These flags were apparently not made in India. Sinn Fein colours and rosettes were also worn. The source of the trouble is clearly indicated by the fact that out of 206 men comprising the last two drafts out from Home, 172 were mutineers at Jullundur.[9]

The Times published a four-paragraph report from their Simla correspondent on 13 July, in which he repeated the allegation that the mutiny had been instigated by Sinn Fein agitators in Ireland. 'A remarkable feature of the affair,' he wrote, 'was the respectful demeanour of the mutineers at Jullundur, who intimated that they would join in suppressing any disorders that might arise outside their own regiment.' The ringleaders of the incidents at Jullundur and at Solon were now awaiting trial by court martial: 'The question of dealing with the remainder is under consideration'.[10]

No time was wasted in setting up the Court of Enquiry into the mutiny, for another telegram from India on 15 July mentioned that it had already commenced its proceedings. This telegram also revealed that the military authorities had changed their minds about censoring the mail of Irish units as they had come to the conclusion that such a course would be inadvisable. Instead, they had appealed to the loyalty and good sense of the men not to pay attention to seditious communications, and had reminded them that 'It is the duty of all British soldiers in these days when seditionists are preaching class hatred and Bolshevism to set an example of strict discipline and unity'. The report prepared by the Court of Enquiry has not been preserved, but an indication of its nature can be gleaned from a telegram sent by the Indian Government to the Secretary of State for India on 21 July, which stated:

> Court of Enquiry at Jullundur has concluded proceedings and its findings are as follows:- The outbreak was a pre-arranged and organized movement. Cause was undoubtedly Sinn Feinism. General Commanding 16th Indian Division concurs in conclusions of the court and recommends that 87 ringleaders be tried by General Court Martial. We will inform you of further progress in matter.[11]

It is apparent that every effort had been made to persuade the Jullundur mutineers to come over to the growing number of loyalists in the Battalion. Joseph Hawes has told how two Irish priests visited Wellington Barracks on Monday, 5 July to talk to the mutineers' committee. In a long, and sometimes heated, discussion, said Hawes, the priests urged them to abandon the mutiny and to escape the consequences of their actions. The breaking of the Oaths of Allegiance was a military crime which could be punished with death and, what was more, it was sinful in the eyes of the Roman Catholic Church. The priests stated their intention of coming back at noon on the following day to find out how many of the men were willing to take their advice. Both Hawes and Flannery have put forward rival claims to have exercised the moral leadership of the Jullundur mutineers at this stage. Hawes alleges that the two Irish priests considered him to be 'a stumbling block to their efforts' on behalf of the authorities, and they attempted to engineer his expulsion from the committee. After they had left, Hawes continues, he said to his old comrades Gogarty, Lally and Sweeney, that the others could join the loyalists if they wished, but he himself was going to stick it out to the bitter end, 'come what may'. According to Hawes, his views prevailed among the rest of the prisoners and when the priests came back the following day they were told that the mutiny was going to continue.[12]

In the series of articles he wrote for the *Irish Weekly Independent* in 1925 under the pseudonym 'One Who Knows', John Flannery did not mention the visit of the Irish priests, which is odd as he professed to have been the unofficial chairman of the mutineers' committee. Perhaps he omitted the incident from his account out of deference to the religious sensibilities of his readers. However, Hawes and Flannery both mention an occurrence two days later, on Wednesday, 7 July, although they differ on some of the actual details. Early that morning, before the sounding of reveille, a large party of Seaforth Highlanders entered the bungalow in which the mutineers were sleeping and ordered them to leave their beds and to fall in outside. Flannery says that these troops were carrying 'entrenching tool handles and other implements', whereas Hawes asserts that some of them had rifles with bayonets fixed, while others were armed with truncheons. When the prisoners were all outside, the officer in charge of the Seaforths told them he was going to call out forty-eight names and he wanted the men he named to fall in separately, five paces in front of the rest. It soon became obvious that the people he was selecting were all the recognized militants and the leaders of the mutiny. Immediately the forty-eight were in position a number of Seaforth Highlanders moved in quickly behind them, forming a line to divide them from the main body of the mutineers. Although it was now clear that the activists were going to be taken away, said Hawes, there was no disorder as they all realized that 'resistance would be useless'. John Flannery, referring to himself in the third person and, as always, stressing the prominent role he played in the matter, wrote as follows:

> For a few moments it looked as if there was going to be trouble. Lance-Corporal Flannery, who was amongst those whose names had been called out, shouted to the main body to control themselves, and let matters take their course. He pointed out to them that they were outwitted, and that it would be useless to offer any resistance, and concluded by telling them to carry on according to the instructions they had received.[13]

The forty-eight were taken away in lorries to an open compound surrounded by a high brick wall. After spending two uncomfortable days there they were marched back to Wellington Barracks and locked up in the Guard Room cells.[14]

In one of his articles in the *Sunday Independent* John Flannery described how, on 10 July, he was taken before 'a board of officers', presumably the Court of Enquiry which had started sitting around this time. In view of the allegations of treachery made later against him by Joseph Hawes and others, Flannery's account of what happened is interesting. The President of the Board, he says, explained to him that they were trying 'to get to the bottom of the cause of the mutiny' and they wanted him to help them. Flannery claims to have replied that he knew nothing at all about it, and to have persisted in declaring his ignorance in spite of their continued interrogation.[15]

As the days passed, says Flannery, the resolve among the mutineers was weakening 'and several were voicing opinions that the best thing they could do was to return to duty'.[16] A final attempt was made by the authorities on 12 July to persuade the prisoners at Jullundur to defect from the mutiny. Joseph Hawes, John Flannery and Tom Tierney have given slightly different accounts of what occurred. Apparently Major Payne, the acting Second-in-Command at Wellington Barracks, paraded all the mutineers who had been left behind when the forty-eight militants were taken away, and offered them a last chance to fall in separately if they wished to join the battalion loyalists. Tierney's recollection is that Payne read out a proclamation signed by the Viceroy promising a free pardon to all the men who availed themselves of this opportunity. Flannery and Tierney agree that the effect of Payne's words was dramatic. Flannery wrote:

> After a few minutes two or three men fell in and gradually others followed suit in threes and fours. Then a large body went over and fell in, until eventually the only man left was Lance-Corporal Willis and a few followers.[17]

Tierney says that there was a 'stampede' to fall in with the defectors and that only a very small bunch of men remained where they stood.[18]

Joseph Hawes, who was writing with the primary intention of glorifying the mutiny, admitted that a number of men had 'ratted' after Payne had spoken – he refers to them contemptuously as falling in 'like a flock of sheep'. However, in Hawes's version of events, the situation is redeemed by Lance-Corporal Willis declaming histrionically to Major Payne, 'I would rather die with the men over in the cells, no matter what kind of a death it is, than to fall in under you with this shower of bastards here'.[19]

During the following week the remaining prisoners at Wellington Barracks were taken by train to Dagshai in the Simla Hills, about ten miles from Solon. On arrival, they were all confined in Dagshai Prison, which Hawes described as being a large building surrounded by a narrow compound and a high stone wall. Each prisoner, he said, was put in a separate cell, fitted with a bare plank bed. Although it was called a prison it was in reality a Military Detention Barracks. An official report in 1911 stated that it had accommodation for fifty-three detainees, and added that 'space inside the walls is rather confined and the cells require lighting. No other sanitary defects'.[20] According to Charles Kerrigan the cells were still inadequately lighted in 1920.

The mutineers found the conditions at Dagshai spartan and grim. Many of them complained about the poor quality and the insufficiency of the rations, and the discomfort of sleeping under blankets on the hard boards without a palliasse or mattress. Above all, they found the routine to be tedious and lonely, as they were locked in their cells for twenty-three hours out of the twenty-four, and were only allowed out to exercise in the prison-yard for two half-hour periods every day.[21] Hawes also asserts that they had no soap or towels, and that neither laundry facilities nor clean shirts were ever provided for them.[22] If this is true it was disgraceful, but Hawes is alone in making the allegations, and in view of the Army's habitual insistence on personal hygiene, especially in tropical climates, it is difficult to believe that he was not gilding the lily.

At the beginning of August, soon after the Court of Enquiry had recorded its findings, a Summary of Evidence was taken in respect of the mutiny at Jullundur. The process lasted for the best part of a week, and every day the mutineers were marched, with a large armed escort, to a building outside the prison where they remained while the prosecution witnesses had their statements taken down in long-hand. Flannery has said that there was no cross-examination at this stage.[23]

It had been decided that the location for the courts martial was to be the gymnasium at Dagshai Barracks, and that the same court would deal with all the cases. In view of this, the Solon mutineers were moved from the military detention barracks at Lucknow to join the men from Jullundur in Dagshai Prison. Now that they were all in one place they had opportunities, during periods of association, for discussing their various experiences. Hawes has said that James Daly told him about the abortive raid on the magazine. Daly's account, as remembered by Hawes, was as follows:

That night a rumour spread in the barracks that British troops were coming in the morning to arrest the rebels. At a discussion in the canteen some of the hotter mutineers suggested taking back their arms and fighting the British. Daly, who was teetotaler himself, said 'I have given my word to Father Baker and I won't break it'. Somebody said 'Are you afraid?' This grieved Daly who said, 'Fall in outside and follow me and I will show you I am no coward'. The mutineers obeyed and fell in behind Daly and Daly advanced up the hill towards the magazine. When they reached between twenty and thirty yards of the magazine, which was still on a ledge over them, a sentry's voice rang out, 'Halt, who goes there?' The men halted and Daly stepped forward a pace and said, 'I'm James Joseph Daly of Tyrrellspass, Mullingar, Co. Westmeath, Ireland, and I demand you to lay down your arms and surrender in the name of the Irish Republic'. Immediately Lieutenants Walsh and McSweeney [sic], who were in charge of the guard, opened fire with their service revolvers.[24]

None of the people who were there at the time have said that Daly halted his raiding party when they were challenged, nor that he called upon the guard to surrender in the name of the Irish Republic. It is impossible to know whether or not those details were added by Joseph Hawes as his own embellishments to Daly's story.

It will be recalled that a copy of the Summary of Evidence which was taken for the mutiny at Solon was obtained by the *Longford Leader* (from Private Thomas Devine) and was subsequently serialized by instalments during the early part of 1923.[25] Most of the witnesses who attested for the prosecution were cross-examined by one or more of the accused men, particularly by those they had purported to identify. By far the most serious aspect of the case was the attack on the magazine, and it is clear from their questions that the identified mutineers were hotly disputing that they had taken any part in it. Even James Daly seemed to be preparing for this line of defence. For instance, after Regimental-Quartermaster-Sergeant Stanton had given evidence that he saw Daly leading the final charge, the Summary reads:

Question by No. 35232 Pte. Daly: How did you recognize me that night in the dark?
Answer: You were wearing a light-coloured shirt, open in the front, which was visible as it was a moonlight night.
Question by No. 35232 Pte. Daly: How far away was I when you recognized me?
Answer: About twenty yards.

Again, when Company-Quartermaster-Sergeant Glenn had identified him as being one of the men who took part in the attack, the Summary shows that Daly challenged his evidence:

> Question by No. 35232 Pte. Daly: How did you recognize me in the charge on the magazine?
> Answer: I saw you fall into the R.C. Chaplain's arms, when Pte. Sears was shot.
> Question by No. 35232 Pte. Daly: How could you have seen me at the magazine when Pte. Sears was shot?
> Answer: Because I was about five yards away from you.[26]

On Saturday, 21 August all the mutineers at Dagshai were paraded in the prison yard and it was announced that sixty-nine of them, thirty-nine from Jullundur and thirty from Solon, were going to be tried by a General Court Martial which would begin its proceedings on the following Monday morning. They were told that the charges would be causing or joining in a mutiny, with the alternative charge of being present at a mutiny and not using their utmost endeavours to suppress it. There would also be additional or lesser charges against specific prisoners. Finally, they were informed that if any of them wanted to call a witness, or witnesses, in his defence, he would be enabled to do so.[27]

Although the mutineers were already aware of the sort of evidence which would be called against them, it was inexcusable that they were only given such short notice of the start of the trial. The Rules of Procedure, then set out in the current volume of the Manual of Military Law, provided that every soldier appearing before a court martial must be afforded a proper opportunity for preparing his defence;[28] a bare two days seems to have been grossly inadequate, bearing in mind that mutiny was one of the gravest military offences, and was punishable with a possible sentence of death. It was equally regrettable that not one of the accused mutineers had any outside person to help him put forward his case. It is most unlikely that any of them would have been able to employ a civilian lawyer, but they were all entitled to the assistance of an army officer, referred to in court-martial parlance as a 'prisoner's friend', who would have been able to represent them at every stage of the trial.[29] It was abundantly clear from the questions asked by some of the Solon mutineers at the taking of the Summary of Evidence that they were challenging the credibility of the prosecution witnesses who had identified them as being members of the party attacking the magazine. Most advocates would

47

agree that a successful cross-examination to establish misidentification requires a fair degree of skill and experience.

Sam Pollock, in his book on the Connaught Rangers mutiny, has said that most of the accused men chose to defend themselves because 'They were suspicious of any officer who might be allotted for their defence'.[30] Neither of the chroniclers of the mutiny has mentioned this. Joseph Hawes has offered no explanation for the lack of representation and John Flannery has merely stated:

> The prisoners were not represented by any solicitor and each man conducted his own defence.[31]

Pollock did not give any indication of the source of his information on the point. If the mutineers had had such a profound distrust of the integrity of their own officers, it is rather surprising to find that at the court martial a major and a captain from the battalion were called as character witnesses for the defence.

In any event, there must have been plenty of officers in other units within the division who could have acted in the capacity of prisoners' friends, had they been asked to do so.

Chapter 5

THE DAYS OF RECKONING

ON 18 August, 1920, Northern Command Orders, issued by Major-General Sir George Barrow at Murree, set out the composition of the court which would try the mutineers.[1] The officer detailed to be president was the 55-year-old Major-General Sir Sydney Lawford, shortly to become G.O.C. Lahore District, who had had a distinguished military career and had commanded the 41st Division during the 1914–18 war. His son Peter Lawford was later to become a well-known film actor. There were six other members of the court, three majors and three captains, none of whom was serving in an Irish regiment. Barrow also appointed as Judge Advocate to the court Major H. B. Tucker, the Assistant Judge Advocate-General on Army Headquarters staff in India. Tucker would have had to advise on matters of law and on the conduct of the trials. He may or may not have been legally qualified, as the Rules of Procedure merely required a Judge Advocate to be 'a fit person'.[2] Major O. F. Lloyd, an officer in the 1st Connaught Rangers, was nominated as prosecutor.

The definition of mutiny given in the Manual of Military Law was:

> Mutiny implies collective insubordination, or a combination of two or more persons to resist or to induce others to resist lawful military authority.[3]

It was an offence under Section 7 of the Army Act,[4] which embraced various forms of mutinous behaviour by persons subject to military law, including causing or joining in a mutiny, being present at a mutiny act and not using their utmost endeavours to suppress it, and coming to the knowledge of any actual or intended mutiny and not immediately informing an officer.

It appears from a document in the War Office files that the courts martial of the thirty-nine Jullundur mutineers, which started at Dagshai on 23 August 1920, lasted for eleven days, and that the accused were tried in three separate groups. The thirty mutineers from Solon were all tried together immediately afterwards.[5] Writing about the trials generally, Sam Pollock has said:

> Hawes, Daly, and some of the others of the leaders, refused, as citizens and soldiers of the Irish Republic, to acknowledge the court's jurisdiction at all, but the trial proceeded notwithstanding.[6]

This proposition is, of course, nonsensical, considering that all the mutineers had chosen to enlist in the British Army, most of them during the previous year, and had voluntarily submitted themselves to British military law. Moreover, as far as is known only two of the people who were present at the courts martial have suggested that some of the accused men declined to cooperate. Private John Lynch said in an interview in 1923, 'We refused to recognize the court and merely answered to our names when called. We let them carry on'.[7] According to Joseph Hawes's account, he and fifteen others, including John Flannery, comprised the second batch of prisoners to be tried. Having described the setting in the courtroom, he went on:

> The procedure was that a witness took the stand and was questioned by the Prosecuting Counsel [sic] as to the part any particular mutineer played. When the Prosecuting Counsel finished, the mutineer or mutineers in question could cross-examine the witness if they so wished. Some of our lads cross-examined some of the witnesses, most of us ignored the court altogether.[8]

Flannery only says that all the prisoners pleaded 'not guilty', and each of them conducted his own defence.[9] In the Solon trial all of the mutineers also pleaded 'not guilty'. In fact, James Daly cross-examined eleven out of the fifteen prosecutor's witnesses and called one witness in his defence, although he did not give evidence himself.

The main part of Hawes's brief reference to his own court martial is devoted to his exposure of the devious behaviour of Lance-Corporal Flannery. After the accused had returned to Dagshai Prison on the penultimate day of their trial, said Hawes, Flannery was seen to be busily writing in his cell and when any of the others approached he reacted in a suspicious manner. The following morning all was revealed. When Flannery was asked if he had anything to say in his defence, he handed in a statement, which, after a discussion among the members of the court, was read out loud. Hawes continued:

> In his statement, Flannery claimed that he had only accepted the part of 'spokesman' for the mutineers for the following reasons: firstly, to keep in touch with the leaders of the mutiny so that he could inform the officers of our actions, and secondly, to keep us from doing anything extreme if it came to a showdown; and he also stated that the actions of the original four of us who started the mutiny, particularly Paddy Sweeney, were not the actions of loyal soldiers.

Hawes says the rest of the prisoners were so enraged by Flannery's statement that they tried to attack him, but were driven back by the escort at the point of the bayonet, and that for the remainder of the trial Flannery had to be given special protection.[10]

Several other ex-mutineers have vilified Flannery for his treachery, including Private Joseph Walsh, whose doggerel ballad in praise of the mutiny spurned him in a phrase:

Now here's to the truth and to those youths that upheld Ireland's cause
Success attend you Sweeney, Gogarty, Lally and that gallant Josie Hawes,
Who always held Ireland's cause at heart as we could plainly see,
For it they were betrayed in Dagshai by the informer Flannery.[11]

Of the thirty-nine Jullundur mutineers thirty-three were convicted, one sergeant, four corporals, eleven lance-corporals and seventeen privates; six were acquitted, a sergeant, a corporal, three lance-corporals and a private.[12] The accused who were found not guilty would have been informed of the verdicts forthwith. On the other hand, in the cases where the court had decided to convict, the President would not have announced any findings, but would merely have asked for evidence as to character, and then invited the prisoners to make pleas in mitigation of sentence if they wished to do so. The reason for this was that, except when there had been an acquittal, neither the verdict nor the sentence of the court was valid until it had been confirmed by proper confirming authority.[13] After hearing the pleas in mitigation, the President would have declared that the proceedings in open court were terminated, and the members of the court would have returned to consider the sentences they should pass. In general, if there was a difference of opinion, the view of the majority would prevail; in the case of an equality of votes on the sentence, the President was allowed a second or casting vote.[14] However, sentence of death could not be passed on an accused person without the concurrence of at least two-thirds of the members of the court.[15]

The sentences passed on the Jullundur mutineers were draconian in the extreme, considering that there had been no violence whatsoever at Wellington Barracks during the incidents which took place there. Five of the accused were condemned to death, including Joseph Hawes and John Flannery. Others received long terms of penal servitude; two for life, two for 20 years, one for 15 years, six for 10 years, four for 5 years and one for 3 years. The rest were awarded either 2 years' or 1 year's imprisonment with hard labour. All were discharged with ignominy and every NCO was reduced to the ranks.[16] It is difficult to account for the discrepancies between some of the sentences. Each of the three men who had joined with Hawes in surrendering themselves at the guardroom on the first morning of the mutiny was dealt with in a different manner. Gogarty was condemned to death, while the other two were given terms of penal servitude, Sweeney for life and Lally for 20 years. Moran, who had followed their example in refusing to perform his duties, received a death sentence. Lance-Corporal Keenan and Private Kelly, who had travelled to Solon to foment the spread of insurgency, were both sentenced to 10 years' penal servitude, yet by any standards they were among the most culpable of all the Jullundur mutineers.

As soon as the President of the court had asked the prosecuting officer for details of the character of any of the accused, the man in question would have known he had been convicted, but when he was returned to Dagshai prison at the end of his trial he would still have been totally unaware of the nature of his sentence. Up to the closing months of the First World War a soldier who had been convicted by court martial of a capital offence did not know until the moment of promulgation, usually about two weeks later, whether or not he had been condemned to death. In May, 1919, however, a new procedure was introduced throughout the British Army whereby if the court had imposed a sentence of death the accused was immediately informed of the fact so that he could prepare himself for the terrible possibility of the firing squad.[17] The method adopted was for him to be handed a confidential letter at the end of his trial, which informed him that he had been sentenced to death, but that this might be revised by higher authority.[18]

Very soon after the Jullundur mutineers had arrived back at the prison after the conclusion of their cases, Lieutenant Smyth, who had been put in charge of them, visited each of the men who had been given a death sentence, accompanied by a sergeant. Hawes has written:

> He came to my cell and handed me an envelope, stamped O. H. M. S., and said, 'I'm sorry, Hawes, to be handing you this'. He also handed one to Gogarty, Moran and Delaney with a similar remark. The envelopes contained our death sentences. We found out later that the same 'postman' had visited Lance-Corporal Flannery in his cell outside the gates. From this on, the death sentence prisoners in the jail were segregated from the other prisoners, each man separately received about a half-hour's exercise under escort in the jail yard.[19]

John Flannery was now being kept in the Guard Room for his own safety. He does not mention this in his account of the mutiny and neither does he refer to the cause of his unpopularity. He merely states that the five of them received the notifications that they had been condemned to death, and adds that there was no recommendation for mercy.[20]

On 4 September, a Saturday, the court began the trial of the Solon mutineers. The evidence against many of them was strong: against others it was almost irrefutable. Men like James Daly, who had made himself so obvious throughout, and Eugene Egan, who had been wounded in the final charge on the magazine, would have been well advised, in their own interests, to have pleaded 'guilty' and to have expressed regret at the tragic outcome of the events. Instead, they joined the rest in challenging all the witnesses who had identified them as taking part in any stage of the mutiny. Understandably enough, most of the cross-examinations were ineffective and often served to make the evidence even more damning. At the close of the prosecution case, in accordance with the authorized court martial procedure, the Judge Advocate asked each of the accused in turn if he wished to give evidence on his own behalf, and if he intended to call any witnesses. All except James Daly and three others elected to testify on oath, and twelve of them said that they wished to call one or more witnesses for their defence.

The twenty-six accused men who gave evidence denied that they had taken any part in the mutiny and no one admitted that he had worn a Sinn Fein badge during the course of the outbreak. Certain of them were to tell a completely different story in press and radio interviews in later years when they spoke with pride of the prominent part they had played as mutineers. With regard to the initial incident at Solon, the march to the Officers' Mess on the evening of 30 June, they claimed in their defence either that they were not there or that they had gone along in all innocence thinking it was a legitimate parade ordered by Captain Badham. Two men said they had drunk so much in the canteen that they did not know what they were doing. Some of the accused maintained that they had been told nothing about the special parades called by Major Alexander and Colonel Wooldridge on the morning of 1 July, or about the instructions given by these two officers that troops wishing to remain loyal should fall in separately. Others said that, although they were present, they were too frightened to demonstrate their loyalty as nobody else took the lead in doing so. The raid on the magazine had had nothing to do with any of them. They all asserted that they were elsewhere when it took place, either out for a walk, in their bungalows or in bed, except for Privates Cherry and Devine who stated that they had only accompanied the raiding party to try to persuade them to turn back. According to Egan's evidence he had just been coming from the canteen when he had been hit in the shoulder by a stray bullet.

Several of the accused, either in their statements or under cross-examination, emphasized their opposition to the mutiny. Egan and McGrath insisted that they had remained loyal throughout. William Daly said he had wanted nothing to do with the mutineers, and Corporal Kelly, Lance-Corporal Hewson and Private Loftus claimed to have admonished them for what they were doing. Private Gorman went further. He told the court that he had done his best to suppress the mutiny single-handed.

Most of the witnesses called by the mutineers had testified as to their previous good character or supported their alibis on the evening of the raid. The one witness called by James Daly was, strangely enough, Lance-Corporal Nolan, the man he had sentenced to death. Daly was obviously at pains to obviate the natural inference that Nolan's trial had been connected with the mutiny, just because it had taken place a short while before the attack on the magazine. In fact, Lance-Corporal Franklin, who had given evidence about the matter for the prosecution, had made it clear that he had only entered the canteen when Daly, standing on a table, was pronouncing the death sentence, and that he had had no idea what it was all about. If Daly had been represented by a professional advocate there would undoubtedly have been an objection to this evidence being given at all. It was clearly irrelevant to the charges on which Daly was being tried and might have been extremely prejudicial as tending to show him a man with a dominating and a ruthless temperament. It is surprising that the Judge Advocate did not confine the evidence of Lance-Corporal Franklin to the fact that he had seen a meeting taking place in the canteen at which a number of the accused were present. As it was, Nolan most probably did Daly's case more harm than good. He said that Daly had entered the canteen that evening and had announced that when the men drew their pay on the following day they were not to salute the officer taking the parade. Then he had begun a 'barrack-room trial' of Nolan for calling some woman 'a common prostitute' because she had offered to give evidence on behalf of a private on some charge which, presumably, had nothing to do with the mutiny. Nolan told the court that he had not been allowed to defend himself against the accusation and that James Daly, the self-appointed judge and prosecutor, had sentenced him to be shot. Lance-Corporal Nolan can have had no reason for liking Daly, and the danger of calling him as a defence witness was apparent at the end of his evidence when he added that soon after his 'trial' the men from the canteen had fallen in under the command of Daly, who had led them away in the direction of the magazine.

The court convicted twenty-eight of the Solon accused and acquitted two. The only evidence against Private McConnell, one of the men acquitted, was that he had stood fast when Major Alexander had ordered the troops who wished to remain loyal to fall in separately. He had, very wisely, declined to give any evidence in his own defence. Private Loftus, the other acquitted man, had been seen wearing a Sinn Fein rosette on the morning of 1 July, and in the evening he had been noticed loitering in the vicinity of the Officers' Mess immediately after the attack on the magazine. Nine mutineers were condemned to death, of whom eight, including Daly and Egan, had been identified as members of the raiding party, and the ninth had taken part in breaking open the rifle-racks in the bungalows. The remaining nineteen accused were sentenced to penal servitude, three for life, three for 15 years, five for 10 years, two for 7 years, two for 5 years and four for 3 years. They were also discharged with ignominy and the NCOs were reduced to the ranks.[21]

The nine men sentenced to death at the Solon court martial were handed their O. H. M. S. envelope by Lieutenant Smyth soon after the trial had ended. They were then moved into cells near those of the condemned Jullundur mutineers. Charles Kerrigan, who had himself received a death sentence, has said that the conditions at Dagshai were good while they were awaiting the moment of promulgation,[22] but Hawes found that the days dragged and he grew weary of prison routine.[23] It must have been a time of considerable tension and anxiety, especially for those who were uncertain whether or not they would have to face a firing squad. John Flannery has written:

> A rumour went round that they would not get any notification of the date of their execution until the firing party would bring them out, and each morning when the condemned men heard the tramp of feet on the stones outside the prison as the sentries were being changed, the first thought that flashed into their minds was that their time had come.[24]

It took about a month for the confirming authority to complete their task. Probably they had no trouble in ratifying the convictions, as they would only have reversed the findings if there had been any serious irregularity in the conduct of the courts martial, but some of the sentences might well have caused them considerable misgivings. Early in October, according to John Flannery, the mutineers were paraded in the prison yard before an officer from the Divisional Staff who told them he was there to read out their sentences now that they had been confirmed by the Commander-in-Chief. First of all, he directed the men under sentence of death to fall in on one side and he informed them that thirteen of their sentences had been commuted to penal servitude for life. Flannery continued:

> Turning to one other – Private Daly of the Solon party – he said, 'I am very sorry, Daly, but your sentence has been confirmed and you are to be shot at daybreak on Tuesday, November the 2nd.'
>   Daly replied, 'It is all right, Sir. I am not afraid and I am proud to die for Ireland, but I am glad my comrades have been spared.'[25]

Flannery's recollection was slightly at fault regarding the commuted death sentence; twelve of them were, in fact, altered to penal servitude for life, and one to penal servitude for 20 years.

The Staff Officer then addressed the mutineers who had been sentenced by the court to penal servitude or imprisonment with hard labour. The confirming authority had decided to reduce twenty-one of their sentences, he said, and to leave twenty-six unaltered. Most of those which were cut down were long terms of penal servitude. The reductions in rank and the ignominious discharges were confirmed in every case.[26]

There is not a scintilla of evidential support for the allegation which has sometimes been made that the authorities exerted pressure on the court to punish the mutineers with the utmost severity. The documents now available show that the War Office made no attempt to interfere with the proceedings either before or after the start of the trials, and if the supposed persuasion had emanated from the High Command in India it is rather surprising that General Sir Charles Munro, the Commander-in-Chief, should have reduced more than half the sentences in the process of confirmation. Had the Government at Westminster wished to exercise any influence they would have done it through Edwin Montagu, the Secretary of State for India. Montagu, however, seems to have been a passive spectator of the events, for he received a private letter from Lord Chelmsford dated 19 October, 1920, in the course of which the Viceroy wrote:

> You have been informed that a Court-Martial has been sitting on those Connaught Rangers who were guilty of mutiny six months back. Nine men [sic] were sentenced by the Court-Martial to death. In the case of eight, this sentence has been commuted, but as regards the ninth, both the Commander-in-Chief and I felt that no course was open to us but to confirm the sentence and the wretched man will be shot. There was no doubt on the proceedings that the man in question was the ringleader in the whole affair, and as this mutiny led – apart from the fact that that mutiny is the most heinous offence that a soldier can commit – also to the death of the two men who were shot dead by the guard at Solon, I feel sure that you will admit that the sentence was well-merited. We should find ourselves in a position of great difficulty in the future with regard to Indian troops in similar circumstances if, in the case of British soldiers, we did not enforce the supreme penalty where conditions justified it. You will, of course, be informed officially of the Court-Martial sentences and the carrying out of the death penalty.[27]

On 25 October, six days after Lord Chelmsford had written his letter, the official notification was sent to the India Office in a telegram from the Army Department of the Government of India.

> The following are the sentences awarded by the Court Martial on the ringleaders of the Connaught Rangers at Jullundur: 14 death sentences, of which one was confirmed (the sentence will be carried out on the 2nd November 1920), 12 were commuted to penal servitude for 20 years. Of the remainder of the mutineers, the sentences vary from imprisonment for one year to penal servitude for 20 years. 62 ringleaders were convicted out of 69 who were tried.[28]

This short telegram contained no less than three important factual errors. The Army Department sent another telegram to the India Office a week later explaining the reasons for Daly's execution:

> Reprieve was not entertained in one case only, as the prisoner was the ringleader throughout and maintained a spirit of flagrant defiance for more than 24 hours; in fact until he was arrested. It should be realized by you that in this case the interests of Ireland have not only to be appraised, but also the possibility of maintaining future discipline in the Indian Army. The Commander-in-Chief is of opinion that if condonation is practised, the example of mutiny set in this case by a British Regiment cannot fail to react with disastrous results on the Indian Army.[29]

Chapter 6

PRELUDE TO MARTYRDOM

THE COMMANDER-IN-CHIEF IN INDIA had a large measure of autonomy from the direct control of the War Office in London, and he was authorized by the Army Act to confirm the findings and the sentences of General Courts Martial, even when they had imposed the penalty of death.[1] It was only if a soldier had been condemned to death for treason or for murder, which were two civil offences, that the approval of the Viceroy was required before he was executed.[2]

As soon as the War Office had been notified of the confirmation of Private Daly's sentence they sent a telegram to Simla drawing the attention of the Commander-in-Chief to an executive order, issued shortly after the Armistice, to the effect that no military death sentence was to be carried out 'without reference to the War Office'. Further, they enquired whether the Viceroy had granted his approval for Daly's execution. The executive order in question was only concerned with sentences of death imposed by courts martial in the field and was not applicable to British troops who were serving in India, but without arguing about the matter the Army Department of the Indian Government sent a telegram in reply stating that the Viceroy had already agreed to Daly's execution being carried out.[3]

After the decision of the court had been promulgated, all the convicted mutineers, including James Daly, had been allowed to start taking their daily exercise periods together in the prison yard. They had been told that the men sentenced to penal servitude and imprisonment with hard labour would be sent back to England as soon as the necessary arrangements could be made.[4] John Flannery was now returned to his cell in the part of the prison where the rest of them were confined, but when he had been back for only one night Hawes protested so vehemently to Lieutenant Smyth that he was moved away again, probably back to the prison Guard Room.[5]

Towards the end of October Daly was taken under escort to the neighbouring Dagshai Barracks, and on the evening of 1 November he was transferred to the prison Guard Room, outside and adjacent to the main gates.[6] There have been various accounts of Daly's final hours before his execution, but the only one on which any reliance can be placed was written by Father Baker, the priest who had tried so hard to restrain the violence during the mutiny at Solon. The others are impregnated to such an extent with hearsay, fiction and fable that they are completely lacking in credibility.

Father Baker had been asked by the Roman Catholic chaplain at Dagshai to minister to James Daly and to prepare him to meet his death for the last two days before his execution. When Daly was moved to the prison Guard Room on 1 November he was very anxious to be visited by some of his friends who were so close to hand but he was told that this would be contrary to regulations. Father Baker contacted Colonel Deacon, the Commanding Officer of the Battalion, and asked him to permit a visit to take place, promising that he would be present himself and would ensure that nothing unlawful occurred. Deacon agreed to send a telegram to the Adjutant-General at Simla requesting that in the circumstances this particular regulation should be waived. Although the application was granted, the necessary message was never transmitted from Simla to Dagshai owing to a breakdown in communications.[7] John Flannery confirms that none of the mutineers were allowed to visit Daly in the Guard Room before his execution,[8] and Joseph Hawes, who had become one of Daly's closest friends during the time they were together at Dagshai, makes no mention of seeing him for a farewell meeting.[9]

James Daly faced up to his ordeal with considerable courage. The day before his execution he received Holy Communion in his cell and made his final Confession to Father Baker. It is very likely that the priest also helped him to compose his last letter home, a copy of which, seemingly accurate, was published in the *Westmeath Examiner* on 19 February, 1921.

My address is in Heaven along with John – and God.

My dearest mother,
I take this opportunity to let you know the dreadful news that I am to be shot on Tuesday morning, 2nd November. But what harm: it is all for Ireland. I am not afraid to die; it is only thinking of you. If you will be happy on earth, I will be happy in Heaven. I am ready to meet my doom. The priest is with me when needed, so you need have no worry

about me, as I am going to my dearest home, Heaven. But I wish to the Lord that I had not started on getting into this trouble at all. I would have been better off. But it is done now and I have to suffer. Out of sixty-two of us, I am the only one to be put out of this world. I am ready now to meet it. God bless you all. Hoping to see you all some day in Heaven. I hope, dearest mother, you won't be terribly put about, but will keep a stout heart. I know it is hard on you, but what can be done. [The *Westmeath Examiner* says that the letter then inquires for Daly's father and other members of his family and friends.] The priest will send my letters home all right. This is the last letter you will get from me. [He then asks God's blessing on his mother and father and all at home.] I hope you will get a Mass said for the happy repose of your fond son Jim, taken from you for the sake of his country. God bless Ireland, and also, you all at home. From your fond son, Jim.[10]

A number of edited versions of the letter have been published at various times, usually omitting the two sentences in which Daly expressed regret for his involvement in the mutiny.

The shooting was to be carried out at dawn on 2 November in the yard at the rear of the prison by a firing-party from the 2nd Battalion of the Royal Fusiliers, which was posted to Aden immediately after the execution to keep the men out of contact with soldiers from any Irish regiments. The officer in charge of the firing-party was probably Lieutenant-Colonel S. G. R. Willis, DSO, of the Royal Field Artillery, or Lieutenant-Colonel Willis of the Devon Regiment. Another possibility is that it was Major R. R. Willis, VC, of the 2nd Battalion of the Lancashire Fusiliers.

Two long tables were set up in front of one of the outer walls, and loaded with sandbags on which the Fusiliers could rest their rifles when they took aim. Between the tables and the prison wall a wooden chair with armrests was placed, ready for the condemned man, and held in position by heavy weights attached to the legs.

Father Baker was with James Daly from the start of the final ritual. He wrote:

At 5.30 a.m. I went into the cell and there I spoke and prayed with him for a short while. He was very calm and resigned and well-prepared. Nearing six o'clock everything was in readiness, and the colonel commanding ordered the prisoner to be brought out. I put on my surplice and stole and had the holy oils ready in my vest pocket. The cell door was opened. There stood Daly, pale, somewhat thin and unwashed, and his clothes so old and dirty. He had on a pair of army boots unpolished, a khaki coat and trousers, a warm jersey below the coat and another thinner jersey below this, all of which had not had a wash since the 2nd of July previous when he was taken. At least this is what I was told, and it looked like it. A prison warder with loaded rifle and fixed bayonet supported him on either side. For some moments we stood on the verandah and then the order was given to proceed.[11]

In a letter he wrote to the *Irish Bulletin* in February, 1921, Private Joseph Walsh asserted that Daly had been offered an injection of morphine before being led out to the prison yard, but that he had refused it. Walsh was one of the Jullundur mutineers who had become a close friend of both James Daly and Joseph Hawes. While they had been all confined at Dagshai before the courts martial Walsh composed a doggerel ballad about the mutiny which was set to music and featured in a radio programme years later. It is now known that morphine injections had occasionally been given to condemned soldiers a short while before they were executed. There is a recorded example of a deserter being doped with '2/3 gms of morphia' prior to being shot at dawn in June, 1915.[12] This was not the only time it happened, as Captain Lawrence Gameson of the Royal Army Medical Corps has recounted his experiences as the doctor on duty when two private soldiers were executed for murder at Lille in 1919. Gameson was instructed by the Provost Marshal that during the preliminaries he must give each of the prisoners a heavy dose of morphia, but they must still be capable of walking to the place where they would be shot, for under no circumstances could they be carried there.[13]

After they had left the Guard Room, Father Baker continued:

I took my place behind Daly, the provost sergeant with several others followed behind, and then came a few officers, and finally the colonel. We passed through the prison gate and turned sharply to the left. Having gone a few paces we were told to halt. The provost sergeant produced a long, black serge bag and attempted to put it over Daly's head. But he shook it off, saying, 'I don't want this, I will die like an Irishman'. There was a commotion among the attendants. Seeing that a scuffle was likely to ensue, I quietly waved the men aside and coaxed Daly to put on the bag, both for his own sake and for the sake of the firing party. Before doing so he begged permission to see some of his friends . . . I looked back at the Colonel and saw from his face that he did not mean to give permission. It was so distressing to tell Daly this. However, he accepted the refusal in a Christian spirit, and the procession moved on again.[14]

Until the first publication of Father Baker's journal the only descriptions of Daly's execution were derived from the reports given by Joseph Hawes and several other mutineers who had been at Dagshai at the time. Hawes claimed that the window of his cell afforded him a clear view of the prison yard;[15] and both Stephen Lally[16] and Valentine Delaney[17] said they had managed to see what was taking place there. Whereas Patrick Hynes maintained that none of the other prisoners ever set eyes on Daly again after he was moved to Dagshai Barracks,[18] Charles Kerrigan thought that the yard was indeed visible from the back portion of the prison,[19] and James Gorman recollects that some of the mutineers watched the execution through small, high windows in their cells, standing on the ends of their bedsteads to do so.[20]

However much Joseph Hawes saw or did not see, there can be little doubt that his description of the execution, written in 1949, was embellished by his customary brand of meretricious embroidery. He says that the procession marched into the yard led by Lieutenant Smyth and Father Baker. They were followed by a squad of about ten soldiers escorting James Daly, who had been blindfolded and was wearing his regimental uniform with a green handkerchief tied loosely round his neck. In spite of his terrible plight, Hawes adds, Daly had surprised his guards by appearing that morning 'washed, shaved and cleaned up generally'. When they had reached the execution-chair and halted, Daly pulled the bandage from his eyes and trampled it underfoot. He refused the order to sit down, exclaiming, 'When I'm shot I want to be shot like an Irishman and fall to the ground'. Eventually he was persuaded to be seated by Father Baker and, turning to the firing squad, lined up ready to perform their awesome duty, Daly said to them:

You men don't know my mind. You might think I'm afraid to die, I'm not, and some day the men in the cells over there may be free, and you might meet them somewhere and say I died a coward. But there is one thing you will never be able to say, unless you tell lies – that you ever put a bullet through Daly's shirt.

With that, according to Hawes, Daly took off his tunic and singlet so that he was only wearing his shorts, boots and puttees, and the green handkerchief still wound round his neck. Having divested himself of these garments he sat back, folded his arms across his chest and told the firing squad he was ready. At this moment the signal was given to the firing squad, the volley rang out, and Daly fell sideways in the weighted chair.[21]

Valentine Delaney added several emotive details to the description given by Hawes. Just after Daly sat down in the chair, said Delaney, 'He looked up in his last moments to the windows of our cells and kissed us goodbye, and we returned the salute.' Delaney also heard Daly's final words before he was shot, 'Goodbye, Mother. We will meet in Heaven. God save Ireland'.

In his description of these grim events Father Baker said that the procession moved into the yard and Daly, who had the black serge bag over his head, was guided to the weighted chair:

When he touched the chair with his leg he said: 'Is this where they are going to shoot me?' and again took off the bag and had a look around and up at the cell windows. There was a rush at him, but I motioned the men off and urged Daly to comply with the regulations. He replied: 'It's all right, Father, I only wanted to have a look around'. Letting me put on the bag, he again pleaded to let at least one of his friends, Private Joseph Hawes, see him. I knew that this would never be granted at such a time, so I begged him to accept the disappointment as a great sacrifice, and to tell me what he wanted to say to Hawes, and I would do so under great secrecy. He said nothing, but his head fell on my shoulder, and, for the first time, he gave way. It was all so heartrending. I then said a few prayers with him, gave him Absolution, and commended his soul to God, upon which, he rejoined: 'May the good God receive my soul!'

He then, without a word, took from his pocket the farewell letter which the other prisoners wrote to him the day before, and which the prison officers were kind enough to have delivered to him. He also took out a couple of cigarettes, a few annas in silver and nickel, and his green silk handkerchief – the token of his leadership. I then happily thought of the scapular of the Sacred Heart which the men had given me the evening before to give to him. I pinned this on his coat over his heart and said the prayer, 'Jesus, Mary and Joseph, I give you my heart and my soul'. I then made room for the medical officer who was showing signs of impatience. However, when the provost sergeant came with a rope to tie him down to the weighted chair, Daly, feeling the rope on his body, said fiercely, 'I will not be tied down'. I said: 'All right', and sent the man away.

The medical officer then came forward and seeing the rosary beads and scapular on Daly, touching them, looked at me as if to say 'take these off'. I said they would not interfere, and so he let them alone. Producing a small white paper target, he pinned it right over the heart and moved aside. The officer in charge of the firing-party then motioned to me and I stationed myself just outside the firing-party with my eyes fixed on this officer. As he let fall a handkerchief the volley was fired, and the bullets found a mark in Daly's heart and passed out of his body with a great spurt of blood. I immediately dashed forward and snatched the bag from his head and anointed him on the forehead. His body leaned a little to the left, his shoulder-blade caught in a corner of the chair, and thus he remained sitting.[22]

In the 'awful' silence which followed the shooting, continued Father Baker, he repeated the prayers for the dead. When he had finished the Medical Officer went up to Daly, felt his pulse, and formally reported to the Colonel that life was extinct. Some prison warders then fetched a coffin from a nearby shed and placed the body into it. Before the lid was screwed down the Medical Officer again tested the dead man's pulse. Finally, the coffin was loaded on to a hearse and taken to the Dagshai cemetery for burial.[23]

Private Daly's death certificate gives his age as 21 years and 6 months, although the court martial records a little less than eight weeks previously had shown him as then being 20 years and 11 months. The cause of death is stated as 'Gunshot wound (sentenced by General Court Martial)'.[24]

A macabre postscript to the morning's events at Dagshai prison has been added by Joseph Hawes. In his account of the mutiny he says that half an hour after the execution Lieutenant Smyth came to his cell to give him Daly's rosary beads and his last message written on the back of an envelope. Before leaving, Smyth told him, 'I have a very hard ordeal for you now, but I know you and your comrades would not like my men to do it'. He went on to order Hawes to take some of his companions into the yard and to clean up Daly's blood from the place where he had been shot. Hawes says that he collected some of his friends and they set to work. He continues:

Jim's blood was in a congealed mess on the ground. He had been hit by thirteen bullets, so he was almost cut in two. There were bits of his flesh and even fragments of bone stuck on the wall. We gathered everything into two small boxes made from timber and gave them to the lieutenant who stated he would see they would be handed to Father Baker to be interred in Jim's grave.[25]

Charles Kerrigan was asked about this incident in an interview in 1987 and he replied that it had never happened. He also said it was untrue that Daly had been almost cut in two by the fatal volley. Even without Kerrigan's refutation, anyone who has the slightest experience of the effects of rifle fire would recognize the absurdity of the suggestion that thirteen bullets fired at short range and aimed at a man's heart could partially sever the top from the lower part of his body.

On 4 November the Viceroy sent a telegram to Edwin Montagu, the Secretary of State for India, informing him that the death sentence on Private Daly had been carried out, and he went on to say, 'The Commander-in-Chief is considering the question of remission of a portion of the sentences in the case of the remaining mutineers who have been convicted. Before taking action I should be glad to have the views of the War Office, as the release of these men may have political consequences'.[26] This query seems to have met with no response as a similarly-worded telegram was sent to Montagu on 12 November.[27] The India Office did not, apparently, consider that this was a matter of pressing urgency as it was not until 24 November that they wrote to the War Office to consult them about it.[28]

A short while after James Daly's execution Montagu sent a querulous letter to Winston Churchill, the Secretary of State for War, which exemplified the dichotomy of control which existed between the India Office and the War Office over soldiers of the British Army serving in India.

Montagu wrote to Churchill on 22 November, 1920:

My Dear Winston,

I must call your attention to a very serious state of affairs which fortunately has passed off without trouble, but which might have led to very great difficulties. I refer to the carrying out of the Court Martial sentence of death on one of the Connaught Rangers in India.

The Commander-in-Chief reported to me, through the Viceroy, in the ordinary constitutional way, his intention of carrying out this sentence. I did not interfere. I might have interfered. I might have thought it expedient, after consultation with my Military Advisers and my Council, to order a postponement or a mitigation; or, what is much more likely, to assure myself that certain aspects of the case had been taken into consideration.

I heard from you privately in casual conversation, that the Commander-in-Chief had reported this sentence also, direct to the War Office. This is surely most unfortunate, for it might well have been that you issued one set of orders direct to the Commander-in-Chief while I issued others.

Edwin Montagu went on to a further complaint. He said that he had applied to the War Office to see the telegrams which had passed between Churchill and the Commander-in-Chief but his request had been refused 'on the ground that they were Secretary of State's telegrams'. He concluded his letter with the comment that they would have to discuss with Lord Curzon, the Foreign Secretary, the whole matter of direct communication between the Commander-in-Chief in India and the War Office as the present situation 'will not do'.[29]

Churchill replied on 23 November.

> My Dear Edwin,
> I will gladly discuss the question of communication between the Commander-in-Chief in India and the War Office. But in the meantime I must mention ... that if you had asked me or my Private Office for a sight of the telegrams, they would have been immediately at your service.[30]

On 24 November, 1920, at Question Time in the House of Commons Churchill was asked whether he could make a statement regarding the sentences which had been imposed on the Connaught Rangers' mutineers, and whether he would consider reducing the severity of the punishment. He replied:

> This case lies within the jurisdiction of the Commander-in-Chief in India and the Viceroy. The proceedings of the trial are still in India and without calling for a special report I am unable to give a detailed answer to the Honourable Member's question, as I am not aware how the sentences of the Court stand at present, nor to what extent they have been varied. I understand however that 14 of the mutineers were sentenced to death, that 13 of the sentences have been commuted, and that the sentence on the remaining soldier was carried out on the 2nd November.[31]

The Army Act provided that a soldier who had been sentenced by a court martial in India to a term of penal servitude or to a term of imprisonment exceeding twelve months should be transferred 'as soon as practicable to a prison or detention barrack or convict establishment within the United Kingdom'.[32] It cannot have been easy, at short notice to organize the passage back to Britain of the sixty mutineers, with their escort, in conditions of close security. During the time the necessary arrangements were being completed the prisoners remained at Dagshai. Meanwhile, consultations were continuing about the possible reduction of the sentences. An internal War Office memorandum, dated 6 December, 1920, prepared for Winston Churchill, reported that the India Office was pressing for a reply as to whether there were any political reasons why the sentences should not be remitted. The memorandum went on to say that as the proceedings had not yet been received by the Judge Advocate General insufficient was known about the cases for an opinion to be given on them. There were, however, two political aspects of the matter:

(a) As regards India, (b) As regards Ireland. As regards (a), you will remember that the Commander-in-Chief advised you that if the death sentence of Private Daly was not carried out, he could not be responsible for the maintenance of discipline in the native units. As regards (b), I presume it is for the Cabinet to say if it is a proper time to show clemency.[33]

A letter was sent by the War Office to the Under Secretary of State for India a few days later, informing him that the Army Council were unable to express any views in regard to the possible remission of the sentences of the convicted mutineers without seeing the proceedings.[34]

In his long account of the history of the mutiny, written in 1949, Joseph Hawes mentioned that Lieutenant Smyth had handed him James Daly's farewell message, jotted down on the back of an envelope, but he gave no indication of what Daly had said in it.[35] During a radio programme, broadcast from Dublin in 1970, Hawes alluded to the farewell message again. This time he spoke of it as a 'note' given to him by Father Baker, and he described its contents for the first time:

He bid me goodbye and told me to pray for him. And he said, 'I'm giving you my beads; pray on my old beads every time that you say your Rosary, to remember me'. And he said, 'Up Balbriggan! Up Balbriggan!' because Balbriggan was burned down by the Tans; so he said, 'Up Balbriggan!' And he said, 'Up the men of Ireland and up the Connaught Rangers!'[36]

Balbriggan was a small town about twenty miles north of Dublin. The previous September the Head Constable there had been assassinated by the I.R.A. while he was having a drink with his brother at a local hotel. A party of Black and Tans had carried out a reprisal raid on the town on 20 September, 1920, looting and burning down four public houses, damaging a lot more property, and killing two suspected I.R.A. men.[37] The actual date of the Black and Tan outrage at Balbriggan was 20 September, a little less than six weeks before Daly's execution, and bearing in mind that letters from the United Kingdom took almost four weeks to reach the Punjab it would have just been possible for Daly to have known about the occurrence. However, there is one strange aspect of the matter. The radio programme in which Hawes publicly revealed the contents of the farewell message also featured an interview with Mrs Teresa Maher, James Daly's sister. She was asked to recall her memories of James at their home in Tyrrellspass when she herself had been about 18 years of age. She replied, 'Well, he used to sing some rebel songs, but I forget them. But I know he always used to be shouting "Up Balbriggan" at the time Balbriggan was burned. He was always used to be shouting [sic] about that at the time.'[38] The reason for Mrs Maher giving such an answer must remain a matter of speculation as she must have been aware that on the day of the outrage at Balbriggan James Daly was in Dagshai prison awaiting the promulgation of the court martial findings and that he never returned home thereafter.

A few days before Christmas, while the mutineers were still awaiting transportation to England, Private John Miranda, who had been sentenced to two years imprisonment with hard labour, died in the prison hospital. According to Hawes his death was due 'solely to the bad conditions prevailing in Dagshai jail'.[39] Sam Pollock, with his usual unquestioning adherence to Hawes's account of the mutiny, said that Miranda died of 'hardship and disease' a few days before Daly's execution.[40] In fact, Miranda's Death Certificate shows that he died in Dagshai on 22 December, 1920, from enteric fever,[41] the medical term for typhoid. This disease is caused by a bacterium which enters a person's body by his eating contaminated food or drinking contaminated liquid. No one has suggested that there was an epidemic in the prison at the time, nor even that any of the other mutineers had been taken ill. It would seem probable that Miranda had been unfortunate enough to have succumbed to an isolated infection.

Chapter 7

SINN FEIN

ALL THE SOLDIERS WHO TOOK PART in the Connaught Rangers mutiny had enlisted or re-enlisted voluntarily in the British Army and had sworn the following oath:

> I [name] swear by Almighty God, that I will be faithful and bear true allegiance to His Majesty King George the Fifth, his heirs and successors, and that I will, as in duty bound, honestly and faithfully defend His Majesty, his heirs and successors, in person, Crown and dignity against all enemies, and will observe and obey all orders of His Majesty, his heirs and successors, and of the generals and officers set over me.[1]

It has been persistently contended on behalf of the mutineers that they were absolved from compliance with their oaths of allegiance owing to the manner in which the British were behaving in Ireland. It is therefore relevant to examine the validity of this argument.

One of the earlier attempts to achieve self-government for Ireland by constitutional means took place in 1870 with the founding of the Home Rule League, which managed to return fifty-six members to the House of Commons at the General Election in 1874. Subsequently, under the leadership of Charles Stewart Parnell, a wealthy, Anglo-Irish Protestant landowner, the Home Rule party succeeded in establishing a lively and forceful parliamentary presence, principally by the use of obstructive tactics designed to draw attention to their cause. The matter was carried no further until the return to power of a Liberal administration in 1886, when Gladstone introduced an Irish Home Rule Bill. This measure was defeated in the Commons at its second reading by the combined vote of the Conservative opposition together with a splinter group from the Liberal party. Parnell was involved in a sensational divorce scandal in 1890 and died a year later.

There followed a period of disarray in the ranks of the Irish Nationalists, during which, in 1893, Gladstone's second Home Rule Bill was
defeated in the House of Lords.

Around 1900 John Redmond, who had been one of Parnell's most
ardent supporters, began to emerge as the new leader of the Home
Rule party in Parliament. Irish nationalists, however, were sharply
torn between those who continued to seek the objective through
constitutional means and a minority like Arthur Griffith who believed
that Ireland would never achieve self-government through legislative
action at Westminster. Griffith, who had become the founder and
editor of a weekly paper called the *United Irishman* in 1898, advocated
the pulverization of the British administration in Ireland by passive
resistance, refusal of cooperation and the withholding of taxes. He
urged Irish Members of Parliament to boycott the House of
Commons and to sit instead in a National Council in Ireland. Such a
body of 'patriotic citizens' did, in fact, meet in Dublin at the end of
1905 and adopted the title of Sinn Fein – the Gaelic words for 'we
ourselves'. But in its early stages the movement had no great political
significance.

After the Liberals had swept into power in 1906 they offered to
introduce a Bill granting Ireland, not complete independence, but a
measure of administrative Home Rule known as 'devolution'.
Although this was unacceptable to Redmond and his followers, they
supported the new government in its extensive reforming programme
relating to English domestic affairs. For the next four years the House
of Lords persisted in rejecting or drastically amending the majority of
the Bills to which the Liberals attached the greatest importance.
Eventually the Upper House brought the conduct of public affairs to a
standstill by refusing to pass the 1909 Budget. Herbert Asquith, who
had become Prime Minister in the previous year, responded by dis-
solving Parliament and seeking a fresh mandate from the electorate.
At the General Election in January, 1910, the Liberals were returned to
power, but with a sufficiently reduced majority in the House of
Commons to leave the Irish Home Rule party with the balance of
power.

The Budget was re-introduced by the Government and, with the
support of the Irish party, it passed successfully through the
Commons. Bowing to the will of the electorate, the Lords also
accepted it without a division. However, the confrontation between
the two Houses of Parliament was not yet at an end as Asquith was
proposing to restrict the powers of the Lords to the delaying of Bills
for a maximum period of two years, rather than rejecting them

outright. It was obvious that the Lords would never consent to such a measure unless they were threatened that if they failed to do so the King would create a sufficient number of new and acquiescent peers to force it through the division lobbies. Edward VII made it clear to Asquith that from a constitutional standpoint he would only be justified in creating the necessary peerages if the Liberals went to the country again and won the election on this specific issue. When King George V came to the throne in May, 1910, he took the same view of the matter as his father had done. In the General Election which followed, the Liberals were returned with a marginally increased majority and the Parliament Act, embodying the intended governmental alterations, passed into law without serious hindrance or delay.

Now that the House of Lords could no longer thwart their programme of reforms, the Liberals proceeded to enact a number of measures which formerly had been, or would have been, stultified by the Upper House. In April, 1912, Asquith brought in a new Home Rule Bill to grant self-government to the whole of Ireland. This aroused bitter resentment among the Protestant counties in Ulster where the vast majority of the people wanted to remain as a part of Great Britain. Under the leadership of Sir Edward Carson, they pledged themselves to oppose the extension of Home Rule to their part of the country, and many thousands of Ulstermen set up a military force called the Ulster Volunteer Force, determined, if necessary, to resort to armed resistance. The Nationalists responded by forming their own military unit, the Irish Volunteers, and at the beginning of 1914 Ireland appeared to be heading for a civil war. Asquith tried in vain to bring the two sides together, but they failed to agree to any suggested compromise and the deadlock remained unresolved. Many people in England were in complete sympathy with the views of Carson and his followers, and in March, 1914, the majority of the British army officers stationed at the Curragh Camp in Kildare made it known that they would prefer to resign their commissions rather than to coerce the surrender of the Ulster loyalists.

This was the position on the outbreak of the First World War in August, 1914. From the start of hostilities John Redmond gave his unstinting support to the Allied cause, encouraging Irishmen to enlist in the British forces and proposing that the Irish Volunteers should take over the defence of Ireland against the Germans. In September, 1914, the Home Rule Bill was passed into law accompanied by an Act suspending its operation until the end of the war.

Redmond's pro-British attitude was by no means universally popular in Ireland, where many of the Nationalists believed that England's preoccupation with the war would provide an ideal opportunity for an Irish rising. The Irish Volunteers now became split into two factions, those who supported and those who opposed John Redmond's policies. Among the latter was Sir Roger Casement, a member of an Ulster Protestant family who had been knighted in 1911 for his work in the British Consular Service and who had retired through ill-health during the following year. He had been a fervent Nationalist for a long while and in the closing months of 1914 he made his way to Berlin, intending to persuade the Germans to land in Ireland and to support a rising of the Irish people. The German High Command rejected Casement's proposal, but permitted him to tour their prisoner-of-war camps for the purpose of forming a brigade from Irish prisoners in them, which would fight with the Germany Army against the British.

In spite of the threats made by the authorities at the prison camps, and their proffered bribes, only a handful of Irish soldiers were induced to enrol. It is now known that the Germans distrusted Casement and never took his scheme very seriously. However, they agreed to supply a quantity of arms and ammunition to enable Sinn Fein to mount a rebellion at any opportune moment. Early in 1916 a ship loaded with obsolete weapons and flying a Norwegian flag sailed from a German port. It was intercepted by a naval patrol off the coast of Kerry. Casement himself did not fare much better, being captured at Banna Strand on the coast of Kerry soon after he was landed from a submarine. Within the space of a few months he had been tried for treason, convicted and hanged.

The Irish Volunteers decided that the planned rising should go ahead even though the consignment of German arms had been lost. On Easter Monday, 24 April, 1916, about 2,000 members of the Irish Volunteers seized various public buildings in Dublin, including the General Post Office, and proclaimed a provisional government. After a week of bitter fighting with British troops, the rebels were forced to surrender. They were tried and were punished with the utmost severity, sixteen being executed and many others deported to prisons and internment camps in Britain.[2] Three of the leaders of the Easter Rising, who were captured and sentenced to long terms of imprisonment, were Eamon De Valera, who had been born in New York but brought to County Clare as a child, William Cosgrave, a licensed vintner and Michael Collins, a former post office clerk. They were released in amnesties a short while later and became the foremost figures in the struggle for Irish independence.

Throughout 1917 and in the early part of 1918 the British High Command were apprehensive of another rising in Ireland with the assistance of the Germans.[3] The policies of Sinn Fein and the Irish Volunteers were now co-ordinated as De Valera had been elected the President of both organizations. Owing to the enormous casualties on the Western Front very few British troops could be spared for garrison duties in Ireland so the Volunteers were enabled to step up the raids they were making on the more isolated police barracks for the purpose of acquiring arms and ammunition. In May, 1918, a number of Sinn Fein leaders were arrested in an effort to curb their activities.[4] Two months later both Sinn Fein and the Irish Volunteers were proclaimed as dangerous associations and thenceforth their meetings became illegal.[5] In spite of these measures, the number and ferocity of the attacks on the Royal Irish Constabulary increased during the summer and autumn.

At the time of the Armistice in November, 1918, the southern and western parts of Ireland were in an extremely disturbed state, but as yet there had been no fatal casualties either among the police or among the Volunteers. Sinn Fein scored a parliamentary triumph at the General Election in December, 1918, capturing seventy-three out of the hundred and five Irish seats in the House of Commons, and winning every seat outside Ulster apart from the four at Trinity College, Dublin.[6] The newly elected Sinn Fein members declined to take their seats at Westminster. Instead those who were not in prison met at the Mansion House in Dublin in January, 1919, and proclaimed themselves to be the first Irish Assembly, the Dail Eireann. They approved a Declaration of Independence and declared that Ireland and England were thenceforth in a state of war with each other, and this would not end 'until Ireland is definitely evacuated by the armed force of England'. Eamon De Valera was appointed President of the new 'Irish Republic'. Michael Collins became the Minister of Finance, and William Cosgrave the Minister for Local Government.[7]

The Irish Volunteers had now adopted the title of the Irish Republican Army, usually abbreviated to the initials I.R.A. They intensified their guerrilla campaign on 21 January, 1919, the day on which the Declaration of Independence was proclaimed in Dublin, when nine I.R.A. men captured a cartload of gelignite in transit for a quarry near Tipperary, and killed the two members of the Royal Irish Constabulary who were escorting it.[8] From that time forth the I.R.A. began to wage open rebellion against the civil and military authorities with a ruthlessness which shocked many of the more moderate supporters of Sinn Fein. Police barracks in remote areas were raided with increasing frequency and were sometimes burned down. Small Royal Irish Constabulary patrols were ambushed and individual officers fired on by snipers. Flying columns occasionally mounted more ambitious attacks.[9] An I.R.A. publication *An tOglâch*, in its issue of 31 January, 1919, stated that soldiers and policemen were to be regarded as members of the invading forces of the enemy and could justifiably be treated as such.[10]

It is a matter of record that before the end of January, 1919, both Dail Eireann as the self-appointed government of the 'Irish Republic', and the I.R.A. as its national armed force, had publicly and unequivocally declared that England and Ireland were at war. It would seem therefore a matter of relevance to observe that most of the soldiers who took part in the Connaught Rangers mutiny had chosen to swear an oath of allegiance to the British Crown between the months of February and November, 1919. Private James Daly himself had attested on 4 April of that year.

Fatal casualties in the Royal Irish Constabulary mounted steadily throughout the spring and the summer of 1919. Some were killed in ambushes and gun-fights; some were murdered in cold blood. On 19 June a District Inspector was shot dead in a crowded street in Thurles, County Tipperary, and nobody came forward to assist the police when they were investigating the crime.[11] A high proportion of the population supported the I.R.A. offensive, which accounted for the fact that after the deliberate killing of a police officer a coroner's jury would often refuse to bring in a verdict of murder.[12] It has been estimated that the I.R.A. numbered 15,000 to 20,000 at this stage, of whom about 3,000 were usually on active service.[13]

Eamon De Valera had been a prisoner in Lincoln Jail when the members of the self-constituted Dail had purported to elect him President of the Irish Republic. A month later, in February, 1919, he had made a dramatic escape, and after a fleeting return to Ireland, he had travelled in disguise to the U.S.A. The attacks on the R.I.C. had continued to escalate during the summer and autumn, and orders had been made proclaiming Sinn Fein, together with its subsidiary societies, as illegal organizations.[14] The I.R.A. had carried out their first direct attack against the military at Fermoy on Sunday, 7 September, 1919, when they ambushed a party of eighteen men on their way to church, killing one private, wounding four more and seizing a quantity of rifles before they made off. After the jury at the inquest on the dead man had declined to return a verdict of murder about 200 infuriated soldiers had raided the town, causing extensive damage.[15]

Three days later the authorities had ordered the suppression of the Dail Eireann and had issued warrants for the arrest of all its members.

The events at Fermoy had marked the intensification of open hostilities between the British Army and the I.R.A. and by the end of 1919 many parts of Ireland were in a state of armed insurrection. The police had, so far, had eighteen of their men killed by the I.R.A. mostly by sniping.[16] The R.I.C. had begun to evacuate most of their isolated barracks with the consequence that considerable areas of the countryside were now completely unpoliced. On 22 December the British Government introduced at Westminster a complicated Bill whereby Ireland would be granted partial home rule with a unified National Council but with separate parliaments in Dublin and Belfast. This scheme was soon abandoned as it was generally opposed by every section of Irish opinion.[17]

Early in January, 1920, an attempt was made by the R.I.C. to arrest all the known I.R.A. leaders, but the operation proved to be a failure because neither the police nor the army possessed an adequate intelligence service.[18] At this time the military were taking over an ever-increasing amount of the duty which had formerly been carried out by the police.[19] The killings by the I.R.A. continued. Two of the murders they considered to be among their most spectacular coups were committed in the early part of the year. The first of these occurred on 21 January when an Assistant Commissioner in the R.I.C. was gunned down in broad daylight not far from a police station. The second was on 26 March when a septuagenarian Resident Magistrate was dragged off a tram on which he had been travelling and shot dead in the roadside beside it.[20] Between January and June no less than 424 R.I.C. barracks had to be abandoned as they were too vulnerable to keep in use. Of the barracks which were still manned, sixteen had been attacked and destroyed, and twenty-nine had been damaged during the same period. Before the beginning of July that year forty-seven court-houses in districts no longer under the direct control of the authorities had been closed down.[21] The I.R.A. was also disrupting mail services and interfering with communications in towns and rural areas.[22] The biggest operation they mounted during the first six months of 1920 was the destruction by fire of the Dublin Customs House.[23] Their selected victims were not invariably soldiers or policemen; it has been estimated that from the beginning of January to the middle of April they murdered seventy-three Irish civilians, including four women.[24] Michael Collins, who had become the I.R.A.'s Director of Intelligence, explained later:

England's shock troops were assassinators. Mine were ambushers, but at times we too assassinated. We had no gaols, and we had therefore to kill all spies, informers and double-crossers.[25]

The Roman Catholic hierarchy in Ireland repeatedly condemned the acts of violence of the I.R.A. In April, 1920, the Bishop of Ross denounced the killing of four members of the R.I.C. as 'callous and deliberate murder'.[26] In a contemptuous reference to I.R.A. tactics the Bishop of Cork in a pastoral letter commented that 'ambushers take very little risk to themselves'.[27] Later, the same Bishop stated publicly that any man who was responsible for killing another in an ambush was a murderer and would be excommunicated.[28]

Casualties in the R.I.C. were mounting steadily in the early part of 1920 and many people feared that it would not be long before they began to resort to counter-terrorism and unauthorized reprisals. On 19 March a party of men in civilian clothing with faces blackened raided the home of Tomas MacCurtain, Lord Mayor of Cork, and shot him dead in front of his wife. MacCurtain, who was just about to be arrested, was Commandant of the 1st (East) Cork Brigade of the I.R.A., and it was generally believed that his murder had been carried out by the police.[29] General Sir Nevil Macready, the military Commander-in-Chief in Ireland, said in April that he had impressed on his senior officers that they were to take no measures that might irritate the Irish population except in retaliation. 'That is to say,' he explained, 'a murder or outrage is committed, and we at once retaliate by a raid for arms or persons in the immediate vicinity.'[30] On 19 June the newly-appointed R.I.C. Commissioner for Munster, Lieutenant-Colonel Smyth, DSO, told his men in an inaugural message, 'Sinn Fein has had the sport up to the present and we are going to have the sport now'. He urged them not to hesitate in shooting civilians on suspicion, even if mistakes were made. 'The more you shoot,' he added, 'the better I like it.'[31]

The R.I.C. had been trained principally as a civil constabulary and they were repeatedly out-manoeuvred in their clashes with the I.R.A. In addition to their losses in combat, a number of their men were continually resigning because of threats to and intimidation of their families.[32] In spite of these dissuasive influences a steady stream of young Irishmen was coming forward to fill the vacancies and the flow was augmented by recently-demobilized British ex-servicemen.[33] At the end of March, 1920, a notice signed by the 'G.O.C. Irish Republican Army' appeared on walls and hoarding-boards throughout the south of Ireland proclaiming that the R.I.C. were spies and traitors and would be treated as such. All prospective recruits to the force were warned that they would be joining it 'at their peril'.[34]

The Rule of Law in Ireland was rapidly becoming non-existent. Over the Easter weekend in 1920, in an operation organized by Sinn Fein and the I.R.A., over a hundred income tax offices in various parts of the country were soaked in paraffin and set on fire.[35] On 26 June, two days before the Connaught Rangers mutiny, the Brigadier commanding the army units in southern Ireland and two staff colonels were captured while on a fishing holiday at Fermoy, and were taken away to be held as hostages.[36]

Between 30 June, 1919, and 30 June, 1920, about eighty members of the R.I.C. and the British forces had been killed, and the authorities showed little sign of being able to regain control.[37] Field Marshal Lord French, Lord-Lieutenant of Ireland, thought that the only solution was the complete elimination of the Sinn Fein movement and the I.R.A. Major-General Tudor, who had become Police Adviser to the Irish Government on 15 May, 1920, fully agreed, and in the meantime he advocated the policy of countering terror with terror.[38]

Chapter 8

THE MOTIVES FOR THE MUTINY

IT HAS ALWAYS BEEN MAINTAINED by the Connaught Rangers mutineers and their eulogists that they took their action as a protest against
the behaviour of the Black and Tans in Ireland. This claim has never
been questioned or investigated and it would seem apposite to examine it more closely.

The Black and Tans were recruited from demobilized British soldiers as an anti-terrorist force and enrolled as temporary constables in
the R.I.C. The nickname of their force, by which it was universally
known and detested, arose from the fact that owing to a shortage of
police uniforms they were clothed in khaki with black caps and belts.
Writing of their invidious reputation, Calton Younger has said:

> They were not the dregs of the English jails, as Irishmen have so often
> alleged, but bored, unsettled, often workless, ex-soldiers, young men
> whose ordinary pity and honour had been dried up by their long and
> merciless ordeal in the trenches.[1]

The first Black and Tan recruits arrived in Ireland on 25 March, 1920,
and after training for several weeks at Gormanstown and Phoenix
Park Depot they were distributed among police stations in various
parts of the country.[2] At the start their numbers were small, but
they had reached a strength of about 500 by the middle of May that
year.[3] Their initial display of lawlessness occurred at Limerick on 28
April when a party of them, for no apparent reason, charged through
the streets breaking windows and assaulting civilians. On that occasion, said Calton Younger, their conduct 'was little more than the
kind of hooliganism which seems to affect large groups of men from
soldiers to football supporters when they visit someone else's
country'.[4]

Richard Bennett has suggested that the outrages started in June, 1920, when, as a reprisal for the murder of three policemen and the wounding of thirteen more by the I.R.A., lorry-loads of Black and Tans 'tore down the village streets firing their rifles at random to the peril of anyone who appeared to be in the way'.[5] He does not, however, indicate his source for this statement. Lord Longford states that the Black and Tans became 'seriously involved' in Ireland throughout the year from July, 1920, to June, 1921,[6] and according to Calton Younger they 'dominated' the Irish scene during the second half of 1920.[7] The *Leitrim Observer* on 13 March, 1920, reported that 'Ex-soldiers partly attired in the uniform of the R.I.C. and in khaki, are doing duty at Carrick-on-Shannon and different towns throughout the whole of the country at the present time'.[8] However, these men were locally recruited Irishmen who preceded the Black and Tans by some months.

Charles Kerrigan has said that at the time of the mutiny the men of the 1st Connaught Rangers were not seeing any newspapers and that their knowledge of events in Ireland was mostly derived from the letters they received.[9] This confirms the belief of the authorities, for in his telegram to the Secretary of State for India on 4 July, 1920, the Viceroy said, 'The men, there can be little doubt, have been influenced by letters from Home in their misconduct, and for the present at any rate it is essential that we should possess knowledge of their correspondence'.[10] It is generally agreed that the mutiny at Jullundur was instigated to a large extent by the reinforcements who had come to the battalion in the last two drafts from England. In the previously-quoted telegram, despatched on 9 July, the Viceroy said:

> We have every reason to believe that the whole affair was engineered by Sinn Fein. Large Sinn Fein flags were hoisted in barracks when the mutiny first broke out at Jullundur. These flags were apparently not made in India. Sinn Fein colours and rosettes were also worn. The source of the trouble is clearly indicated by the fact that out of the 206 men comprising the last two drafts out from Home, 172 were mutineers at Jullundur.[11]

In this telegram the Viceroy inferred that the Sinn Fein flags and rosettes were brought into India by the two recent drafts. The mutineers have claimed, however, that they were made in the barracks out of strips of coloured material purchased in the cantonment bazaar. The 1st Connaught Rangers' returns for the relevant period show the arrival of the following reinforcement drafts:

December 1919	13 officers	15 O.R.s
January 1920	4 officers	2 O.R.s
February 1920	4 officers	
March 1920		180 O.R.s
June 1920		125 O.R.s[12]

It would seem that even the last draft to arrive in India would have sailed from England just before the start of the period in which the Black and Tans began their reprehensible activities.

None of the mutineers has ever revealed the details of the information they were being given in letters from home, or the identities of the people who were sending it to them. The Nationalist Press in Ireland, understandably enough, was reporting events in an extremely emotive manner, and it is highly probable that the correspondence from the relatives and friends of the men reflected a similar attitude. On 10 January, 1920, the *Westmeath Independent* published a two-column month-by-month summary of the happenings in the country during 1919.[13] The report was prefaced by the words:

With a retrospect [sic] Irishmen, on the whole, have reason to be proud. Of persecution and oppression they have had their share but, seemingly, it is characteristic of our national spirit to thrive under such conditions, and the outlook for the country during the New Year should suffice to make the least optimistic among us feel happy.

The resumé of the year's events which followed was interspersed with reports of tyranny and repression by the authorities. For example, in January there had been 'huge protest meetings all over Ireland to demand release of political prisoners'. In March the Westmeath County Council had condemned 'the scandalous treatment of Irish political prisoners'. In May a concert and lecture in Athlone had been stopped by British troops with bayonets fixed. In August at Kilbeggan soldiers had dispersed a meeting at bayonet point. In September there had been searches, raids and indiscriminate arrests by members of the R.I.C. In October the police had made repeated baton charges on a crowd in Mullingar. In November Irish civilians had been tried by military courts martial. And in December there had been a swoop on Irish political leaders and those arrested had been 'deported' to England in naval vessels.

The *Westmeath Independent* circulated in the area of the homes of several of the leaders of the mutiny, including James Daly. On

24 January, 1920, the paper ran a story under a banner headline 'DEPLORABLE' and the sub-heading 'Terror in Southern Town, Soldiers Out Of Hand'.[14] The long and graphic account began:

> The Munster town of Thurles, the seat of the Great College of the Holy Ghost, Rockwell, and the official residence of the Archbishop of Cashel, had a terrible experience on Tuesday night last, when police and soldiers got out of hand and ran amok. Houses were promiscuously fired into, hand grenades exploded, and the people reduced to a state of general consternation. It was a night of horror for the citizens.

It is apparent from the account given by the newspaper that the trouble arose from an incident at eleven o'clock that evening when a constable returning home from work was shot three times on his doorstep and was rushed to hospital 'in a critical condition'. The apparent object of the combined military and police operation was to search for the perpetrators of the crime and for their weapons. There was no allegation that any civilians had been killed or injured but the intention of the authorities may well have been to intimidate the local inhabitants.

Readers of the Nationalist newspapers in Ireland were left in no doubt as to the justness of their cause. At the end of January, 1920, the *Westmeath Independent* printed in full the text of a statement issued by Cardinal Logue at a full meeting of Irish Roman Catholic bishops.[15] It accused the Government of disregarding the national feelings and the national rights of the people in Ireland, and of being occupied almost exclusively 'in the arduous work of political repression'. The statement went on:

> We would represent to the advocates of military rule in Ireland that government by force, which was never right, is today wholly obsolete ... We have therefore to declare that the one true way to terminate our historic troubles and establish friendly relations between England and Ireland, to the advantage of both countries, is to allow an undivided Ireland to choose her own form of government.

The same issue of the paper reported that the Archbishop of Cashel had sent a £50 contribution to Eamon De Valera, who was campaigning in the United States of America to raise money and support for Sinn Fein.[16] In an accompanying letter with his gift the Archbishop spoke of Irish homes being raided by the armed forces of the British Crown, and streets being 'paraded by an army of occupation'. He wished De Valera every blessing in his 'noble efforts to right the wrongs of centuries, and to free Ireland from the blighting influence of foreign rule'.

Throughout the spring of 1920 the Irish Press was reporting raids and arrests by both the military and the police and also the impassioned words of the Nationalist leaders. In an article at the beginning of April Erskine Childers condemned the raiding of private homes by the military. In many recent instances, he alleged, women occupants had been locked up under armed guards while their property was ransacked. He continued:

> Imagine the moral effect of such a procedure on the young officer and men told off for this duty. Is it a wonder that discipline is relaxed and unpardonable irregularities occur – looting, insolence, drunkenness, cruel severity to women, wanton and causeless destruction? All these things have been happening . . . What right has England to torment and demoralize Ireland?[17]

When some Sinn Fein prisoners at Mountjoy gaol went on hunger strike in the middle of April, the *Westmeath Independent* told its readers that 'Ireland looked on aghast at the unconquerable spirit of her sons fighting this unequal fight against the powers of brute force'.[18] A week later the same paper, in reporting the Budget, declared that Ireland was being plundered and bled from London for the benefit of Englishmen.[19]

For several weeks before the Connaught Rangers mutiny the level of anti-British vituperation in the Nationalist Press was increasing. The *Westmeath Independent* asserted that Ireland had been subjected to military invasion and was being governed by brute force and unadulterated coercion.[20] The *Irish Statesman* gave this message to the British nation:

> You may pack this country with troops as full as it will hold, you may by shooting, bombing, bayoneting, or by a sufficient threat of brute force, hold the people down; but you will never be able to govern in any civilized sense of the term, for you will never win that consent of the governed which is the only sanction of government worthy of the name.[21]

The Nationalist papers reported with pride the raiding of police stations and the gutting of tax offices, and even commended the

I.R.A. on one occasion for their 'coolness, daring and audacity'.[22] It was never suggested in the Irish press at any time during the first half of 1920 that the R.I.C. were not suffering more casualties than they were themselves inflicting on the I.R.A. The *Times Index* for the months January–March that year gives the names of eleven police officers who were murdered;[23] in the same *Index* for the months of April–June the number has risen to twenty-five.[24]

If the Black and Tans were really the main incentive for the Connaught Rangers mutiny it seems strange that they were never specifically mentioned in the resultant courts martial. When Hawes and his three comrades surrendered at the very start of the mutiny they gave the reason for their action as being that they were 'in sympathy with Ireland'.[25] During the next few days various other explanations were offered by mutineers at Jullundur. Some said they were protesting at the treatment of the Irish people; others said their protest was about the way Ireland was being governed. A number stated that they were demanding the complete withdrawal of the British Army from Irish soil;[26] similarly Private James Daly, as the self-appointed spokesman of the mutineers at Solon, had told Captain Badham that they would refuse to work again until every British soldier had been removed from Ireland. It might not be a mere coincidence that when the Dail Eireann had been inaugurated in Dublin on 21 January, 1919, the members had declared that the state of war against England would continue 'until Ireland is definitely evacuated by the armed forces of England'.

It is impossible to be certain how much information about the creation or the activities of the Black and Tans had reached the 1st Connaught Rangers by the last week in June, 1920. Later on, when the claim was first put forward that the mutiny was principally a protest against Black and Tan atrocities in Ireland, the outrageous conduct of this unit had become notorious and they were regarded with universal abhorrence. The possibility cannot be disregarded that the mutineers were seeking a plausible justification for the betrayal of their oaths of allegiance, and at the same time, no doubt, enhancing their own renown among their fellow countrymen.

No other Irish regiment during that bitter and emotive period experienced a similar outbreak to that which occurred in the 1st Battalion of the Connaught Rangers. The question must therefore be asked, why did this happen at Jullundur and Solon? During the summer of 1919 G. N. Molesworth had been posted to the Adjutant-General's Branch at Army Headquarters in Simla, where he was placed in charge of the section concerned with the discipline of British troops. He has said of the Connaught Rangers mutiny:

> For some time Sinn Fein has been actively campaigning for Home Rule for Ireland. There is no doubt they had cells in this battalion, which had been working without the knowledge of officers and senior NCOs, or possibly with the connivance of some of the latter, for a considerable time. In the general upset which followed World War I in India, they seemed to have decided that the time had come to strike. What they intended to do, or what hopes they could have had of anything more than a demonstration, is uncertain.[27]

There was a suspicion at that time that support for Sinn Fein was strong in other regiments too. On 26 July, barely a month after the Connaught Rangers mutiny, Field-Marshal Sir Henry Wilson, the Chief of the Imperial General Staff, received a telegram informing him that Lord D'Abernon, the British Ambassador in Berlin, considered that the 1st Battalion, Royal Irish Regiment should be withdrawn from Allenstein, a town in Eastern Prussia, because 'They are full of Sinn Fein and cannot be relied on, nor is their conduct doing any good to our prestige'. Ten days later Wilson asked Lord Curzon, the Foreign Secretary, for permission for the withdrawal of this battalion, adding to his message 'It is urgent in every sense'.[28]

In September, 1921, the Assistant Adjutant-General reported to Wilson that he had been speaking to the Commanding Officer of the 1st Battalion, Royal Dublin Fusiliers, who was 'concerned about his men if things get bad in Ireland'. The Assistant A.G. continued:

> The loyal men whose people are in the affected areas will feel they ought to be with their parents and (the commanding officer) thinks it should be considered whether Irishmen should not be given indefinite leave, or some other arrangement be come to, to enable them to look after them. It is a difficult question, but conditions are exceptional and are a strain on the men's loyalty and discipline. The Irish Guards are worried about their men too, from the fact that they cannot proceed to Ireland on furlough this winter.[29]

Nothing has come to light which indicates that the Connaught Rangers mutineers were in contact with the Nationalist movement in India. Indeed, several of them were asked years later in radio interviews if at the time of the mutiny they had sensed any rapport between the Irish and the Indian people, and usually replied that they had not considered the matter. Kerrigan stated that he had had little contact with Indians except for dhobi-wallahs who worked in the barracks, and John Flannery made no secret of his distrust of the 'natives'. Nevertheless, there were others who perceived an affinity of interest in the aspirations of the two nations. On 28 February, 1920, Eamon De Valera had issued a statement in which he urged India, Ireland and Egypt 'to combine to fight for and obtain their freedom'.[30] A journal in Poona extolled the conduct of 'these Irish soldier patriots', and compared them contemptuously with the Indian troops who had 'shot down their innocent countrymen and children at the order of General Dyer'.[31] The mutineers were also praised by a Delhi paper which commented that 'the Irish people can preserve their honour, defy the orders of the Government, and defeat its unjust aims'.[32]

As far as is known only one of the members of the court martial which tried the mutineers has left a record of his conclusions in regard to the causes of the mutiny. Lieutenant-Colonel J. C. W. Francis was serving as a captain in the 19th Hussars at the time the trials took place. In a confidential letter, written on 21 November to Colonel F. W. S. Jourdain, he said:

My general impression [of] the cause was:
1. The unrest in Ireland.
2. Letters from home.
3. Very poor discipline indeed of the entirely unintelligent sort.
4. Extremely bad relations between officers and men.
5. Want of satisfactory occupation and activity.
6. The hot weather.[33]

It would be as well to look at these six factors individually.

With regard to the unrest in Ireland and the letters from home, there is not much to be added to what has been said already. Sam Pollock in his book on the mutiny has stated, with his customary paucity of research, that the mutineers had learnt from their correspondence about the shameful deeds committed by the Black and Tans and the Auxiliaries.[34] In fact the Auxiliaries, a special gendarmerie recruited from ex-army officers, were not formed until the end of July, 1920, and did not start to operate in Ireland until the following month.[35]

The next two points mentioned by Francis, the poor discipline in the battalion and the bad relationship between the officers and men, are corroborated by other sources. After listening to a broadcast feature about the mutiny in December, 1963, Colonel F. W. S.

Jourdain, who had served as a regular officer in the 1st Connaught Rangers, wrote to a friend, 'My candid opinion was that the officers in that battalion at that time were not good enough, and if they had been they would have foreseen the trouble and most likely have prevented it'.[36] In a letter to Field-Marshal Sir Gerald Templer, dated 20 May, 1971, Colonel Jourdain said that from the information he had received from officers who were present at the mutiny he had formed the opinion that 'the senior officers were quite out of touch with their men and the junior officers were kept in their place and not asked for their opinions'. He went on:

> Although there were evidently one or two captains with the battalion at the time of the mutiny in 1920, for most of 1919 at Dover the battalion had five majors and no captains. As a subaltern, I was Adjutant myself until August (when I was sent off to North Russia as an intelligence officer), so I remember that anomalous situation very well. The Commanding Officer (Deacon) was already in India and due to take over the battalion on its arrival there in October or November. In the meantime a certain Major Payne was in command, but one could not communicate with him effectively after, say, 6 p.m. In the circumstances it was a great misfortune, to put it mildly, that the company commanders of our 1st Battalion were not sufficiently close to their men to have some idea of what was going on in their minds and to have tried to help them in the circumstances which were admittedly difficult for both officers and men.[37]

In a letter to *The Times*, written in August, 1969, Colonel Jourdain explained why, in his opinion, the disproportion between the number of majors in the battalion and the number of captains had aggravated the discontent of the men. The majors, he said,

> could be a little awkward at times. Looking back, I am sure that because of the deficiency in captains things were out of balance and that this had its effect on the battalion as a whole. The companies would have been better and happier concerns if they had been commanded by officers who had been subalterns more recently than majors.[38]

When a military unit is afflicted with low morale or laxity of discipline, the malaise often emanates from the very top. Lieutenant-Colonel Deacon had only commanded the 1st Connaught Rangers since their arrival in India; already, according to W. G. Robertson, one of the subalterns in the battalion, he had become most unpopular with all ranks.[39] Robertson and MacWeeney also blame Deacon for his irresolution at the start of the mutiny. They both believed that if he had reacted with more firmness he might have crushed it in its infancy. Brigadier C. I. Jerrard, who had been a 2nd Lieutenant in the 51st Sikh Regiment stationed at Jullundur in 1920, was able to form an objective view of Lieutenant-Colonel Deacon's Battalion. Years later he said:

> I had met several of the Connaught Rangers junior officers on courts of enquiry, and also Major Payne who, to my inexperienced eye, appeared to be good. I was not very impressed with the others who appeared to have a 'chip on their shoulders' and had too much to say against their Colonel and Adjutant, which was not good, especially to an outsider like myself. We played a lot of football against the Rangers, but their officers were never present, and their teams were run by NCOs. We gained the impression that the officers were not in close touch with the men.[40]

The last two factors mentioned by Lieutenant–Colonel Francis when he listed the causes of the mutiny were the 'want of satisfactory occupation and activity' for the troops, and 'the hot weather'.

It is known that during the sweltering summer months on the plains of the Punjab in 1920 the temperatures rose to unusually high levels. In that sort of heat it was customary for British troops in India only to parade from six o'clock until eight o'clock each morning and to be relatively free for the rest of the day. The *Regimental History* of the Connaught Rangers states that the training in the 1st Battalion was broken off that year before the hot weather began, and that two companies were sent away to hill-stations. The author of the history is critical of Colonel Deacon's decision to keep the newly arrived drafts on the plains, and although he makes no direct reference to the lack of 'occupation and activity' of the men remaining in Wellington Barracks, he draws attention to the fact that the mutiny broke out after two of the hottest days of the year and at a time when there were few experienced NCOs available for duty.[41]

Sam Pollock has alleged that during the month of June the men of the 1st Battalion who were left in Jullundur were made to undergo 'rigorous training exercises' throughout the day in which they marched or doubled, wearing tight jackets done up to the neck and carrying full packs, haversacks, pouches, entrenching tools, rifles, bayonets and ammunition. He adds,

It was suspected by some of the men that this spell of Active Service conditions was deliberately designed to keep them out of mischief – maybe even to wearying them beyond the stage at which they might react violently to the news from Ireland: the news of the doings of the Blacks and Tans.[42]

If this exhausting routine had been taking place it is difficult to understand the conclusion formed by Lieutenant-Colonel Francis after hearing all the evidence at the trials that the boredom and inaction of the troops were factors contributing to the outbreak of the mutiny. Presumably Pollock obtained his information from his chief source, Joseph Hawes. If so, it is worth noting that Hawes, in his own account of the mutiny, has not said a single word about it. The truth of the allegation was not accepted by Brigadier-General Jerrard who was, of course, in Jullundur at the time, and who commented:

I do not remember any field exercises being carried out at high noon during that summer and in view of the fact that it reached temperatures of 120 and the army was far more sun-conscious than they were in 1940–44, and I very much doubt if any such parades ever took place, especially by British troops who were treated most carefully in this respect.[43]

In the early 1970s, when the Connaught Rangers mutiny was once more becoming a matter of considerable interest, Desmond Mac-Weeney remarked in a private letter to Colonel Jourdain that the truth of what had occurred was 'very far from the appalling nonsense given out by Hawes & Co. and reproduced, especially in Kilfeather's book and to some extent by Sam Pollock'.[44]

Chapter 9

THE BIRTH OF A LEGEND

NEARLY ALL OF THE SURVIVING MUTINEERS were returned to England in various troopships during January, 1921. On their arrival, those who had been sentenced to terms of penal servitude were sent to the civil prison at Portland, and those sentenced to imprisonment with hard labour were sent to the military prison at Woking.

The War Office in London only received a full report about the mutiny in the middle of January and it came to them, not from the Indian High Command, but from the India Office. Brigadier-General Childs, the Director of Personal Services, wrote a memorandum to the Adjutant-General saying, 'I am rather coming to the conclusion that we have been deliberately ignored in this case by the Commander-in-Chief in India'. The India Office were still pressing them, he went on, for their views on possible remissions of the sentences which had been imposed, but since they had not yet been sent a copy of the court martial proceedings it would be impossible for them to express an opinion. He pointed out that the Indian authorities seemed unaware of the fact that when the sentenced soldiers had been returned to England, the power of remission passed automatically from the G.O.C. India to the Army Council. 'I personally should strenuously oppose any further remissions,' he said, 'other than which have already been made by the G.O.C. when confirming the proceedings'.[1]

The Director of Personal Services was a senior officer on the General Staff, with particular responsibilities in matters of discipline and welfare. As Brigadier-General Childs had held the appointment since 1916 he must have had ample experience of the difficulties created by the bipartite control exercised by the War Office and the Indian High Command over British regiments serving in India. He was succeeded at the end of January by Major-General Ready, who wrote a minute for the Adjutant-General on 31 March telling him that all the mutineers except five were now in England. As the India Office were continuing to enquire about the possible remission of the sentences, he suggested that the last five men should be sent back as soon as possible so that none of the prisoners would remain under the jurisdiction of the G.O.C. India. Ready continued, 'I do not think that any of the sentences should be interfered with at present. At a later date we should consider remissions of some of the longer sentences awarded.'[2] The Adjutant-General replied that before he discussed the subject with the Secretary of State for War he would like to know if the Judge Advocate General had received the court martial proceedings yet, and if so, whether he had made any recommendations.[3] In fact the proceedings did not reach London until the first week in April, although the Indian High Command claimed that they had been despatched during November of the previous year.[4]

At the beginning of May the Judge Advocate General's office made their report. They stated that they could see no reason for any reduction in the sentences of imprisonment with hard labour. With regard to men then serving terms of penal servitude they said, 'In some cases the more severe sentences are obviously due to the more prominent part taken by those particular men. In other cases it is rather more difficult to see why the court differentiated in punishment when the men with whom they were dealing appear on the face of the proceedings to have committed exactly the same acts. But probably they were largely influenced by the appearance and demeanour of the prisoners at their trial.' The report suggested that none of the penal servitude sentences should be reviewed until a minimum of three years had been served, and added, 'Nearly all these men are Irishmen; and it would appear eminently undesirable that any of them should have their sentences remitted and thus be enabled to find their way back to Ireland to add to the unrest. Our proposal is that all the sentences should be reviewed in September, 1923.'[5]

The report was approved by the Adjutant-General and the Secretary of State for War, who agreed to follow its proposals. Major-General Ready was still anxious that the last five mutineers should be sent home from India so that one single authority could deal with all the sentences together.[6] A letter was sent by the War Office to the Under-Secretary of State for India on 21 May, 1921, telling him the proceedings had been reviewed and that the Army Council had decided 'not to take any action at present to remit the sentences of any of the soldiers convicted by Court-Martial' in connection with the mutiny. Nothing was said about the proposal to review the sentences in September, 1923. The letter went on to request that 'the five soldiers named in the attached list' should be sent back to England immediately to complete their sentences.[7] One of the men whose names were listed was Private Miranda who had died of enteric fever at Dagshai the previous December. However, the other four arrived at the military prison in Woking in the middle of June.

John Flannery only deals with the period after the mutineers reached England in the briefest terms. They were divided into groups, he says, and were sent to prisons in various parts of the country where 'they claimed treatment as political prisoners but were not strong enough in numbers to enforce their demands'.[8] Joseph Hawes, on the other hand, has dwelt at some length on the experiences of the mutineers when serving terms of penal servitude, and has treated this as the final phase of their tribulations. On arrival at Southampton, according to his account, they were all taken to Portland chained together, except for Lance-Corporal Flannery who, presumably for his own protection, was sent by himself to a prison in the Isle of Wight. While the rest of them were confined at Portland they were treated like the other civilian inmates, apart from the fact they could avail themselves of certain minor privileges as military prisoners. After a few weeks and without any preliminary warning, they were transferred to Maidstone Prison where they were put into a separate wing, consisting of a detached, two-storied concrete building. It was usually damp, he says, and it had no form of heating. They slept in hammocks, slung across the cells from one wall to another.[9]

Hawes emphasizes the militant attitude of the mutineers towards the prison authorities. One morning soon after their arrival at Maidstone, he says, they found that one of their number, Private Lynch, was missing. Although they did not know it until later, he had been removed to the punishment cells for committing a disciplinary offence. The mutineers expressed their intention of refusing to do any work until they had been told what had happened to him. They were charged with disobedience and were immediately brought before the Governor, who referred the matter to the visiting prison magistrates. At their trial a few days later they were all sentenced to fifteen days on a diet of bread-and-water followed by three months' solitary confinement in the punishment block. After the three-month period had passed they were returned to the separate wing where they had been accommodated previously. Soon after their return, Hawes says, a few of them refused to work in protest against the loss of their privileges, and they were marched back to the punishment cells. Again they came up before the visiting magistrates and this time they were awarded twenty-eight days on bread-and-water, followed by six months' solitary confinement. Hawes claims that he and others went on hunger-strike and they had to be forcibly fed. He continues:

> After this six months' punishment ended discipline relaxed a little, probably due to the fact that they could not break us. Most of the year 1922 was uneventful except for minor incidents. Individual mutineers were occasionally up on charges for breaking prison rules, but we made no effort at any organized resistance to authority until the latter part of 1922.[10]

James Gorman has given a somewhat different account of the enforcement of discipline at Maidstone Prison. He agrees with Hawes that during the early days the mutineers refused to join their working parties until they were told what had become of Private Lynch, and also that they were brought before the visiting magistrates for their disobedience. However, he says they were punished with fourteen, not fifteen days on bread-and-water, followed by fourteen days, and not three months, solitary confinement. This discrepancy might well result from a genuine error of recollection between himself and Joseph Hawes. It is more difficult to find an innocent explanation for their dissimilar accounts of what took place thereafter. Gorman says that the next mutineer to get into trouble was Private Devine, who was working on the laundry party and who threw a Black-and-Tan prisoner into a tub of boiling water, 'so that he could have been skinned, the same as you could skin a pig'. Devine received the not immoderate sentence of twenty-eight days on bread-and-water for this offence. For the rest, says Gorman, 'we got a few other minor bread-and-waters — three or four days'. He makes no mention of any protracted spells of solitary confinement, hunger-strikes or forced-feeding.[11] Charles Kerrigan considered that the conditions at Maidstone were 'fair enough' as the mutineers were employed in the prison workshops; they were given ordinary meals and they were allowed the normal periods of exercise. He admits that he benefited from his periods in the prison-school and learnt 'sums and reading and writing and things'.[12] It should be added that Art O'Brien, the Sinn Fein representative in London, in the course of a note to Michael Collins soon after the mutineers had arrived at Maidstone Prison, wrote, 'Men say they are well treated by warders. All in good health'.[13]

The heroic legend of the Connaught Rangers mutiny, and also the martyrdom of James Daly, was inspired to a large extent by the writings of Joseph Hawes and John Flannery, but others have added their contributions. Private Joseph Walsh started early to publicize the story. In February, 1921, while he was on board ship returning to England as a prisoner, he wrote a letter to the *Irish Bulletin* in which he said:

> I was one of the 350 men of the Connaught Rangers who laid down their arms at Jullundur, India on the 28th June, 1920, as a protest against the way the Government was treating Ireland. Out of the 350 who laid down their arms, the authorities picked 62 men who they thought were the ringleaders and had them tried by mock courtmartial. The remaining 288 men returned back to soldier. They tried to get us to surrender. They used every means in their power, so at last they told us it looked 'so terrible [sic] bad in the eyes of the natives of India', so they tried force. The South Wales Borderers used both bayonet and ball-ammunition, but it was no use. We meant death before surrender.

He ended with the words, 'If ever God spares me to go free, I will open the eyes of the world, as regards what I and my comrades have suffered, but it is all for Erin.'[14]

Walsh is the only person who has asserted that there was some sort of skirmish when the relieving troops were taking over Wellington Barracks. According to every other account the mutineers offered no resistance at all. Indeed, it has never been suggested elsewhere that fighting occurred in Jullundur at any stage of the mutiny. Walsh might, of course, have been referring to the incident when Major Payne attempted to make the Jullundur mutineers take down a tent just after the mutiny and summoned the help of a guard from the South Wales Borderers to force them to comply with his orders.

The legend of the Connaught Rangers mutiny attained its full flowering after Hawes and Flannery had published their versions of what had taken place. By April, 1952, the *Irish Press* was saying, 'If comparison is possible, these Connaught Rangers were among the bravest men in the fight for Ireland's freedom'.[15] In an introduction to a two-part feature on the mutiny in 1970, the Provisional Sinn Fein paper *An Phoblacht* described it as 'a great story', and 'an inspiring epic'. Dealing with the beginning of the events, the first article stated:

> Private Hawes took complete charge of the revolting Rangers and thus a new chapter in the history of Ireland was opened. The men under the command of Private Hawes were as brave and true to Ireland as were any of the Wild Geese who had served in Continental armies. Indeed they were braver because they had neither support nor backing. They were on their own against the full might and power of an empire. Their

deed will be remembered because it brought glory and fame to the land of their birth for which these men were prepared to give all.[16]

The second article concluded, 'The story of the Connaught Rangers Mutiny is one of the great stories of our history. These men should never be forgotten by the Nation they served so faithfully'.[17]

The death of James Daly received a fair amount of attention in the Irish papers from the outset. Early in December, 1920, the *Westmeath Examiner* published in full his last letter home, and an account of his execution, under the headline 'Young Irish Soldier Shot In India'.[18] It was stated that Daly had joined the Royal Irish Regiment in 1915 and had been wounded while serving on the Western Front. The truth is that he joined up in the Royal Munster Fusiliers at Mullingar in 1917, but he was then under-age and his mother arranged for him to be discharged. He enlisted again, this time in the Connaught Rangers, in April, 1919. According to the records he was entitled to the British War and the Victory medals; these were forfeited, however, when he was sentenced to death. In February, 1921, the *Westmeath Examiner* alluded to the execution again, when they quoted extracts from a letter sent to Daly's parents by 'an old comrade' of their son's, who was himself serving a five-year prison sentence for his part in the mutiny. He told them that they could have the satisfaction that 'James had died a martyr and a saint', and the writer went on:

Just as the bullet – the fatal bullet – struck him the priest rushed forward and gave him the last anointing. Your poor boy just raised his lovely eyes to Heaven once more – then died. I am also proud to tell you that your dead son's bravery amazed those who had any association with the sad details of his execution. An officer in the Machine Gun Corps told me that James was the bravest man he had ever seen.[19]

The sanguinary details of James Daly's execution, true or fictitious, evoked a morbid fascination. In April, 1922, another Westmeath paper interviewed a lance-corporal, just released from Maidstone Prison, who claimed to have witnessed the scene. The corporal said:

He got a very cruel death . . . They brought him out in the yard and shot him opposite the prison windows. They left his heart and some of his bones there in the yard and they picked them up and gave them to the priest to have them buried. He met his death bravely.[20]

In time the rhetorical inexactitudes which have been accorded to James Daly himself were extended to cover the whole episode for which he was executed. On 1 July, 1950, the *Irish Weekly and Ulster Examiner* published an anonymous article on the Connaught Rangers mutiny, which said of Daly, 'He was aged nineteen and a half years, was a native of Tyrrellspass, had fought at Ypres, wore wound stripes and decorations'. The writer may not have realized that, if these facts were all correct, Daly would have been just over 14 when he was serving in the second battle of Ypres. The article went on to describe the attack on the magazine at Solon:

> The magazine was on a hill and was then held by some officers and some bandsmen, Englishmen. The defenders had machine guns; Daly's men were unarmed. The attackers were met by a withering fire in which two were killed. Father Baker, regimental chaplain, dashed between the fire and the attackers, holding a crucifix aloft, and asked Daly to order a retiral. Daly spoke to the Chaplain and ordered a retreat.[21]

The patriotic verses and ballads about the mutiny which appeared from time to time in Irish newspapers and journals sometimes stretched poetic licence to its limits. For example, a tribute to James Daly in the *Westmeath Examiner* in 1951 contained the following lines:

> We have many a deathless name on Ireland's muster roll
> Of true men who have fought and fell for freedom's hallowed goal –
> Who on the scaffold and the field have died to set us free,
> And win for the suffering mother-land the boon of liberty.
>
> One name among that noble throng our million hearts will stir,
> 'Tis the name of bold young Daly, Martyr of Gallandor [sic]
> When the news from Ireland travelled far beyond the ocean's swell,
> How the tyrant might of England had made our land a hell . . .
>
> They led him to the sacrifice hemmed in by circling steel,
> And by the open graveside they order him to kneel –
> But proudly and unflinchingly he faced the firing squad,
> And he answered 'I'm an Irishman, I kneel to none but God'.[22]

The *Irish Press* in 1952 provided the words and music of a long ballad glorifying the mutiny, which their readers were encouraged to sing. The opening stanzas were:

Come all ye loyal Irish folk and
    listen unto me,
While I relate the cruel fate of
    men beyond the sea.
How gallant Connaught Rangers
    beneath the burning sun
Of India revolted and faced the
    English gun.
A soldier home on furlough;
    Young Joseph Hawes of Clare,
The burning and the murders of
    Black and Tan beheld.
He saw the frightful carnage of
    Cromwell's khaki horde,
By men all dressed in khaki;
    the uniform he wore.

The ballad then tells how Hawes organized the mutiny at Jullundur
and it continues:

Surrounded by the English troops
    and called upon to yield
They proudly shouted 'Never!
    No loyalty we feel;
For England or the Empire we never
    more will stand,
No more we owe allegiance to
    the King of Black and Tans!'

The ballad finishes with the execution of Private Daly.

Jim Daly faced the firing-squad,
    full gallant, proud and true,
And thirteen English bullets his
    body cut in two.
The noble blood of Dalach, the
    Royal blood of Niall,
Was soaked up by the burning sand
    – his soul his maker claimed. [23]

By the time the mutineers were all confined in English prisons, the
situation in Ireland had undergone a serious deterioration and events

were moving precipitately towards a climax. The rule of law had broken down and casualties were mounting on both sides. The whole country was beset with murder, arson, reprisals and intimidation. Under the Restoration of Order in Ireland Act, which came into force in August 1920, trial by jury was virtually suspended, the public were excluded from courtrooms, and many civil offences became triable by court martial. The British Government had now become determined to match, or even to outdo the terror-tactics of the I.R.A. The principal units on which they relied were the Black and Tans and the new Auxiliary Division of the Royal Irish Constabulary. The Black and Tans numbered about 2,000 men in the autumn of 1920.[24] They were still members of the police force but were becoming more and more remote from effective police control and habitually engaged in looting, arson, thuggery and murder. The Auxiliary Division, known as the 'Auxies', had come into being in August, 1920, and was recruited exclusively from ex-officers of the British armed forces. Each member held a rank equivalent to a sergeant in the R.I.C., but they were much more highly paid than the ordinary police. The Auxies were, in fact, a special corps of para-military policemen. They operated in their own companies and were under the overall command of a regular army brigadier. Although some of their companies became first-class fighting units, Charles Townshend wrote, 'many succumbed to drunkenness and gained a reputation as perpetrators of the calculated and destructive reprisals'.[25] Speaking of developments in Ireland, a Conservative M.P., Edward Wood, later to become the Earl of Halifax and a leading British statesman, said in the House of Commons, 'It is idle to deny that, making whatever allowances we like, there have been happenings by a section of the Crown's officers of which every Englishman must be ashamed'.[26] A contrary view was taken by the Prime Minister, Lloyd George, who commented in a speech in October, 'We have murder by the throat ... We had to reorganize the police, and when the Government was ready we struck the terrorists, and now they are complaining of terror'.[27]

For their part, the I.R.A. were continuing their campaign of isolated attacks, ambushes, assassinations and intimidation – and were carrying out their own atrocities. They habitually burnt down houses belonging to the Anglo-Irish and to people of known Unionist sympathies, sometimes molesting the owners, and sometimes even murdering them. Girls who went out with members of the R.I.C. were seized and the hair was cropped from their heads.[28] Any civilian who gave or was suspected of giving information about I.R.A. activities to the authorities was liable to be killed. Mrs Lindsay, an old lady in her 70s who had warned the police of an ambush being prepared in the vicinity of her house, was kidnapped and shot.[29] A young woman called Kitty Carroll, the sole support of her elderly parents and her invalid brother, was dragged outside her home and murdered on the grounds that she had informed.[30] Between the beginning of January and the middle of April, 1921, no less than seventy-three civilians, including four women, were killed by the I.R.A.[31] These repeated acts of terrorism began to worry some of the Nationalist leaders. Erskine Childers, who was responsible for Sinn Fein's publicity, wrote to Michael Collins, then the Director of Intelligence for the I.R.A., proposing that the execution of women for spying should be forbidden from then on, owing to the bad image that was being created. Further, he suggested that the I.R.A. should disclaim responsibility for the murder of Kitty Carroll, and should pretend that Mrs Lindsay was still alive as a prisoner.[32]

Although the Connaught Rangers mutineers had taken every possible step to disassociate themselves from the British Army and from the British Government's policies in Ireland, they must have realized that in the eyes of the Irish Nationalists they bore the stigma of having enlisted voluntarily in the hated forces of the Crown, and of having taken the oath of allegiance to King George V at a time when the Dail Eireann had already declared that Ireland and England were at war with each other.

In their propaganda the I.R.A. were professing their sense of solidarity with the many demobilized British ex-servicemen then in Ireland. On 21 May, 1920, the *Irish Bulletin* stated:

> Ex-servicemen in Ireland are men enlisted from the people. They fought for four years against Prussianism. They return to Ireland and find their own people under a Prussianism as bitter as that they helped to defeat, and they naturally join their people in the struggle against oppression. The vast majority of ex-servicemen ... are steadfast supporters of the Republican Movement.[33]

The truth of the matter was revealed by Jane Leonard in her informative study of the attitude of the I.R.A. towards ex-servicemen during this period. She discovered that 'Ex-servicemen formed a civilian target for attack by the I.R.A. in 1920 and 1921. At least eighty-two were murdered prior to the Truce of July, 1921. Between January and April, 1921, alone, almost a third of all civilians killed by the I.R.A. were ex-soldiers'.[34] Miss Leonard goes on to say that 'The resentment and rejection of ex-servicemen by the nationalist community after the

First World War had its roots in the long-standing prejudice against Irishmen who joined the British forces'. She cites the example of one demobilized soldier who received a threatening letter telling him, 'You are a marked man. You wore the English khaki.'[35] This was still the prevalent mood in the country when the mutineers were released from prison, and may well have been one of the factors which had motivated them to embellish the gallantry of the mutiny, and to magnify the hardships of the punishment they had suffered for supporting the Nationalistic cause.

Throughout 1920 Field-Marshal Viscount French, the Lord-Lieutenant of Ireland, had maintained that the I.R.A. would not be crushed, and order would never be restored without the introduction of martial law. This view was shared by Major-General Tudor, the Police Adviser to the Irish Government. The Cabinet in London had hesitated to take such a drastic step until it was seen that other measures had not proved to be sufficient. After the events of what became known as 'Bloody Sunday', Lord French succeeded in getting his way. Early in the morning of Sunday, 21 November squads of I.R.A. men broke into eight houses in Dublin and murdered twelve British officers whom they claimed were secret service agents, an allegation refuted by the military authorities. Most of the victims were taken completely by surprise and some were shot in the presence of their wives.[36] Two weeks later the British Government issued a proclamation declaring that, as Ireland was now in a state of armed insurrection, the Irish garrison was to be placed on active service and martial law introduced, but would at first be limited to the four most lawless counties in the south of the country.[37] It was not long before martial law was extended to other counties and eventually it was applied in the whole of Ireland.

In the latter part of 1920 the Cabinet had been endeavouring to devise a constitutional settlement by which Ireland would be divided into two separate Home Rule areas, the North with its parliament in Belfast, and the South with its parliament in Dublin. Both parts would be granted limited powers of self-government whilst remaining inside the United Kingdom. National unity was to be preserved by a Council of Ireland. The response to the scheme was unfavourable. The Sinn Fein leaders made it clear that they would not acknowledge the validity of the Belfast parliament, and the Unionists in the north were reluctant to accept the authority of the proposed Council of Ireland.[38]

During the early months of 1921 the struggle in Ireland entered its most ruthless phase with a constant sequence of outrages being committed by the I.R.A. on the one side, and the Black and Tans or the Auxiliary Division of the Royal Irish Constabulary on the other. Although the I.R.A. were still capable of waging a continuous guerrilla campaign, their casualties were mounting and an increasing number of their men were seeking refuge in the hills. From the British point of view, their own forces were making a certain amount of headway, but there seemed to be little prospect of breaking the deadlock in the immediate future. The financial expenditure involved in maintaining an army of around 40,000 troops in a defensive, inactive and largely ineffectual role was causing the Government to turn their attention to the possibility of a negotiated settlement with Sinn Fein, and to set their hopes on their projected scheme for the division of Ireland into two semi-autonomous dependencies.[39]

Whether or not they supported the proposal for partitioning their country, the majority of the Irish people were longing for the restoration of peace. The Galway County Council was voicing a widespread feeling in December, 1920, when it passed a resolution deploring the I.R.A.'s campaign of terrorization and killing, and, equally, the reprisals exacted by the British forces. They asked the Dail to appoint three delegates and to empower them to arrange a settlement which was honourable to both nations.[40]

The desire for a truce was increasing.

Chapter 10

THE TREATY

THE GOVERNMENT OF IRELAND ACT, establishing partition, came into force in May, 1920. One of the first steps in making the measure effective was to be the holding of General Elections for both the Belfast and Dublin parliaments. When the results were declared, the Unionists had gained a massive majority in the North, whilst in the South the Republican candidates were returned unopposed in all but the four Trinity College Dublin seats. The obstacle to a settlement still seemed to be insurmountable. The British were making it clear that there could be no question of the establishment of an Independent Irish Republic. They were emphatic that a negotiated peace must be based upon Ireland's membership of the Commonwealth and her continued allegiance to the Crown. For their part the Dublin government decided to recognize the legality of the parliament in Belfast and the separate administration of the six northern counties.

Nevertheless, negotiations took place and a Truce was signed on 11 June, 1921. A few weeks later the British military command in Ireland ended all raids and reprisals, and the Government ordered the release of a number of Sinn Fein leaders from prison in England. The great majority of the people in Ireland welcomed the Truce wholeheartedly, but there were exceptions. A group of hard-line Republicans led by Eamon De Valera were adamant that they would not accept a settlement under the proposed conditions, and the I.R.A. refused to call off its campaign of killings and ambushes. During the summer months of that year Richard Mulcahy, Chief of Staff of the I.R.A., admitted that they had suffered a military defeat,[1] and Michael Collins reconciled himself to the fact that Sinn Fein would never achieve their objective of driving the British forces from the shores of Ireland.[2] This was the situation when, at the beginning of July, a Dail conference at the Dublin Mansion House, presided over by De Valera, agreed to implement the terms of the Truce. The I.R.A., after a last spate of activity during which they killed twenty people in thirty-six hours, suddenly ceased their operations.[3]

In the middle of July negotiations began in London between the British Government and an official Sinn Fein delegation on the contentious subject of Ireland's constitutional future. Lloyd George wanted the twenty-six counties of the south to have a modified Dominion status within the British Commonwealth. De Valera, who assumed control of the Irish party, persisted in his assertion that there should be one government for all thirty-two counties and that the Irish nation should be granted, not Dominion status, but 'a certain treaty of free association with the British Commonwealth group'.[4] The Dail was convened in Dublin on 16 August to consider the position, and unanimously rejected Lloyd George's proposals. The existing Irish Ministry therefore resigned and De Valera was elected President of the Republic of Ireland. He wrote to Lloyd George:

> If a small nation's right to independence is forfeit when a more powerful neighbour courts its territory for military or other advantages it is suffered to confer, there is an end to liberty.[5]

Lloyd George replied that if De Valera intended that Ireland should repudiate completely both her membership of the Commonwealth and her allegiance to the Crown, there was no point in prolonging the discussions. On the other hand, he continued,

> If your real objection to our proposals is that they offer Ireland less than the liberty which we have described, that objection can be explored at a conference.[6]

After a further exchange of letters Lloyd George invited De Valera to send over a delegation to a fresh conference, the object of which would be to ascertain 'how the association of Ireland with the community of nations known as the British Empire may best be reconciled with Irish National aspirations'. De Valera accepted the invitation, but decided not to go to London himself. He nominated five delegates, including Arthur Griffith, his Minister for Foreign Affairs, and Michael Collins, his Finance Minister. Erskine Childers accompanied the party in the capacity of their chief secretary.[7]

The conference began at 10 Downing Street on 11 October and after weeks of negotiations little progress had been made. On 30

November Lloyd George issued the Irish delegates with a draft treaty which incorporated what he described as being his 'final terms'. The Irish party travelled back to Dublin for urgent discussions with De Valera and the rest of the Irish Cabinet. Sharp differences of opinion now emerged. Griffith, Collins and other members of the delegation felt certain they would be able to win no more concessions from the British; others thought they should continue to persevere. De Valera himself still wanted a form of external association with the Commonwealth, and remained steadfastly opposed to any settlement by which Ireland would owe allegiance to the Crown. The Cabinet meeting proved to be wholly inconclusive and the delegates travelled back to London angry, confused and divided among themselves as to whether to re-open negotiations.[8]

The new discussions took place on Sunday, 4 December. Arthur Griffith, the leader of the Irish party, would have been willing to sign the draft Articles of Agreement there and then without further haggling, but he had been forbidden to do so in Dublin. Michael Collins, the most formidable and respected of the delegates, was satisfied with the offer of Dominion status, provided it was applied to a unified Ireland consisting of all thirty-two counties and having a single parliament. As the hours wore on it became obvious that, although the British Cabinet Ministers were willing to modify the wording of the oath of allegiance, they would compromise no further. When Griffith still demurred, Lloyd George told him bluntly, 'If that is your last word, your answer means war, as desired by you'.[9] However, the British had not given up hope even then of achieving their purpose peaceably. On the following morning Lloyd George summoned Michael Collins to 10 Downing Street for a private discussion. There were negotiations in the afternoon during which the Irish obtained some minor amendments to the draft treaty. Eventually, early in the evening, Lloyd George issued an ultimatum that the delegates must decide immediately without referring the matter to the Dail, whether or not they would agree to accept his Government's proposals. The alternative, he informed them, was a renewal of the war.[10]

The Irish withdrew for a private discussion. The offer before them was that the twenty-six counties of Ireland would have:

full dominion status, subject to one or two modifications, especially in regard to the Navy, and her position in the Empire would be the same as that of the great self-governing Dominions. In particular there would be no question of any veto by Great Britain upon purely Irish legislation.[11]

After several hours of agonized heart-searching, and without contacting Dublin by telephone, the delegates decided to accept the proposals. They signed the Articles of Agreement in the early hours of the morning on Tuesday, 6 December, and thereby assented to the creation of an Irish Free State with Dominion status within the British Commonwealth of Nations.

The news that the Treaty had been signed was welcomed by most of the people in the twenty-six counties, who only wanted to return to a normal and peaceful life.[12] It was also greeted with relief by the public bodies, the Unions, the farmers' organizations and the Church. The Archbishop of Cashel in a public statement said, 'The people of Ireland, by a vast majority, are in favour of the Treaty, and in a democratic country the will of the people is the final court of appeal.'[13] Notwithstanding the mood of the country, the attitude of the Dail was uncertain. The crucial debate on the settlement began on 14 December and dragged on in a spirit of bitterness and acrimony until the vote was finally taken on 7 January, 1922. The result reflected the narrow balance of opinion. Sixty-four members voted in favour of the Treaty and fifty-seven voted against it, a slender majority of seven. Two days later, De Valera resigned from the Cabinet and Arthur Griffith was elected President in his place.

Immediately after their delegates had signed the Treaty the Government in Dublin started to press for the release of all the Irish who had been interned or imprisoned in connection with the recent troubles. The British Cabinet decided early in December that those who had merely been interned should be released at once, but, in the case of the Irishmen who had been convicted of offences, the matter should be put off pending the negotiation of a mutual amnesty.

On 27 January, 1922, E. J. Duggan, the Irish Minister for Home Affairs, sent Lionel Curtis at the Cabinet Office in London a copy of the draft Amnesty Proclamation which had been prepared by the provisional Government in Dublin. Curtis had been acting as Lloyd George's adviser in the framing of the Treaty, and had now been appointed 'Adviser to the Colonial Office on Irish Affairs'. In a covering letter Duggan stressed that the draft had only been approved by his Government 'on the understanding that the Amnesty on the British side will be extended so as to cover the cases mentioned by us in committee'. He asked Curtis to put the document before the Cabinet, and he went on:

You might consider at the same time, say, what decision has been come to regarding the release of prisoners convicted in England and Scotland, as well as the Connaught Rangers and the special cases in Ulster. I might mention that in view of the forthcoming Act [of Indemnity] the release of these prisoners is a matter of great urgency.[14]

The draft Proclamation granted a general pardon 'in respect of all acts, committed in Ireland and elsewhere, in connection with the recent hostilities, by members of any of the several units of the British forces, or any servants, supporters or retainers of the said Government of Great Britain, and all other persons who co-operated with them in any capacity whatsoever'.[15]

The British Cabinet considered E. J. Duggan's letter at a meeting on 30 January and agreed to accept the substance but not the form of the draft Proclamation. With regard to the rest of Duggan's proposals, Winston Churchill, the Colonial Secretary, said he concurred with the view of the Irish Government that prisoners convicted in Britain before the Truce ought to be liberated. Churchill thought that the Connaught Rangers mutineers should be treated as falling into this category and they, too, should be set free. It is plain that his opinion was not shared by all his colleagues, as the Cabinet Minute reads, 'Strong objection was taken on the grounds of military discipline to the release of the condemned Connaught Rangers as part of a political amnesty'. It was therefore decided that the matter should be examined by Sir Laming Worthington-Evans, the Secretary of State for War, 'with a view, if possible, to their liberation in connection with the impending disbandment of the regiment'.[16]

The next day Lloyd George sent a forthright note to the War Minister headed 'Urgent', setting out his own views on the subject. 'I fear,' he wrote, 'I can suggest no good military reason for releasing men convicted of such a serious military offence.' He continued:

The Irish Provisional Government will undoubtedly desire for political purposes to advertise their release to the widest possible extent. The Army will know that men convicted of one of the gravest military crimes have been released in response to political pressure. I fear this must have a bad effect on discipline and may lead to mutinies in future cases when troops are asked to support law and order against extreme labour or other disaffected persons. They will feel that, however severe the sentence, short of death, it is sure to be remitted once peace is restored. I must therefore advise you most strongly against release. Remission is another matter. The sentences were certainly most rigorous. I should be glad to see a revision carried out on sympathetic lines.[17]

Sir Laming Worthington-Evans presented his report to the Cabinet on 21 February.[18] He said that after careful thought, he had come to the conclusion that there were no military grounds whatever for recommending the release of the Connaught Rangers mutineers who were at present serving sentences of imprisonment, since organized mutiny was one of the most serious offences which a soldier could commit. Ordinarily, when a man was released prematurely very few people knew anything about it. In the case of the Connaught Rangers it would be different, as it was certain to be very widely advertised by the Irish Provisional Government 'as an example of their power and clemency'. The Army would then draw its own conclusion that political pressure could set aside the verdict of a court of law and could be used to save a criminal from the consequences of his actions. It was essential that soldiers should continue to look on mutiny as the most serious of military offences and one that would be punished with the utmost severity. 'Grave effects may be anticipated,' he warned, 'if the Army ceases so to regard mutiny, especially in the event of a civil emergency. Cases may well arise where troops are called upon to support the civil power, when the restoration of law and order will depend on their loyalty and nothing else.' He went on to remind the other members of the Cabinet that after the Connaught Rangers had mutinied the Commander-in-Chief in India had insisted, in the interests of discipline, on one death sentence being carried out and the others being commuted to penal servitude for life, and in one case for twenty years. The War Minister concluded his report by saying:

> I would point out the grave difficulties that may be anticipated in India in enforcing discipline among our Indian troops if it becomes known that British soldiers guilty of the most serious military crime have their punishment reduced as a result of political pressure. While I am most strongly opposed to any action that could give colour to such a suggestion, I am prepared, if the Cabinet approve, to acquiesce in the sentences being reviewed; they are undoubtedly severe, and to that extent merit revision.

He suggested a scale of substantial reductions. For instance, a life sentence would be varied to 7 years, terms of 20 years to 6, 15 years to 5, and 10 years to 4. Men who were serving 3 years or less would be released from prison immediately. The Cabinet assented to his proposals but agreed that no public announcement should be made about their decision.[19]

The impending disbandment of the Connaught Rangers and other regiments recruited in the counties which would now form the Irish Free State was announced in Army Orders early in March, 1922. This prompted the author and ex-Irish Nationalist M.P. Stephen Gwynn in his weekly column in *The Observer* to appeal for the release of imprisoned mutineers. Gwynn had a special interest in the matter because he himself had enlisted in the Connaught Rangers as a private in 1915, although he was then 51, and later had served with the Regiment as an officer on the Western Front. The argument he put forward was that other Irishmen who had actually fired on English troops and police officers were being freed from custody under a general amnesty covering the events of the last few years in Ireland, and it was unfair for the condemned mutineers to be kept in prison any longer. From a strictly military point of view, he said, their actions had been indefensible, but what they had actually done was to make a political protest by demanding to leave an army which was being used against their own country. There was, of course, the disciplinary aspect, but this would no longer apply with the disappearance of their Regiment. He went on:

> In a couple of months there will be no more Connaught Rangers, no more Dublins, Munsters, Leinsters, Irish Horse; you are done with them. The Provisional Government have, as they were bound to do, forced the release of those who took part with them in active rebellion, not only in Ireland but in Great Britain. But these unlucky soldiers are nobody's children, and there is enough vindictiveness in the world, and in the army tradition, to advise that when so many have escaped, somebody at least should be made to suffer.[20]

Before the Irish Free State could become formally established it was necessary for the relevant legislative measures to be enacted by both the Dail and the Parliament at Westminster. During the interim period the Provisional Irish Government continued to hold office, with Arthur Griffith as President and Michael Collins as Chairman. In the months which followed the signing of the Treaty the situation in Ireland was far from tranquil. A minority of the I.R.A. were still determined to pursue their struggle, politically and militarily, for the abolition of the border with the six counties and the creation of a unified republic comprising the whole country. They were opposed to the holding of a General Election until they had attained their objectives, and many of them favoured the imposition of a military dictatorship under their own leaders. In January, 1922, the I.R.A. set up an Executive Army Council and Military Action Committee. Very soon they were organizing armed raids across the border, assassinations and the seizure of hostages. In the face of this belligerence the Provisional Government started to recruit a national army; the membership was confined to men who had declared themselves to be supporters of the Treaty. It was recognized, however, that it would be some months before this new force could be adequately trained and equipped.

The supervision of Irish affairs now came under Winston Churchill as Secretary of State for the Colonies. Churchill hoped that the preliminaries to the establishment of the Irish Free State would be completed during the summer of 1922. Like the rest of the Cabinet, he had confidence in Michael Collins, with his personal prestige, his charisma and his proven courage, to control the extremist elements among the Nationalists and to persuade them to accept the agreed terms of the settlement. Time was to show that they had overestimated the authority of Michael Collins and underestimated the influence of Eamon De Valera. The prospect of civil war was already being raised by De Valera soon after he retired from the Presidency. In one speech he had said that, if the Treaty was accepted, the fight for freedom would still go on and the Irish people, instead of fighting foreign soldiers, would have to fight the soldiers of an Irish Government set up by Irishmen.[21] On another occasion he put it more emotively, declaring that if the people voted in favour of the Treaty at the forthcoming election, the members of the I.R.A. 'will have to march over the bodies of their own brothers; they will have to wade through Irish blood'.[22] In April Churchill issued a warning that the British would not be able to withdraw their troops from Ireland 'until we know that the Irish people are going to stay by the Treaty. Neither will we be able to refrain from stating the consequences which would follow the setting up of a Republic'.[23]

On the night of 13 April a force of I.R.A. men, comprising the Republican Army Executive and 120 volunteers from the Dublin Brigade, took over the buildings of the Four Courts, the principal courthouse in Dublin, and declared it to be 'the military headquarters of the Irish Republic'. The following day they sent the Dail a document containing their 'peace terms', which included a demand for the disbandment of the Civic Guard, the new Irish police force, and an undertaking that no elections would be held while the threat of war with England still existed. They said that these terms were 'probably the last hope' of saving the country from a civil war. Elsewhere in Ireland parties of I.R.A. and their anti-Treaty supporters took over various public buildings. The partly-formed national army put up little effective opposition to these incursions and there were very few casualties.

The General Election took place in the twenty-six counties on 16 June, 1922, and the results showed a substantial majority in favour of accepting the Treaty. A new Government was then formed in Dublin, headed by Arthur Griffith and Michael Collins, who both remained in their previous offices. Now that the constitutional situation had been determined the Cabinet at Westminster was impatient for the Irish pro-Treaty forces to regain possession of the Four Courts, and they were even prepared, if necessary, for British units to undertake the operation, supported by tanks and aircraft. However, the Provisional Government preferred to use its own troops. Early in the morning on 28 June pro-Treaty soldiers began an attack on the building, using infantry and artillery. A bitter struggle ensued and it was only after three days that the remnants of the garrison finally surrendered. While the siege of the Four Courts was still taking place, De Valera and other Republican leaders announced their support for the I.R.A., and for an armed insurrection throughout the country.

At the beginning of June Winston Churchill had received a request for the release of the imprisoned Connaught Rangers mutineers from the Reverend Dr Collins, a Dublin clergyman who had served as an army chaplain and had been decorated with the Military Cross. Dr Collins wrote:

> I wish to petition His Majesty's Government to grant a free pardon to the Connaught Rangers found guilty of mutiny in India in 1920. Should the forthcoming General Elections in Ireland result in a majority for the Irish Free State, I know that such an act would strengthen very much the position of the Government in Ireland ... A number of the men who were condemned to long sentences of imprisonment have had no direct evidence brought against them to warrant such a severe sentence. I have been to Solon and Simla and have heard the official version, and I have also been Chaplain to some of the prisoners and hence have heard both sides.[24]

Churchill took Collins's letter seriously and sent it to the War Minister with a request that he might be given the advice of the Army Council in drafting a reply. After discussing the matter, the Army Council suggested that Dr Collins should be told:

(a) that the Cabinet have carefully considered the cases of the Connaught Rangers mutineers and have directed that drastic reductions are made in their sentences with the result that some of them have been released; (b) that no further reduction of their sentences, which were inflicted not for a political offence, but for one of the most serious of all military crimes, can be considered.[25]

A few weeks before the Four Courts were stormed by the new Irish Free State Army, the Connaught Rangers had been formally disbanded, the 1st Battalion in the Punjab and the 2nd Battalion at Dover. In a farewell letter to the Colonel of the 1st Battalion, Major-General Sir Herbert Uniacke, the Commander of the Rawalpindi District, spoke of the sadness he felt that a Regiment with such a fine military record extending over the last 129 years should come to the end of its existence. 'You recently, for a brief period, fell on troublous times,' he wrote,

> but have won through with every credit to yourselves, and the Battalion stands now a well-disciplined, well-trained body of men that anyone should be proud to command. This state of efficiency would not have been attained unless the officers, NCOs and men had given the most loyal support to the Commanding Officer, and I consider the way in which all ranks have played the game during the past twelve months is beyond praise. Now when the Battalion is about to be struck off the muster roll of the British Army you may pass away as a body of fighting men, fit for service anywhere, with your heads held high, confident that you have upheld the old reputation of the Rangers.[26]

The Regimental Colours of the 1st and 2nd Battalions were received by King George V in St George's Hall, Windsor Castle. On 13 June the *Irish Times* had published a short poem. 'To the Colours of the Rangers', which began:

> You'll hang in the Castle of Windsor,
> And dust will enshrine every fold
> On which are emblazoned the honours
> We gained in the battles of old;
> But none will write on you the legend
> How we strove to be worthy your fame;
> You will fade, and our deeds – all forgotten –
> Fade quicker than even a name.[27]

After disbandment of the Connaught Rangers there was a feeling among the relatives and friends of the mutineers that there was no justification for prolonging their punishment. Towards the end of July Churchill received a personal letter at the House of Commons from a man called Denis Hammon, who gave an address at Athlone in County Westmeath. Mr Hammon said:

> I have been asked to write to you directly asking you to release the unfortunate Connaught Rangers who are presently imprisoned in Maidstone Convict Prison. Some of these come from the neighbourhood of this town and their friends are very anxious that they should be released. I think it is in their favour that beyond insubordination there is no other charge against any of these men, many of whom at the time were mere boys ... there seems no reason for further imprisonment as the Connaught Rangers have been disbanded.[28]

Mr Hammon was sent what was becoming the stock reply by the Colonial Office telling him that the sentences had already been drastically reduced and pointing out that mutiny was considered to be 'one of the most serious of all military crimes'.[29]

The Irish Civil War, which lasted for approximately ten months, was fought out on a single issue between the supporters and the opponents of the Treaty, the principal protagonists being on the one side the Free State troops, and on the other an irregular rebel force. They were equally unprepared for the struggle, both in organization and in strategical planning. As the area of fighting increased Michael Collins, at his own request, was temporarily relieved of his political duties and was appointed Commander-in-Chief of the Free State Army for the duration of the hostilities. The force at his disposal, besides being under-trained and ill-equipped, was very small numerically, but the Provisional Government Cabinet authorized a substantial increase in its size until the emergency was over. Although De Valera joined the General Staff of the Irregulars he played very little part in the conduct of military operations. He realized that with the majority of the people in the twenty-six counties being in favour of the Treaty the odds were weighted against the insurrection. During the summer he wrote in his diary, 'Any chance of winning? If there was any chance, [it is our] duty to hold on to secure it. If none, duty to try to get the men to quit – for the present. The people must be won to the cause before any successful fighting can be done.' In a letter to a friend he said, 'There can be no glory and no enthusiasm ... worst of all, there seems to be no way out of it.'[30]

Most of the fighting took place in the south and the west of the country. After the early engagements there were few pitched battles; the Irregulars reverted to the guerrilla tactics at which they excelled, and the Free State Army mainly occupied towns and fortified posts. During August, 1922, the pro-Treaty party lost two of its principal leaders. At the beginning of the month Arthur Griffith died suddenly from a cerebral haemorrhage. Ten days later Michael Collins was killed in an ambush in West Cork when taking part in a tour of inspection of his troops in the area.

The Minister for Local Government, William Cosgrave, took over from Michael Collins as Chairman of the Provisional Government and also became President of the Dail in place of Arthur Griffith. Cosgrave was a staunch supporter of the Treaty. He had had a lifelong association with the Irish Nationalist movement and had been a founder-member of Sinn Fein. With his political background and his service in the Volunteers during the Easter Rising, his credentials for the task which lay ahead of him seemed admirable. In Cosgrave's years of ministerial office he had created for himself the reputation of being an able administrator; it was yet to be seen whether or not he also possessed the qualities of a national leader.

Chapter 11

'A GRACIOUS ACT'

A MEETING OF THE DAIL at the beginning of September, 1922, voted in favour of the constitution of the Irish Free State, and thenceforth the country was ruled by a National instead of a Provisional Government. But the Civil War still continued, amid increasing criticism of the Army's ineffectiveness against the guerrilla tactics of the Irregulars. Under the Public Safety Act, passed by the Dail in the last week of September, special military courts were set up to try terrorist offences, including the unlawful possession of firearms, and were given the power of passing sentence of death. In the debate on the measure, William Cosgrave said:

> Although I have always objected to a death penalty, there is no other way I know of in which ordered conditions can be restored in this country, or any security obtained for our troops, or to give our troops any confidence in us as a Government. We must accept the responsibility.[1]

In a joint pastoral letter the Irish Roman Catholic Bishops urged the public to support the new administration, and condemned the armed resistance of the Irregulars, declaring,

> They carry on what they call a war, but which, in the absence of any legitimate authority to justify it, is morally only a system of murder and assassinations of the national forces – for it must not be forgotten that killing in an unjust war is as much murder before God as if there were no war.[2]

An offer to assist the Irish Government came from an unexpected quarter. In the latter part of August twenty-eight of the mutineers in

Maidstone Prison petitioned the War Office to release them so that they could join the Irish Free State Army and fight against the anti-Treaty forces. When he was submitting their petitions to the Adjutant-General, the Director of Personal Services wrote in a covering note:

> In these appeals they are almost identical in saying that the deaths of Michael Collins and Mr Griffith make them feel that their duty lies in supporting the Provisional Government of Ireland against the rebels, and they all, with one exception, give this as the reason that they are asking for reconsideration of their sentences ... I would point out that in nearly all of these cases where petitions are submitted there is attached a schedule of offences committed during their penal servitude, which shows that these men have continually given trouble, collectively and individually, in the prison in which they are situated.[3]

The Judge Advocate General added the comment, 'I do not advise that further clemency should be extended to these men who in addition to their original offence have given much trouble in prison.'[4]

The twenty-eight mutineers wrote out and signed their petitions separately. Joseph Hawes said that, as an Irishman in India, he had mutinied as a protest against the way his country was being treated by the British Government, but that that state of affairs no longer existed. He wanted to join the Irish Free State Army because of 'the desolation and misery caused to my country by a Spanish adventurer De Valera and his followers'.[5] Several of the prisoners laid stress on their loyalty to the Crown. Patrick Cherry and John Oliver, both of whom had taken part in the raid on the armoury at Solon, ended their petition with the words 'God save the King', and Cherry said that he wanted a chance 'to make known my loyalty to His Majesty which I had the misfortune to break'.[6] Thomas Devine, another Solon mutineer, maintained that he wanted a chance to demonstrate his loyalty to the British Empire.[7]

A number of mutineers, in their petitions, spoke of their admiration for Michael Collins. One commented upon the ruinous policy of the rebels compared with 'the glorious policy of the late Messrs Collins and Griffith'.[8] Almost universally, they condemned the revolution, Lance-Corporal Hewson saying that the conduct of the rebels filled every Irishman with disgust.[9] Private Kearney denounced the atrocities committed by 'the renegade De Valera'.[10] The only petitioner who did not seek release for the purpose of joining the Irish

Free State Army was Private Mannion, who stated that his wife was destitute and he wanted to be free because he was her sole support.[11]

On 19 October, 1922, the Conservatives withdrew from the coalition government, which had been in power since December, 1918, and declared that they would fight the next General Election as an independent party. A few days later Lloyd George resigned as Prime Minister to be succeeded by Andrew Bonar Law who formed a Cabinet of Conservative Ministers. Stephen Gwynn had been acquainted with Bonar Law in the past and he considered that this was an opportune moment to make another appeal for the release of the mutineers. On 31 October he sent the new Prime Minister a letter saying that these men had demanded to lay down their arms and quit the Army because of the news reaching them from Ireland. Although he did not complain because they had been punished for their behaviour, it seemed unjust to him 'that the amnesty which closed the political events of which their mutiny was a part should not have been extended to them'. If they were treated with clemency now, he was sure it would have no obvious political value. The Nationalist ex-soldiers in Ireland would be pleased, but they had no political influence. 'Some believe,' he concluded, 'in the efficacy of an action which is done simply for justice, or to heal a service of injustice.'[12]

Apparently Bonar Law was not unimpressed by the letter as he referred it to the War Minister, the Earl of Derby, for his personal opinion. Derby reported on 12 December:

> The question of remission of sentences was brought before my predecessor. He went very carefully into the matter, and with evident reluctance the then Adjutant-General prepared a memorandum in which he consented to certain reductions of the sentences.[13]

The War Office informed Stephen Gwynn on 14 December that the Secretary of State for War was unable to give a definite reply to his letter until he had had an opportunity of giving the matter his further personal attention, but he doubted, from his own knowledge of the cases against the mutineers, if he would be able to recommend any reductions in the sentences, additional to those that had already been made.[14]

The campaign for the release of the imprisoned Connaught Rangers was being maintained with unabated vigour by the Nationalist forces in Ireland. On 9 October, 1922, the *Freeman's Journal* published in full a letter from Private Michael Kearney at Maidstone Prison to his mother in County Clare. Kearney, aged 22, had been sentenced originally to 15 years' penal servitude for his part in the raid on the armoury at Solon. The readers of the *Freeman's Journal* might have been surprised if they had known that in his petition to the War Office, about six weeks previously, Kearney had referred to De Valera as a 'renegade' and had stated that he wished to join the Irish Free State Army 'to fight for the preservation of the Empire – the greatest Empire in the world'. His letter to his mother was written in an educated, though embroidered, style and bore the imprint of substantial editing. He began naturally enough, by enquiring about 'the loved ones at home', and went on to say:

> What news can a poor prisoner send from his dungeon, one who is absolutely cut off from the world, whose daily life is a monotonous succession of the same routine, nothing but an anticipation that those for whom he gave his liberty and veritable existence – for this is a 'living tomb' – might at least obtain his emancipation by a generous interest in his case. I am tired of expectation, wearied of false hope, and no longer dream the dreams which time and experience have proved to be simply delusions ... We hope and are disappointed, trust and are deceived, persevere and are brought to the verge of misanthropy by experiencing the blackest of all vices, base ingratitude. The past has seen our hopes baffled; the present, surprise at the indifference of those for whom we suffered, and still suffer, the loss of 'one of the most precious gifts that Heaven has given to man' to quote the Spanish Cervantes ...[15]

It reads more like a political oration than a letter from an absent, homesick private soldier of that period to one of his parents, but it was sufficiently emotive, no doubt, for its intended purpose, and a covering note urged the public not to forget 'the brave lads who, in their own way, struck a blow to forward Irish freedom'.[16]

There was an anonymous letter on the correspondence page of the *Poblacht na h'Eireann* at the beginning of December from a woman who said that both her husband and her brother were serving sentences for the mutiny. They had been, she explained, Republican soldiers and that was the reason they had laid down their arms in India. They were now being kept in prison merely 'for love of their country'. She appealed for their release in time for Christmas as she had to keep six small children and a crippled father-in-law, and she was almost penniless.[17]

It was not only Irish Nationalists who were agitating for the liberation of the mutineers. In December the War Office received an appeal on their behalf from five officers, all of whom had served in one or other of the battalions in the Connaught Rangers. They were an impressive group consisting of a General, a Brigadier, a Colonel, a Major and Captain Stephen Gwynn. They said they had met together in Dublin 'to discuss the matter of the interests of the two Nations', but it seems that their principal concern was the fate of the members of their regiment who were still in prison. They stressed that they did not seek to justify the mutiny, nor did they criticize the sentences. However, they felt that the acts of indiscipline which had occurred 'had their origin in Irish political events', and they suggested that all the prisoners should now be pardoned. A few days after the appeal reached the War Office a Lieutenant-Colonel who had commanded the 2nd Battalion of the Connaught Rangers sent a telegram from Ireland to say that he wished his name to be added to it.[18]

William Cosgrave became the first elected President of the Executive Council of the Irish Free State on 6 December, 1922. Ten days later he wrote to Bonar Law to tell him that among the immediate legislative measures to be introduced in the Dail was an Amnesty Bill 'to give legal effect (so far as that may now be necessary) to the undertaking given by the late General Collins with regard to the British Military engaged in Ireland during the period prior to the Truce'. He went on:

We had hoped that this Bill would be regarded as non-contentious, but we find that the case of the Connaught Rangers and other prisoners, whose names are given on the enclosed schedule, now held by your Government, is occupying the public mind very considerably and also the minds of many members of our Parliament. We have reason to believe that the question of these prisoners will be raised when the Amnesty Bill is brought forward, and that it will be urged that while we propose a complete amnesty for the British Military in Ireland, the British Government, by its continued detention of the prisoners referred to above, have granted only a partial amnesty to our nationals.

Cosgrave 'earnestly requested' the British Prime Minister to give the matter his attention.[19]

Bonar Law replied immediately, promising that Cosgrave's letter would receive the attention of the British Government as quickly as possible. But, he added, the Secretary of State for War had just been abroad and so he would be unable to make a more definite response until the following week.[20]

The problem of whether or not the Connaught Rangers should be released, with its conflicting political and military aspects, was evidently regarded by the Cabinet as being of the utmost importance. The Earl of Derby, in a memorandum to the Adjutant-General on 18 December, wrote that he had been shown by the Prime Minister a letter from the Irish Government in which they indicated that they were about to introduce an Amnesty Bill for the benefit of British soldiers, 'but they felt that it was impossible to do so while we were still keeping in prison for a political offence the men who had mutinied in the Connaught Rangers'. The Prime Minister had told him that, although Conservative MPs would probably support the War Office view, 'it might be extremely difficult to face the House of Commons on the matter'. Derby said he had informed the Prime Minister that the Military Members of the Army Council could not go back on the opinion they had already expressed, and that if in the end the Cabinet were forced to give way, he thought it only just 'that it should be known to the country that it was by order of the Cabinet and not by the consent of the Army Council'. The Prime Minister had then referred to the various recent cases of mutiny which had occurred when the Army was being demobilized. He had asked Derby to send him notes on any such cases in which the mutineers had been forgiven, as these would afford a useful precedent. Derby said that he told the Prime Minister that such cases were dissimilar to the Connaught Rangers mutiny, but he would prepare the notes as directed.[21]

The Adjutant-General replied to this memorandum on the same day. He said there had been a great many mutinies during the period of demobilization, but it would take some time to locate the relevant files. All the sentences were reviewed in 1919 and there had been a general exercise of clemency ... With regard to the mutiny of the Connaught Rangers, he had been informed by General Childs, the Director of Personal Services, that he had interviewed a large number of officers from the battalion concerned,

> and there is no doubt in his mind that the mutiny, grave as it was, was conducted by the men taking part in it with only one instance of violence, viz: an attack on the guard room, and beyond that the men behaved with great restraint, and with no violence. In fact, they themselves assisted in removing their arms etc. to the stores and merely refused to go on parade.

The sentences had already been reviewed and reduced, the Adjutant-General went on:

If, however, the Cabinet choose to make a *beau geste* to mark the commencement of the life of the new Free State, they will, I hope, make it clear that they do so on their own authority and not by the advice of the Army Council.[22]

William Cosgrave's letter to Bonar Law was discussed by the Cabinet at a meeting on 19 December, and the Home Secretary was asked to examine the cases of all the prisoners, other than the Connaught Rangers, to whom the President had specifically referred.[23] The Army Council met to consider the matter on the same day. The Earl of Derby, in a letter, informed the Prime Minister what had taken place:

I explained the political position to them as you had put it to me. They quite saw the force of the argument from a political point of view, though from a military point of view they adhered to the view that was given to you by the Adjutant-General yesterday. I have told them that I do not ask them to agree with the political view and that they will not be asked to justify it.

He suggested that if clemency were to be shown it must emanate directly from the King, on the advice of the Government.

This is therefore simply to inform you that if you now think it advisable, either with or without the concurrence of the rest of the Cabinet, to advise His Majesty to exercise his clemency by the grant of a King's Pardon, I, as head of the office concerned, will support you in any such action.

Derby ended by saying that the pardon should be announced as being granted by the King 'on the advice of his Ministers'.[24]

By the end of December, 1922, all the British troops had been withdrawn from the Irish Free State, except for the small garrisons which remained at certain ports under the terms of the Treaty. The Civil War continued, but the Government forces were gradually gaining control of the entire country. The rebels were now fragmented into isolated pockets of resistance, mostly in County Cork and in the south of County Tipperary. They were becoming increasingly short of arms and money, and a number of their leaders had been captured. Early in the New Year the powers of the military courts to impose capital sentences were extended, and during the month of January no less than thirty-four executions were carried out.

The Amnesty Bill was due to be debated in the Dail on 4 January, 1923. A short while before this date the Irish Ministers added a new complication to the proposed release of the Connaught Rangers mutineers when they began to press the British Government to pardon a man called Joseph Dowling as well. Dowling was, in fact, an ex-Connaught Ranger who was serving a life sentence for treachery. He had been captured on the Western Front early in the war and was one of the very few prisoners-of-war who had volunteered to join Roger Casement's abortive Irish Brigade. During the massive German counterattack in the spring of 1918, in which the B.E.F. suffered 300,000 casualties and were forced back to a precarious line some fifty miles from the Channel Ports, Dowling had been caught on the coast of County Clare where he had just been landed by a German submarine. It was suspected by British Intelligence that the Germans were trying to organize an insurrection in Ireland in order to divert troops from the fighting in France, and that Dowling's mission had been connected with an attempt to land arms for the planned rising.

At a meeting of the British Cabinet on 29 December, 1922, it was agreed that the Secretary of State for the Colonies should send an emissary to the Irish President to tell him that they were willing to advise the King that the Connaught Rangers mutineers should be given a free pardon, 'but that they were prepared to make this concession with great reluctance and only if it would, without further concession, secure the passage of the Amnesty Bill through Parliament . . .'[25]

The Permanent Under-Secretary at the Colonial Office was chosen as the emissary to carry this message to Dublin. He sent a telegram to Whitehall on 3 January to say that the Irish Government felt that the release of the Connaught Rangers would provide sufficient impetus to ensure the passage of the Amnesty Bill through the Dail the next day, and that they would do their utmost to make certain it was not defeated. In the same telegram he suggested that the Home Secretary should consider the freeing of the mutineers at once, as 'it was important that the release could not be ascribed to political pressure brought to bear as a consequence of the debate upon the Bill in the Dail'.[26]

Whilst all this was taking place the Earl of Derby who, as Secretary for War, was one of the Ministers principally concerned, was on holiday at the Grand Hotel, Cannes. Surviving documents show that he kept in constant contact with Kenneth Lyon, the Principal Private Secretary at the War Office, by letter, telephone and telegram. In the course of a long despatch, written the day before the Amnesty Bill was to be debated in Dublin, Lyon told him of the latest developments in the negotiations for the freeing of the mutineers. He wrote:

> I have just been informed of the final decision regarding the release of the Connaught Rangers and the question of Dowling, the assistant of Roger Casement, and the Irish Ministers during the last two days were very strongly of opinion that Dowling and the Connaught Rangers cases were exactly parallel and if the Connaught Rangers were released, Dowling should be released too. After discussion with the Home Office and Colonial Office, it was decided to instruct our representative in Ireland to inform the Irish Government that the British Government could see no parallel between the two cases, and that the British Government would be very much embarrassed if Dowling were released because we had in custody still British subjects convicted of similar offences and now undergoing life sentences. If we were to release Dowling there would be no reason for not releasing the others. This message was conveyed to the Irish Government with the intimation that if they did not accept the release of the Connaught Rangers without Dowling, the British Government would withdraw their offer to release the Connaught Rangers.

Lyon then recounted how further discussions had taken place between Tim Healy, the veteran Nationalist, who was now Governor-General of the Irish Free State, and some of his Ministers on the one side, and representatives of the British Government on the other. Eventually, the Irish Government had agreed to accept the British proposal, but they had still remained 'unconvinced of the necessity for not releasing Dowling and they would not pledge themselves that Dowling's case would not be raised in the Dail. They would, however, endeavour to differentiate the cases of the Connaught Rangers and Dowling to the Irish Parliament'. Having reached this understanding, Lyon continued,

> Orders were given last night for the release of the Connaught Rangers, a submission to the King being made by the Home Secretary. In communicating the decision of the Government to release the Connaught Rangers to the Governor-General, the Secretary of State for the Colonies impressed on him that the decision was only taken on the definite understanding that the release of the Connaught Rangers alone would give sufficient impetus for the [Amnesty] Bill being carried through, and upon the assurance that the Free State would do their utmost to ensure its passage.[27]

Derby commented in his reply:

> With regard to the Connaught Rangers, I wish you would look up the Cabinet decision, because as far as my recollection goes it was distinctly agreed that the prisoners should not be released until the Indemnity Bill had passed through the Irish House of Commons. Dowling is on quite a different footing, and I shall certainly oppose his release, though it is not a matter for resignation if I am overruled.[28]

Introducing the Amnesty Bill in the Dail on 4 January, 1923, William Cosgrave said that its purpose was to indemnify all the people who had supported the British Government during the last few years, by carrying out orders, or being responsible for acts, which would be or might be the subject of legal proceedings. He went on:

> I am glad to be able to announce the release of the Connaught Rangers, which is agreed to be a further proof of the British Government's desire to efface bitter memories of the recent trouble. The difficulties in the way of a complete amnesty were known, having regard to the way with which the case was viewed from the severe standpoint of the British Army, and in ordering the release of these prisoners the British Government gave proof that it has acted in the spirit of goodwill towards us and towards the Irish people everywhere.[29]

Early in the debate, as the Irish Ministers had anticipated, the case of Joseph Dowling was raised. One Labour Member of the Dail, Cathal O'Shannon, whilst not opposing the Bill, invited the President to tell them whether there was any likelihood of some other prisoners still in British custody being released as well. 'I think, if my recollection is right,' he said, 'that Dowling, who landed on the coast of Clare in 1918 is still in prison . . . I would like an assurance that the Government is not passing the matter over without consideration.'[30] He was supported by Darrell Figgis, who said that Dowling had behaved with courage and should not be forgotten. Figgis suggested that there might be a large number of other Irishmen in English prisons who had served their country, or were suspected of having done so, and their cases had been overlooked altogether.[31]

At this point Mr Kevin O'Higgins, the Minister for Home Affairs, intervened to say that at the time of the earlier amnesty the British Home Office had supplied the Provisional Government with a complete list of all the Irish political prisoners who were then being held in English prisons. The Connaught Rangers mutineers and Joseph

Dowling were in a class on their own as they came under military jurisdiction. The British military authorities were anxious to establish the principle that a political amnesty could not apply to members of the armed forces.

A forthright speech was made by a backbencher, William Sears, a relative of Private Sears who had been killed in the raid on the magazine at Solon. He expressed his satisfaction at the release of the mutineers, and added:

> I think there is no act that the English have done for the last twelve months to my mind, which indicates more their change of mind and change of attitude towards this country. I think their case was particularly difficult for the British Government. They released the prisoners they had in the convict prisons in England immediately after the Treaty was signed, but in regard to the Connaught Rangers they were in a very difficult position. These men were out in India and had sworn allegiance to England when they joined up, and they not alone fought against England, but they broke that pledge, so that the English could have charged them with a double offence. Therefore, I think their release is a token of a very good spirit and I have great pleasure in supporting the Bill on that account.[32]

In the course of his reply to the debate, William Cosgrave surmised that any soldiers committing the same offence as the Connaught Rangers or Joseph Dowling in the Irish Army would be given much more severe punishments than these men had received. In all the circumstances, he considered that the British Government were performing 'a gracious act' in granting the mutineers a pardon.[33] The Amnesty Bill was then passed without a division.

The news of the release of the Connaught Rangers was universally welcomed by the Irish Press, although an article in the I.R.A. journal *Poblacht na h'Eireann* asserted that they had been freed 'not out of justice or clemency but for the sake of political effect'. The writer reported that on 8 January, while the Dublin Government was celebrating the return home of the mutineers, five soldiers in the Irish Free State Army were executed with their approval, because they had committed a similar offence by 'returning to their allegiance to the Republic'. The article enquired, 'Could anything illustrate more clearly the hideous foundation of treachery and vile hypocrisy upon which the Free State is based?'[34]

Chapter 12

THE HOMECOMING

IN HIS ACCOUNT OF the Connaught Rangers' mutiny, John Flannery only makes the briefest reference to the ultimate release of the mutineers from prison. A few of them serving short sentences, he says, were freed at the time of the Anglo-Irish truce, and, 'after protracted negotiations', the remainder were liberated on 4 January, 1923.[1] His reticence is understandable if there is any truth in the statement made by Joseph Howes that when the mutineers arrived back from India at the start of the sentences, Flannery was separated from the rest, allegedly for his own protection, and sent off alone 'to the prison of the Isle of Wight'.[2] When reporting the release of the men in January, 1923, several Irish newspapers stated that four Connaught Rangers had been serving their sentences at Parkhurst, the large convict prison on the Isle of Wight, and the *Irish Independent* gave their names as McGowan, Devers, McGrath and Shallow, and went on to say that John Flannery had originally been sent to Parkhurst but had been moved 'at his own request'.[3] The prison records show, in fact, that Flannery was released from Parkhurst with the other four on 6 January, 1923.

Hawes has described his experience when the pardon was granted. About six weeks earlier, he says, he and some other mutineers had decided to make a final protest at Maidstone by smashing everything on which they could lay their hands. Before their plan could be put into operation, the authorities heard what was afoot and the ringleaders were promptly transferred to other prisons. Hawes himself had been sent to Shrewsbury Gaol. Late at night on 3 January the Chief Warder had come to his cell to inform him he was to be freed. He had then been taken before the Governor who had given him the option of leaving the prison there and then or staying until the following morning. Hawes had chosen to spend that night in his cell and had travelled next day to Holyhead, where he met the party of mutineers who had just been released from Maidstone and were waiting to embark on the overnight ferry to Dublin. Hawes added significantly than there was no sign of Lance-Corporal Flannery,[4] but that is not surprising as the five prisoners in Parkhurst were not discharged for another two days.

According to the prison records a total of thirty-two Connaught Rangers were released from Maidstone on 4 January. Eight mutineers had been freed the previous March, six from Maidstone, one from Liverpool and one from Manchester.

On their arrival in Dublin some of the mutineers told reporters how they had received news of their pardon at Maidstone Jail the previous morning. They had assembled for the usual eight o'clock parade to be searched by warders. Then an order had been given that when the rest of the prisoners fell out to join the working parties the Connaught Rangers were to stand fast. None of them knew the reason for this and some thought they were going to be transferred to another prison. Presently the Governor had appeared and, reading from a typewritten document, he announced that all mutineers who were still at the prison were to be set at liberty immediately and that their release would be unconditional.[5] James Gorman's recollection is different. He says that as soon as the cells were opened that morning the Governor had come in and told them they had been pardoned.[6] The subsequent events emerged from various interviews given by the men. They were provided with train and boat warrants for their journey from Maidstone to Dublin, and each of them was issued, free of charge, with a civilian suit, a shirt and a set of underwear. During that day they were addressed by two Roman Catholic chaplains, both of whom had 'pointed out the evils of intemperance and requested them not to harbour any ill-feelings towards their jailers'.[7] According to one of the Irish national newspapers, when the regular chaplain at Maidstone was told that the Connaught Rangers were going to be released 'he regretted their departure, as they had been exemplary Catholics while they were there and had set a great example to the criminals'.[8] This statement does not accord with the descriptions some of the mutineers gave of their behaviour in the prison, nor is it consistent with the number of disciplinary offences which were entered on most of their record sheets.[9]

The mutineers left the prison late in the afternoon, accompanied by one of the Roman Catholic chaplains, to begin their journey home. The fact of their departure was apparently well known in Maidstone because the *Irish Independent* reported that 'the inhabitants of the town lined the route and stood spellbound as they marched four deep from the gloomy portals to the railway station'.[10] Another Irish paper stated that the Prison Governor had joined the men when they were about to board their train, and wished them the best of luck in the future, adding, 'keep out of trouble. I'm glad to see the back of you'. They agreed that he had every reason to make the last remark because they had always 'roused him considerably'.[11]

Few of the mutineers could have anticipated the adulation they were to receive following their release. When the train from Maidstone arrived at Victoria Station they were met by a small group of prominent members of the Irish Self-Determination League who took charge of the entertainment while they were passing through London. Charles Kerrigan has said that some of them were given a conducted tour of London, riding on the top decks of buses.[12] They foregathered at Euston Station during the evening and found that a number of London Irish Nationalists were waiting to see them off on the next stage of their journey. A complete coach on the Holyhead boat-train had been set aside for them, marked with the notice 'Reserved for Connaught Rangers', and as they pulled out of the station the cheering crowd on the platform started to sing 'God Save Ireland'. One of the mutineers said later, 'We were sent off like gentlemen'.[13]

After they had left London their celebrations must have continued as James Gorman admitted that 'By the time that we were in Holyhead there wasn't much of the train left together'.[14]

The Irish newspapers differed in their reports as to the numbers of mutineers who were released from Maidstone Prison, and the number who travelled on the overnight boat from Holyhead to Dublin on Thursday, 4 January. Most of them stated correctly that thirty-two had been freed at Maidstone and gave the same figure as the size of the party arriving in Dublin on the following morning. It seems to have been generally accepted, too, that four of the mutineers from Parkhurst made the crossing from Holyhead a day later. The *Evening Herald* reported that thirty-two prisoners had been released from Maidstone the previous day but only twenty-nine of them had arrived in Dublin that morning, and went on to mention various other English prisons where individual mutineers had been detained.[15] The name John Flannery does not appear in any of the lists of prisoners returning home, but he and some of the others probably travelled independently.

The arrival of the boat from Holyhead at the Carlisle Pier, Dun Laoghaire, on the morning of Friday, 5 January was 'a remarkable and inspiring scene', said the Dublin *Evening Telegraph*.[16] Owing to the fact that it was still very early the waiting crowd was small, but nevertheless it was vociferous. As soon as the ferry had berthed the official Reception Committee, which included four members of the Dail and the Chairman of the Irish Self-Determination League, went on board to congratulate the Connaught Rangers on their release from prison and to welcome them home. To the cheers of the onlookers the mutineers then filed down the gangplank. 'Attired in civilian clothes, the men all looked well, despite their experiences,' said the reporter from the *Evening Herald*, 'the youthful appearance of the majority – some of them mere boys – was the subject of comment amongst those on the pier'.[17]

Special compartments had been reserved for the party on the train from Dun Laoghaire to Dublin, and once again they left the station with the cheers of their admirers ringing in their ears. When they reached Westland Row, the terminal station in the city, there were more jubilant crowds, more cheering and more emotional fervour. It was the sort of triumphal acclaim accorded to returning heroes. They were taken from the train to the Grosvenor Hotel nearby where a special celebratory breakfast had been prepared in their honour; 'the first decent meal' they had eaten, said *The Freeman's Journal*, 'after two years of prison feeding'.[18] After they had finished their breakfast the majority of the mutineers set out for their homes, but about a dozen of them stayed on at the hotel 'where they were visited by large numbers of people during the day and everything possible was done for their comfort'.[19] Telegrams had been sent to the relatives of the men travelling from Dublin by train that morning to various parts of Ireland so that a suitable reception would greet them on arrival at their destinations. To forestall any critical comment that the released Connaught Rangers had not been welcomed by a Government Minister or a civic dignitary, *The Freeman's Journal* published a statement, no doubt officially inspired, which explained:

It was in deference to the feelings of the men, and with a desire to spare them excitement and strain, that the reception in Dublin was of such a private nature.[20]

The Irish newspapers which covered the homecoming were in agreement that the sympathies of the mutineers in the civil war were wholeheartedly on the side of the Free State. When the train from Maidstone arrived at Victoria Station, said the *Catholic Herald*, '"Long Live the Irish Free State" was the cry of the released men as they stepped upon the platform'.[21] The *Irish Independent* reporter wrote:

The attitude of the ex-prisoners towards the situation in Ireland is summed up in the following statement by one of them – 'We believe we should stand by whatever policy the majority of our countrymen have declared for'.[22]

After their celebration breakfast at the Grosvenor Hotel the mutineers who were not staying in Dublin 'left for their homes with parting good wishes for the success of the Free State', said the *Evening Telegraph*.[23]

These reports must have been particularly galling to the anti-Treaty Republicans, who had always regarded the Connaught Rangers mutineers as being adherents of their own political viewpoint. They were very sensitive after the general pardon about the rumours that some of the liberated men had enlisted in the Irish Free State Army. On 13 January *Poblacht na h'Eireann*, the official newsheet of the I.R.A., made the announcement:

> In view of the recent release from imprisonment of the Connaught Rangers who took part in the Mutiny in India as a protest against the British War of Aggression on the Irish Republic, we take this opportunity of informing our readers that of all the men who took part in the Mutiny in India only one had joined the 'Free State' Army, and he is the man who turned King's Evidence against his comrades. The remainder of the gallant band, we are proud to say, remained true to the ideal of Irish Independence for which they suffered so much.[24]

Presumably the paper was referring to John Flannery as the one man who had enlisted, as he was the only mutineer to be accused by the rest of 'turning King's Evidence'. In fact there is nothing to suggest that Flannery ever joined the Free State Army, although it is known that a number of others did so.

The feteing of the returned Connaught Rangers continued after they were back in their own towns and villages. The attitude of the public was typified in the experiences of the 21-year-old Private William Coman at Cashel, a small cathedral town in County Tipperary, just over a hundred miles south-west of Dublin. The reception accorded to Coman was described in the Clonmel paper, *The Nationalist*, at the end of January. After dealing briefly with the exploits of the mutineers, the report went on:

> It is right that Ireland should remember such men for they are an honour to their country. Their pluck and pride of race are proverbial. Since Mr

Coman's return to his native Cashel congratulations have been showered on him, and, prompted by the feeling of the people, many of his friends decided on organizing a fund in order to give the public an opportunity of marking their appreciation of his heroism and patriotism. Cashel feels an intense pride in counting as one of her sons a member of that gallant band of Connaught Rangers.[25]

On a Sunday afternoon a ceremony took place in Coman's honour. A fife and drum band paraded through the streets playing national airs and a large crowd assembled round a platform at the open space in the centre of the city. The meeting was presided over by Francis Phillips, the Chairman of the Urban Council, who seems to have used the occasion for a passionate and emotive peroration. In a three-and-a-half column report *The Nationalist* quoted the speeches almost verbatim. Phillips spoke of the mutiny in histrionic phrases. 'In dark and dangerous and desperate days', a young man in their midst, whilst serving in the uniform of His Majesty King George 'under the torrid sun of India', had 'grounded arms when his country's life and liberty were at stake (hear, hear)'. These gallant Connaught Rangers had vowed, 'Never, while Irish blood courses in our veins, shall we shoulder arms to win laurels for the British Crown while Dark Rosaleen is in chains (hear, hear)'. These men had known the penalty for mutiny was death, but 'they dared the bristling bayonets of Britain because they had the spirit that came down to them from their ancestors.' He concluded:

> We can learn a lesson from the deeds of these true patriots. It was the doings of such men that have made the Irish cause indestructible. We have now an opportunity of showing our admiration for one of these heroes – a Cashel man (applause).[26]

The next speaker, the Right Reverend Dean Ryan, was not to be outdone in rhetoric, and he too extolled the valour of the mutiny, in which the Connaught Rangers had decided 'to dissociate themselves from England's services and to consecrate themselves to the service of the Green Flag of Ireland (applause)'. He told his audience:

> We have reason to congratulate ourselves that one of our own kith and kin, born and reared in the parish, proved himself a hero on that heroic occasion (applause). I say that around that young boy's head there is today, and there will be to the end, the halo of the patriot of Ireland, and he deserves the homage and respect of all who love Ireland (hear, hear).[27]

As soon as the eulogies were finished the meeting passed on to the ultimate event, which William Coman must have found to be especially pleasing. *The Nationalist* described what took place in one short paragraph:

> Dean Ryan opened the subscription list with a donation of £1, and his example was immediately followed. Pound notes and ten shilling notes were handed in spontaneously and even poor women gave as much as 2s. 6d.[28]

For several weeks after the mutineers had arrived at their homes, the local papers in their counties published accounts of their experience. A number of them indulged in some mild exaggeration and they had a general tendency to overstate their own involvement in the leadership of the mutiny, particularly during its early stages. Several complained about the treatment they had received when the mutiny was over. Eugene Egan, who had been wounded, though not seriously, in the raid on the magazine at Solon, said he was not properly looked after in hospital and 'it was only by a miracle he did not die'.[29] According to John Buckley, when the mutineers had been awaiting their courts martial in the prison at Lucknow, they were told by a General that if they caused any trouble they would be shot without a trial.[30]

The most sensational of the allegations were made by Private Valentine Delaney and were prominently reported in the *Western People* and the *Roscommon Journal*. Delaney, describing himself as one of the leaders of the mutiny, said that on one occasion in Dagshai Prison the mutineers were lined up along a wall and given five minutes to surrender or be shot. 'As we refused to surrender,' he went on, 'the soldiers rushed towards us with fixed bayonets and revolvers and were going to shoot us down, when our chaplain, a Belgian priest, threw up his hands and said, "If you shoot these men you'll shoot me also".'[31] Delaney complained of the 'barbarous' treatment that he and the others had received in prison at Dagshai, Poona and Maidstone. At Dagshai they had refused to work after Daly was executed.[32] As a punishment they were 'maltreated into unconsciousness', and confined to their cells for three days, handcuffed and without food. In Poona, where they again refused to work, about twenty of the prison staff had beaten them on the head with truncheons, knocking some of them unconscious.[33] After his stoicism in enduring such brutalities as these it was not surprising that Valentine Delaney should be honoured and lionized on his return to his native town in County Roscommon.

At the time the pardon was granted, the civil war had entered its final phase. The Republican insurgents, with their military position palpably beyond hope, were increasingly affected by demoralization and despair. In a vain effort to restore their flagging spirits Liam Lynch, Chief of Staff of the I.R.A., issued a statement claiming that they were in a stronger military position than ever before. 'This war will go on,' he said, 'until the independence of our country is recognized by our enemies, foreign and domestic. There can be no compromise in this fundamental condition. Victory is within our grasp if we stand united and firmly.'[34] Throughout February and March, 1923, there were more and more surreptitious demands for a ceasefire from the Republican side, and when Liam Lynch was shot dead in a skirmish with Irish Free State troops on 10 April it was hoped by many that the last obstacle to a negotiated peace had been removed.

On 20 April Frank Aiken, who had been Commandant General of the Northern Division of the I.R.A., was appointed to succeed Liam Lynch. He immediately proposed to the 'Republican Government' and the Army Executive that they should sue for peace, on condition that the 'Sovereignty of the Irish nation and the integrity of its territory are inalienable'.[35] After a tense discussion the proposal was carried by a substantial majority. On 20 April a joint meeting of the self-styled 'Republican Government' and the Army Executive directed Aiken to order the suspension of the I.R.A. offensive, and authorized De Valera, as 'President of the Irish Republic', to issue a Proclamation setting out the terms upon which they would be prepared to negotiate a peace settlement with the Irish Free State. This approach was coldly received by the Free State Government which was not disposed to open negotiations with any pre-conditions imposed by the Republicans. However, preliminary talks did take place, but they foundered both because De Valera refused to acknowledge the presently-constituted Dail as being the legitimate government of the country, and because he doubted his ability to persuade the I.R.A. to surrender their arms.

In spite of De Valera's intransigence, the writing was on the wall. A further joint meeting of the 'Republican Government' and the Army Executive in the middle of May directed Frank Aiken to order a ceasefire and to entrust his men to deposit their arms in secret dumps. The ceasefire came into effect on 24 May, 1923, and the same day De Valera issued a proclamation to the I.R.A., telling them, 'Further sacrifice on your part would now be in vain and continuance of the struggle in arms unwise in the national interest. Military victory must be allowed to rest, for the moment, with those who have destroyed the Republic'.[36] Neither De Valera nor Aiken intended the peace to be permanent; they were both hopeful that, in more propitious circumstances, arms could be re-issued to their men and the struggle could be renewed.

The orders for the ceasefire were generally obeyed by members of the I.R.A., whose operations against the Irish Free State Army and the police were then discontinued but who remained in readiness for a further call to service. Eamon De Valera, disguised with a beard and a moustache, went into hiding.

In the summer of 1923 a campaign was started on behalf of the other imprisoned Connaught Ranger, Joseph Dowling, with the object of assimilating his case with those of the mutineers and getting him pardoned as well. The *Mayo News* on 7 July published a long letter from Colonel Maurice Moore, a member of the Free State Senate, denying that Dowling had been guilty of treachery. It was true that Dowling had been enlisted in the British Army, the Senator wrote, but that did not make him an English soldier and he owed allegiance 'to the Government of the United Kingdom, not England'. He had joined the Irish Brigade to fight for Irish freedom in company with fifty-three other British Army prisoners in German prisoner-of-war camps. With startling naivete the Senator quoted the regulations applicable to Irishmen joining Sir Roger Casement's Brigade, one of which read:

> The Brigade shall be clothed, fed and officially equipped with arms and ammunition by the German Government and shall be stationed near Berlin and be treated as guests of the German Government.[37]

Predictably, the campaign failed and Joseph Dowling, whose original death sentence had been commuted to penal servitude for life, remained in prison.

The euphoria surrounding the release of the Connaught Rangers gradually subsided, leaving, for a number of them, an anti-climax in which they sought to adjust themselves to civilian life with no money, no jobs and no qualifications. A General Election took place in the Irish Free State during August, 1923, which the Republicans contested, but in which the pro-Treaty party were returned to power. William Cosgrave was reinstalled as President and was entrusted with the massive task of restoring his country from the ravages and bitterness of the Civil War.

As for Eamon De Valera, he had emerged from his hideout to address an election rally and had been arrested by soldiers of the Free

State Army. Although he had been imprisoned for the next year he had remained a potent factor in the Irish political scene as the acknowledged leader of the Republican movement.

The ex-mutineers were not forgotten in the newly-born Dominion. Someone was working for them or they were working for themselves. On 19 June, 1924, at Question Time in the Dail a backbench Member asked the President whether it was the intention of the Government 'to make any provision by way of pension or gratuity in respect of men of the Connaught Rangers who were convicted in India for their Irish sympathies, and if he will see that the men who have been unable to secure employment since their release from prison are placed upon equal terms with the dismissed or resigned R.I.C. men'. Mr Cosgrave replied that there was no statutory authority for making any payments to the mutineers, but that if he was informed of the details of any of them who was suffering from hardship he would see what could be done about it. In answer to a supplementary question, he agreed that their 'noble action' had been of great service to Ireland.[38]

A group calling themselves 'The Committee of Ex-Connaught Rangers' had been formed with John Flannery as Secretary. They had organized a meeting in Dublin on 3 July, 1924, which had passed a resolution that:

> This public meeting of the citizens of Dublin place on record our appreciation of the services rendered to the cause of Ireland by the Connaught Rangers on grounding arms in India, June, 1920, as a protest against the conditions prevailing in Ireland during the Black and Tan Terror, and we demand that these services shall be adequately recognized.

Flannery, who seems to have been the moving spirit in this group, sent a resolution to the President two days later 'on behalf of the Committee of ex-Connaught Rangers'. In a covering letter he drew the President's attention to the fact that the mutiny 'rendered a service to the Cause of Ireland' which at that time had a far-reaching effect but that the mutineers had never been adequately compensated for their action and sacrifices.

He concluded:

> They are now absolutely in want and they desire me to ask you to receive a Deputation from them, with one or two others, on their behalf at your earliest convenience to explain the details of their case.[39]

Flannery received a fairly prompt reply from the President's office telling him that his letter would be placed before Mr Cosgrave at the first available opportunity, but that, owing to the great pressure on the President's time, the suggested interview could not be arranged for any date in the immediate future. He was informed, however, that it might be possible for an interview to take place when the Dail adjourned for the Summer Recess. In the meantime, Flannery was asked for a brief memorandum on the points he wished to raise at the interview.[40]

On 19 July John Flannery wrote again, this time addressing his letter to Mr Cosgrave not as President, but as Minister of Defence, an additional office which he had recently assumed. Flannery said that he wished in particular to forward six cases of hardship. Firstly, 'poor old Peter Smith of Windmill Lane, Drogheda', the father of Peter Smyth (Flannery spelt the name incorrectly) who had been killed in the raid on the magazine at Solon. According to Flannery, the father was now 'over 60 and unable to work' and had been mainly dependent on his dead son for support. He had tried unsuccessfully to obtain help from the British Government. Flannery then mentioned five other cases collectively, John Oliver, William Burland, Thomas Devine, John McGowan and himself. All of them were at present 'idle and practically destitute'. He went on:

> We feel that some compensation ought to be made us for loss of service, imprisonment etc. In Oliver's case his service in the British Army was $16^1/_2$ years, in my own case I had $12^1/_6$ years. McGowan is suffering from a tubercular throat which he contracted in prison. Some of us have not even the dole to fall back upon. In my case I have an aged mother and a younger sister to look to me, who have now unfortunately nothing for them. Only for a widowed sister – burdened with two children – in receipt of £1. 16/- per week from the British Govt. owing to her husband dying from the after-effects of war, we were now all starving today. Surely some compensation is due the Connaughts for their action, and each man to be compensated according to his service in British Army. The five cases mentioned are in need of immediate assistance.[41]

Without waiting for a reply, Flannery followed this up with another letter to the President on 22 July asking that the Irish Free State should give immediate consideration to the claims of the ex-Connaught Rangers 'who grounded their arms in India in the interests of Ireland and who were subjected to the rigours of the British law for their action'. The men believed, he said, that the President and his Ministry were 'kindly disposed and recognize the "great service" rendered to the Irish Cause by their action and therefore hope, not alone for the reception of the deputation on the points necessary to discuss, but they also believe that your Government is anxious to do something decent by way of recognizing their "great service"'.

Flannery mentioned in particular his personal suffering and sacrifice and reminded the President of the men who had been killed in the fighting at Solon. Enclosed in his letter he sent a list of the mutineers showing the sentences they had all received, and also a form on which three of the men had set out the particulars of their own hardship.

John McGowan, who had been in the British Army for seven years before the mutiny said,

> I served in the Nat. Army for 10 months. I am in a bad state & I was suffering from glands in prison caused through my incarceration. I am not able to do much, so if I got any assistance I could try to start for myself. I am sleeping out & I am near starved. I applied for the Guards (the Civic Guard) but was not taken, and several other jobs.

John Oliver, who had had fifteen and a half years' service in the Connaught Rangers had also served for a short period in the Irish Free State Army, but had not had any employment since his discharge. 'I'm without parents, friends or home,' he said, 'and owing to incarceration in prison I'm suffering from weakness and ill-health.'

The last of the three, Thomas Devine, had enlisted in the Connaught Rangers in 1915. He was one of the men whose death sentence had been commuted to penal servitude for life. On his release from prison he said he had joined the Free State Army, but had been discharged at the end of the Civil War and had been unemployed ever since and dependent on his father.

Flannery concluded his letter to the President with the words, 'You will see the urgent need of help for us . . . Trusting you will favour us with an early reply and interview'.[42]

Chapter 13

JOHN FLANNERY'S CAMPAIGN

DURING THE SUMMER MONTHS of 1924 printed handbills appeared on walls in Dublin and other towns urging support for the mutineers. They bore the following announcement:

> Connaught Rangers who grounded arms in India in June, 1920, as a protest against the ill-treatment of the people of Ireland by the Black and Tans are now cast adrift without any provision being made for them.
>
> Jailed by the British Government. Cast aside by the people of Ireland. Irishmen! Is this your return for their manly action? Look out for Public Meetings. Communications to be addressed to Sec. Ex-Connaught Rangers Committee, 35 Upper Gardiner Street.[1]

It was noticeable that John Flannery and his committee often avoided describing the events at Jullundur and Solon as a mutiny, preferring to depict their actions at that time somewhat innocuously as being a mere 'grounding of arms'.

Flannery had obtained the support of certain prominent social crusaders in Dublin for his campaign, including the President of the Tenants' Association, the Secretary of the Council of the Unemployed and several leading members of the Gaelic League, the Trade Union Congress and the Dublin Trades Council. On 27 August he organized a large evening meeting at O'Connell Street in the centre of Dublin to protest at the way in which the released prisoners were being treated by the Irish Free State Government. Several spectators praised the conduct of the mutineers in glowing terms, a representative of the Gaelic League saying, 'The stand made in India by the Connaught Rangers in hostile surroundings will rank as one of the most glorious episodes in Ireland's fight for freedom'.

In his own speech Flannery read out a message he had received from the Ministry of Finance informing him that 'the case of the Connaught Rangers is still under consideration but nothing definite has yet been decided on'. He also disclosed, with disgust, that the Government had offered immediate enlistment in the National Army to any released Connaught Ranger who was medically fit.[2]

At the conclusion of the demonstration a resolution was passed, with unanimous approval, which declared:

> This mass open air meeting of Dublin citizens hereby registers emphatic protest against the treatment which is being meted out to the men of the Connaught Rangers who so gallantly stood for Ireland in India and in protest against the wholesale infamies of the 'Black and Tans' here in 1920, and we urge by demanding that authority at once come to the assistance of these men by raising them from want, misery and starvation, as it is a scandal that bravery and chivalry be so treated.

And further:

> We deplore the suggestion of the Free State Government which endeavours to conscript these men into the National Army by starving them into submission, and demand instead that the high-pensioned employees of Government and other services be displaced to make room for the ex-Connaughts and others deserving of employment.[3]

Copies of this resolution were sent off next day to the British Prime Minister, President Cosgrave and Tim Healy, the Governor-General of the Irish Free State, by John Flannery. It is apparent that Flannery was also actively engaged at this time in distributing notices and posters, as he received a letter in September from Annie Smyth, whose brother had been killed at Solon, assuring him that she had given out all the 'bills' he had sent her. She apologized for not being able to offer more help with 'the Movement', but explained that she was a single girl looking after an elderly father in their home at Drogheda, and her only brother was now dead. 'I need hardly tell you,' she wrote, 'his death came as a great blow to us; in fact my mother died a few months after him. It just broke her heart. And then to think that we never got a penny from either Government makes me think that it is not worth while doing anything for Ireland.' She wondered how the Movement was progressing because she had not read much about it in the papers recently. 'I think it is awful the way the Government is treating you,' she said, 'and I think it is up to the people of Ireland to do all they can to assist you.'[4]

It seems completely unjustifiable for the British Army not to have accepted liability for the death of Private Smyth. All the available evidence led to the conclusion that he had not been taking part in the raid on the magazine, at any rate the probability was very much in his favour. In fairness he should have been classified as having been killed accidentally in the course of his military service, and his next-of-kin should have been compensated accordingly.

One of the reasons for the Irish Government's delay in meeting a deputation from Flannery's committee was their uncertainty as to which ministerial department would be best suited to adjudicate on the claims that were being so vigorously pressed by and on behalf of the mutineers. Having failed to evoke any immediate action from the President himself, Flannery next turned to the Minister for Justice, in all probability because he had been chairman of a committee which had investigated the claims for compensation made by the dismissed or retired members of the Royal Irish Constabulary when they had been replaced as the national police by the Garda Siochana.[5] On 19 September Flannery wrote to the Minister on behalf of the Ex-Connaught Rangers Committee:

> Dear Sir,
> A Deputation of four has been selected by our Committee to wait on you on Monday 22nd inst. at the hour of 12 o'clock noon, for the purpose of laying our case before you orally and seeking your help in having something definite done for the men of the Connaught Rangers who 'did noble work for Ireland' in India in 1920. It is unnecessary to point out that the matter is now hanging on a long time and should be considered and finally disposed of.[6]

However, the Ministry for Justice did not intend to be pressurized by John Flannery into authenticating the claims put forward by the mutineers. Indeed, there seemed to be an evident disinclination among Government Departments in Dublin to assume a primary responsibility in the matter. Flannery received a prompt and courteous reply to his letter, informing him that the Minister for Justice had ascertained from the President's Department that they were going to arrange to see a deputation from the Committee during the course of the following week. The Minister had asked the Department to communicate with Flannery to arrange an appointment as soon as possible, and in the circumstances it seemed unnecessary for a deputation from the Connaught Rangers to visit the Ministry of Justice on the following Monday.[7]

Flannery responded with another letter addressed personally to the Minister for Justice, thanking him for the interest he had taken but saying, 'I would respectfully point out to you that the hardships and privations of myself and comrades are of a nature which calls for immediate relief, as hunger and want is our lot'. He complained that during the previous July the President's Department had informed them that the claim put forward by the ex-Connaught Rangers was under consideration, and he had been promised that the President would arrange to receive a deputation during the following week – 'a similarity of phraseology,' he said, with the undertaking they had now given to the Minister. He went on:

> Thus you can see the matter is merely receiving evasive attention and not alone that but the President's Dept. appears to think that the subject is one which only requires bluff to hold off; as a matter of real fact the ex-Connaughts cannot exist longer on air, but require recognition for 'noble services to their country' and the necessary help to feed their dependents and themselves.[8]

As it happened, a deputation chosen by the Ex-Connaught Rangers Committee was received on 24 September at the Government Buildings in Dublin by Seamus Dolan, the President's Secretary. Flannery took with him to the interview Frank Larkin, President of the Tenant's Association, and Dermott Stewart of the Dublin Trades Council. Larkin acted as the principal spokesman. He told Dolan that what they were demanding for the released prisoners were the same rates of compensation as those that had formerly been paid to resigned or dismissed members of the Royal Irish Constabulary. 'There is a distinct obligation on the Government to help these men,' he said. 'The British ex-servicemen have been given a grant as well as a pension by the British Government after the World War, for services rendered to their country. This is a suggestion of what might be done for the ex-Connaught Rangers who served Ireland in India.' He then cited two examples of the 'abject poverty' in which some of the mutineers and their next-of-kin were existing. Flannery was living in one room with four other people, and Smyth of Drogheda was 'almost prepared to go to the workhouse'. He finished by declaring that all these men should be helped immediately and they would then become loyal citizens of the Irish Free State. Next it was the turn of Dermott Stewart. He said that he would like to concur with the plea just made by Frank Larkin. The Dublin Trades Council regarded the claims of the Connaught Rangers 'as very exceptional, requiring exceptional treatment'. With regard to the possibility of the released prisoners joining the National Army, he suggested unrealistically that 'after their strenuous military service, with the hardships of the climate, their long service and their imprisonment' none of the men would be fit enough to enlist. Flannery was apparently content that the necessary points had been made as he confined himself to thanking the other two for coming with him, and expressing gratitude to Seamus Dolan for receiving the deputation. Dolan replied that he would put the case for the ex-Connaught Rangers as strongly as possible before the Executive Council of the Government.[9]

Two days after the deputation had visited the President's Secretary, Flannery wrote a letter to the *Irish Independent* from his address in Dublin:

> Dear Sir,
> Will you please allow me, through your valuable paper to publicly notify the men of the 1920 Mutiny in India belonging to the Connaught Rangers that the Government has decided to give the matter of recognition to the men its practical sympathy, and it is absolutely necessary that I should have their names, addresses, service, rank, possible amount of pension had they continued service, and the number of their dependents. As many of my comrades are scattered, and some hold ranks in the Civic Guards and the National Army, I hope with your help to get in immediate touch with them. I am in touch with a good number but there are others who have changed their old addresses.[10]

Flannery's letter was published in the *Irish Independent* on 27 September. It seems only to have elicited a moderate response, for he wrote to Seamus Dolan a week later, sending him a list of twenty-one names, including his own and those of the men killed at Solon. By the side of the names, Flannery has set out how many dependents each man was trying to support and the number of years he had served in the British Army at the time of his conviction. The names of three men who actually started the mutiny, Joseph Hawes, Stephen Lally and Patrick Gogarty, are omitted from the list, as is that of Joseph Walsh who played a prominent part after it had developed. Flannery had added under the heading of 'Remarks':

> Flannery and Oliver forfeit life pensions, thirty pounds gratuity and credits. Generally, most of the men forfeited this gratuity with their pensions, while a number forfeit disability grants (malaria, sunstroke or heart affection (sic)). The dependents of the executed and killed call for special treatment.

Seamus Dolan wrote to the Minister for Finance about the compensation of the Mutineers on 21 October, enclosing a copy of the notes he had made when he saw the deputation on 24 September, and the list of names he had been sent by John Flannery. He said in his letter, 'The total number of men involved is 52, and from the letters I have received and the statement made by the Deputation I am satisfied that a good proportion of them are in very bad circumstances, in fact, as members of the Deputation stated, in dire want. In addition to the 52 men above mentioned, there are the dependents of the three men who lost their lives.' Dolan admitted to having some difficulty in suggesting the best way in which the matter should be handled, but he believed that the mutineers should get some help, as most of them had forfeited gratuities and credits and some had lost life pensions. 'I would suggest,' he went on, 'that by way of immediate relief for the men "in dire want" that a sum of £200 be made available at once, and when you have decided how far you will go to meet the general claim put forward, a small committee of three might be set up to examine the circumstances of each case.'[11]

The Minister for Finance's Secretary replied that his Minister had given Seamus Dolan's letter careful consideration, but had come to the conclusion that this was not a matter with which he could deal properly in the first instance. He suggested that the case of the Connaught Rangers should be taken up and considered by some other Minister who would, if he thought fit, then make a recommendation to the Ministry of Finance; he thought that any such recommendation should come from the Minister for Justice or the Minister for Defence.[12]

Whether or not a committee was appointed to consider the claims of the mutineers at that time is not ascertainable from the records of the Irish Government, though it appears certain payments were made during the next few months, probably to the men who were considered to be 'in dire need'.

John Flannery's assumption of the leadership of the mutineers was by no means either generally acknowledged or universally welcomed by the others, many of whom still regarded him as a self-seeking double-crosser. This was evidenced by a letter Joseph Walsh sent to the *Irish Independent* towards the end of October, 1924, approximately two months after the same newspaper had published a letter from Flannery asking all the mutineers to send him their present addresses. Walsh, ignoring the existence of the ex-Connaught Ranger Committee, said he had been asked to appeal to every mutineer to celebrate the fourth anniversary of the death of their comrade James Daly by attending a Mass on the morning of 2 November. 'It is a pity that his remains are not buried in the land he loved so much,' Walsh continued. 'The remnants of that gallant little force who hoisted the green, white and gold on top of a soldier's barracks, and who defied both bayonet and ball on a far, far foreign shore, are forgotten by many, and some had to emigrate. What are left may seem to be forgotten, but we ourselves should not forget Daly.' He ended by inviting his old comrades from the days of the mutiny to write to him so that he could exchange their addresses with the others.[13]

On 16 February, 1925, Flannery turned up at the President's Department in Merion Square, Dublin, without having an appointment. He handed in a letter addressed to Mr Cosgrave, from Mary Larkin of the Tenant's Association which stated:

Bearer Mr John Flannery of the Connaught Rangers is in the position which calls for immediate relief. His Mother's rent and other debts have accumulated, and it would be a merciful act to give him a grant to help him out. He is waiting for a reply or an interview, should it be convenient for you to see him in person.[14]

It would appear from later correspondence that Flannery was seen on this occasion by one of the secretaries but not, understandably enough, by the President himself. However, the visit did have some effect because Cosgrave wrote to Ernest Blythe, the Minister of Finance, two days later telling him he had received a number of letters from Connaught Rangers about grants or compensation. Some small payments had been made to them out of the Special Fund, he said, but apparently they were dissatisfied because they thought they ought to be compensated on the same scale as dismissed or resigned members of the Royal Irish Constabulary. The President suggested the creation of a small committee of two Parliamentary Secretaries and a Minister to consider the claims of these men. He ended, 'I do not know whether this is the best way of dealing with the cases, but in any case the whole matter is unsatisfactory at present going from one Minister to another and to the Private Secretaries as well.'[15]

Flannery kept up his pressure on the Government to comply with the demands he was making for himself and for the other mutineers. On 21 February he called again at the President's Department and handed in another letter from Mary Larkin addressed to William Cosgrave. This time she said:

Re: Connaught Rangers.
Kindly see Mr John Flannery re. above. It is deplorable that no attention
is being paid to his repeated applications for consideration to himself
and comrades. Something ought to be done immediately.

Mary Larkin added a postscript, 'Flannery will wait to see if you have a
reply'.[16]

In an effort to put a stop to Flannery's appearances at the offices of
their Department, the secretary who had seen him on his first visit
wrote to him on 23 February telling him, 'As I informed you last
week, the President has made certain representations to the Minister
of Finance regarding the position of ex-Connaught Rangers. When
Mr Blythe's decision is forthcoming you will be immediately
informed'.[17]

About this time the *Sunday Independent* published the first instalment of their seven-part feature, 'The Connaught Rangers Mutiny;
It's History and Sequel' by 'One Who Knows'. When introducing the
series the paper said, 'The full facts of the grounding of arms by
members of the First Battalion of the Connaught Rangers while
stationed in India have never been published. They form a very
important and interesting part of history. They have been collected
and written in narrative form by one who was in close touch with
every phase of the *émeute* and who has personal knowledge of the
matters and persons referred to. This narrative has been purchased by
Independent Newspapers Ltd for exclusive publication.'[18] Their description of the happenings at Jullundur and Solon as an '*émeute*' was a
particularly inappropriate term, as it means a popular rising rather
than a mutiny.

It must remain a matter of speculation why John Flannery chose to
write under a nom de plume, as he was certainly neither a modest nor a
reticent man. One possibility is that at a time when he was parading
his destitution he did not want to disclose that he had sold his story to
one of the largest newspaper groups in Ireland. It is more likely that he
realized that his account of the mutiny, with its constant emphasis on
his own supremacy and control, would be more convincing if it
appeared to be written by an unbiased observer. Doubtless he was also
anxious to terminate the accusations of duplicity which were being
made against him. On the other hand, his reason might have been
simply that he was afraid of being subjected to physical assault if he
had used his own name in the articles.

In tracing the origin of the mutiny, 'One Who Knows' says that it
started when four privates at Jullundur decided to soldier no more 'as a

protest against the tyrannies of British rule in Ireland'. He gives the names of the four correctly as Lally, Hawes, Sweeney and Gogarty, in that order, without according any precedence to Joseph Hawes, or even mentioning that it was his idea in the first place. The account admits that, when the privates told Lance-Corporal Flannery of their plan, he, being an experienced soldier, 'knew that their action amounted to mutiny, and he pointed out to them that the consequences would be very serious for them'. They had refused to heed his warning and gone off to the Guard Room. Rightaway, apparently, Lance-Corporal Flannery 'thought the matter over' and from then on he took charge of the mutiny. Naturally, no reference is made to Flannery visiting the Guard Room and endeavouring to persuade the prisoners there to abandon the protest and return to their duties.[19] There was only one illustration accompanying the first article of the series, and that significantly was a head-and-shoulders photograph of John Flannery. It was used again in a later instalment when it appeared with a photograph of Private James Daly.

Ernest Blythe did not reply to the President's letter of 18 February until 3 March. He said then that before any action was taken in regard to paying compensation to the ex-Connaught Rangers he wanted to put before Mr Cosgrave an objection which he thought should not be overlooked. He continued:

> Unless sufficient money can be found in the Special Relief Fund it will be necessary to go to the Dail and have the money for compensation voted. Whether the proposal met with opposition there or not, it would be certain to receive a good deal of publicity and I think that the British Government might reasonably feel aggrieved at our action. Our proposal is simply to provide compensation for men who voluntarily joined the British Army and who, having mutinied, were dismissed for disciplinary reasons. Their case is not at all on all fours with that of the R.I.C., for men do not ordinarily enlist in the British Army with the intention of making a career of it in the way that men formerly joined the R.I.C. Their vested interests are not the same and they have not the same prospects of pension on retirement.
>
> I feel therefore that we are under no obligation to provide compensation in these cases, and in view of the possible objection of the British Government I think it undesirable that we should do so otherwise than through the Relief Fund.[20]

William Cosgrave was an able politician and he was sufficient of a realist to appreciate the likely reaction in England to a parliamentary debate on the compensation of a group of ex-soldiers who had been discharged with ignominy from the British Army. The relationship between Britain and the Irish Free State was becoming increasingly cordial and the President had no wish to cause any offence to the Government at Westminster, or to reopen past controversies. At the same time he was aware of the intense nationalistic sentiment which still pervaded in his own country. Flannery's persistent and vociferous campaign had already won him appreciable support both inside and outside the Dail, and would not be slackened until his claims had received favourable consideration from the authorities. Unfortunately, the Special Fund, which was used for the relief of financial hardship 'brought about by services rendered to the State', was running out of money. If payments could have been made to the mutineers from this source, they would have scarcely been noticed by the general public, and there would have been no need for an emotive debate about the matter in the Dail. Accordingly, a memorandum was sent by the President's Department to the Ministry of Finance pointing out that the Dail Special Fund was now very much depleted, in fact it was 'nearly exhausted'. The President therefore suggested that Mr Blythe should 'consider the question of reimbursing the fund by means of a Financial Vote'. The mutineers were only mentioned specifically in the last paragraph of the memorandum:

> Regarding the question of the claims of the ex-Connaught Rangers, the President thinks that it would be well to set up a Committee such as was previously suggested in order that they might make recommendations for payment of gratuities ranging from £25 to £100.[21]

A Committee of four was appointed soon afterwards with Seamus Dolan, the President's Secretary, as Chairman, 'To examine and report upon the claim for compensation from the Government of Saorstat Eireann put forward by certain ex-members of the Connaught Rangers'.[22]

A meeting appears to have taken place on 8 March between the Minister for Finance and representatives of the mutineers, but no record can be traced of what transpired at it. Presumably Ernest Blythe told the representatives about the recently-formed committee, and probably added that until it had brought out its report he was unable to make any announcement. The next day John Flannery wrote to the President:

Dear Sir,

In re: Connaught Rangers,

My comrades are very disappointed with Mr Blythe's answer at yesterday's meeting, and ask me to seek a short interview with you tomorrow
Tuesday at 11.30 o'c A.M. I will attend at that hour, and trust it will not
inconvenience you to see me.[23]

Someone has written a note at the top of this letter to the effect that
Flannery called at the President's Department on 10 March but he was
told that Mr Cosgrave was engaged, and that the claim of the ex-
Connaught Rangers was still under consideration.

At Question Time in the Dail on 25 March Alfred Byrne asked the
Minister for Finance what progress, if any, had been made by the
Committee which was inquiring into the Connaught Rangers' claims
for compensation. Ernest Blythe replied that it was proceeding with
its work, and added, 'The appointment of the Committee does not
mean any more that there is a case for inquiry, and it must not be
assumed that the inquiry will result in the payment of compensation'.[24] The Minister's answer angered John Flannery who, turning
from insistence to vituperation, wrote another letter to the President
on 27 March, in which he said:

Dear Sir
My Committee directs me to forward you attached resolutions passed
at a meeting held yesterday. 'The Connaught Rangers (1920 Mutiny)
Committee have heard with pain and disappointment the reply of Mr
Blythe to a question concerning the men and their dependents on
25.3.25, and consider that they have been fooled by the Ministers and
Whips, chiefly led by President Cosgrave and Mr Blythe, and they call
upon the Government Party to resign a seat in the north side of Dublin
City, to contest the matter of the Connaught Rangers in public as the
Proposed Inquiry is both a farce and a humbug.'[25]

This letter does not seem to have been answered by anyone in the
President's Department. Perhaps their patience with John Flannery
and his committee was becoming exhausted. The matter of compen-
sating the mutineers was raised again in the Dail at the end of April
when a member asked Mr Cosgrave whether any decision had yet
been reached about giving the convicted Connaught Rangers identical
treatment to that which had been accorded to ex-policemen in the
Royal Irish Constabulary. Mr Blythe replied for the President. He said
that the mutineers' claims were still being considered by the Committee which had not yet furnished its report.[26]

For the next six months the Government issued no statements concerning the progress or the findings of Seamus Dolan's committee, and the possible compensation of the mutineers was not mentioned again in the Dail until Question Time on 12 November, when Alfred Byrne asked the President if he could state the results of the inquiries made about their claims. William Cosgrave replied:

> From the report presented by the Committee appointed to enquire into this matter, it does not appear that the circumstances are such as to sustain any claim for compensation from the Government and after careful consideration, the Minister for Finance is not prepared to recommend that any payment from Government funds in respect of such a claim should be made. Such of the men concerned, however, as are not employed on Government work already will be offered an opportunity of obtaining such employment, provided that they have not already refused Government employment or having obtained it have lost it through causes within their own control. Steps have been taken with a view to ascertaining the names of the individuals to whom this concession should apply.[27]

As there were no supplementary questions it would seem that the members of all parties were satisfied that Cosgrave had dealt with the problem in a reasonably fair manner. Indeed, the subject was not referred to again in the Dail during the following few months.

John Flannery must have been aware of the finality of the Government's decision as he and his committee became quiescent for several years. It may well have been that the President's proposal to the Ministry of Finance was followed and gratuities were paid to the mutineers in most need out of the Dail Special Fund. In his memorandum Cosgrave had suggested that the amount of such payments should range between £25 and £100, which was not, perhaps, over-generous if they were to be final awards.

A different aspect of the matter was raised in the Dail on 8 December, 1926, when two members, Mr Laidhin and Mr Lyons, asked the Minister for Defence to introduce legislation for the benefit of ex-Connaught Rangers mutineers now serving in the National Army, which would enable them to count their time in prison after the mutiny towards their total period of military service for pension purposes. The Minister replied that he was not prepared to introduce any legislation on the lines suggested. Mr Lyons said that these men must surely expect 'to get some compensation for the work they carried out when they helped, as best they could, to establish the Free

State'. The Minister remained adamant, and reminded the House of the statement made by the President on 12 November the previous year. In any case, he said, there was at present no pension scheme under the Military Service Act. Mr Lyons concluded the discussion by protesting, with more sense of rhetoric than practicality, 'Then those who fought for Ireland fought in vain!'[28]

Chapter 14

THE REWARD

THE CONTROVERSY AS TO WHETHER OR NOT the Connaught Rangers mutineers should be compensated from the national purse never became a major party political issue in the Irish Free State. Throughout the 1920s William Cosgrave and his pro-treaty adherents continued to dominate the parliamentary scene. In 1924, on his release from prison, Eamon De Valera assembled a small Republican faction opposed to the policies of the Government, but refusing to contest elections. They modified their attitude in 1927 when they started to put up candidates for Parliament, at the same time stressing that they regarded the oath of allegiance to the Crown as being 'an empty political formula'. From then on De Valera's Fianna Fail party became firmly established as the effective opposition party in the Dail.

Flannery's committee still remained in existence, and although they became less vociferous after 1925, the claims of the mutineers for recognition and reward had been publicized sufficiently for others to pursue the campaign on their behalf. At Question Time in the Dail on 10 November, 1927, Frank Kerlin, a member of Fianna Fail, asked the Minister for Finance, still Ernest Blythe, if the Government would reconsider their previous decision and would now grant gratuities or pensions to the ex-Connaught Rangers who had taken part in the mutiny; also to the dependent relatives of the men who died as a result of it. Blythe reminded him that the matter had been fully examined by a committee and no new circumstances had arisen to justify any modification of the views they had put forward in their report. Mr Kerlin inquired if it was the considered opinion of the Cabinet that the mutineers had no claims whatsoever on an Irish Government. The Minister replied, 'No more than many Irish civilians who, at heavy material loss, and great risk, gave assistance during the national struggle'.[1]

During 1927 a new society called the Connaught Rangers Mutineers Association had been formed, which was seemingly quite independent of John Flannery's ex-Connaught Rangers (1920 Mutiny)
Committee.[2] Whereas Flannery's group met at his own home, the
new Association established its headquarters at the Kevin Barry Memorial Hall in Parnell Square, Dublin.

Kevin Barry was one of Ireland's national heroes from the final
struggle for independence, whose name and whose exploits had been
commemorated in a popular patriotic song. He had been hanged on 1
November, 1920, the day before James Daly was shot at dawn.
Attempts had been made to identify them with each other, but in fact
they had little in common except the tragically young age at which
they were executed and the courage with which they both met their
deaths. At the time of his arrest Kevin Barry was an 18-year old
medical student serving in the Irish Volunteers in Dublin. A ration
party from the Duke of Wellington's Regiment had been in an army
lorry waiting to load up with bread from a baker's shop when Barry
and several other youths, all in civilian clothing, were walking past
along the pavement. They suddenly produced revolvers and opened
fire at point-blank range, killing three of the soldiers in the back of the
vehicle. Afterwards they made good their escape, but Barry was
discovered hiding under another lorry nearby, still in possession of a
loaded revolver. There is a widespread belief in Ireland that, although
he was tortured, Barry refused to disclose the names of his confeder-
ates. He was convicted of murdering one of the dead men and of being
an accessory to the murder of the other two. A number of people felt
that Barry should not be hanged because of his youth.[3]

The Connaught Rangers Mutineers Association devoted their activities to 'obtaining justice' for the survivors of the mutiny, and getting
the bodies of the mutineers who had been shot brought back to
Ireland.
    During the latter months of 1928 the Irish Government was in-
tending to make new provision for the compensation of dismissed or
retired members of the Royal Irish Constabulary. This prompted John
Flannery to write a letter to President Cosgrave on 21 September
saying:

A special meeting of the ex-Connaught Rangers (1920 Mutiny) Committee was held at the above address on the 17th inst. and it was

unanimously decided that I write to you and ask that you use your influence to have the ex-Connaught Rangers (who were convicted in India in 1920 for their National Sympathy) included in the R.I.C. bill, which the Minister for Finance is introducing next month. I am sure there is no necessity for me to repeat here, the stand made in India by the Connaught Rangers? Suffice to say that when the people of Ireland were standing with their backs to the wall, fighting the hereditary foe for their very existence, the Connaught Rangers were the one and only Irish Regiment who had the moral courage to challenge the right of that mighty Empire to persecute their fellow-countrymen and women, who were fighting for a noble and righteous cause. These men are now in dire need and they look to you, as head of the Irish Free State, to come to their aid, and let the people of other countries see that Ireland does not forget those of her sons who came to her aid in her hour of need, and who did not forget to remember that they were Irishmen although they were serving in the ranks of the English Army. I trust that you will give this your kind consideration, with a view of easing the intolerable position which we find ourselves in today, because of our loyalty to Ireland. I will conclude by hoping that you will let me have a reply as soon as it is convenient for you to do so.[4]

The letter was signed 'J. Flannery Sec.'. It was sent by the President's Department to the Ministry of Finance with a covering note asking for material with which to draft a reply. Presumably Flannery was written to in due course and told that the position had not altered since it had been stated by Ernest Blythe at Question Time in the Dail the previous November.

There is reason to believe that the Flannery Committee was keeping in close touch with certain members of the Dail who were sympathetic to their claims. Three weeks after Flannery had sent his letter to the President, Frank Kerlin asked the Minister for Finance in the Dail if representations had been made to him to have the ex-Connaught Rangers mutineers included in the forthcoming Bill affecting ex-members of the R.I.C. Ernest Blythe replied that although representations of such a nature had been received, the circumstances had not altered since his last statement on the mutineers' claims. He denied the suggestion Mr Kerlin then made that the Committee of Inquiry set up by the Government to consider the compensation of the mutineers had recommended that the men should be paid grants or gratuities.[5] The day before Ernest Blythe had answered these questions a note had been prepared for him by his department, which had set out the findings of the Committee of Inquiry, and the undertaking given by the President in November, 1925, that the mutineers, with certain exceptions, would be given the opportunity of obtaining Government employment. The note continued:

> Considerable difficulty has been met in making any progress in affording employment to the men concerned, chiefly because it has been found extremely difficult to secure accurate information as to the persons affected or as to the type of man in question or his suitability for Government employment. Further, the claims of ex-National Army men for Government employment have had to take priority.[6]

Frank Kerlin was nothing if not persistent. In the Dail on 20 April, 1929, he repeated his plea that the mutineers should receive compensation from the Government. He said he had read extracts from the evidence of the courts martial in India – presumably he was referring to the Summaries of Evidence taken before the trials – and that 'they all bore out the opinion that in the mutiny the men were actuated by patriotic motives'. Ernest Blythe answered, with what was becoming his stock reply, that the committee which had investigated the matter had come to the conclusion that the mutineers had no better claim to compensation than many civilian Irishmen who had taken risks and suffered losses. Mr Fahy, another member of Fianna Fail, suggested that all the ex-Connaught Rangers who had taken part in the mutiny should be granted the amount of the pensions they would have received if it had never occurred. He was supported by speakers from all parties who had praised the heroism of the mutineers.

The India Office in London was following with close attention the controversy in Dublin regarding the compensation of the Connaught Rangers mutineers. The Military Secretary at the time was a distinguished soldier, General Sir Claud Jacob. An ex-Indian Army officer, he had spent the first thirty years of his military service almost entirely on the North-West Frontier, and after several years in France and Belgium during the war he had returned to India as Chief of Staff in 1929, an appointment he was holding when the mutinies had taken place at Jullundur and Solon. A Minute was prepared for him at the India Office, summarizing Kerlin's question in the Dail on 24 April, 1920, Ernest Blythe's reply, and the subsequent all-party tributes to the mutineers. In the space reserved for his own comment at the end of the Minute the Assistant Military Secretary had merely written two exclamation marks, before passing the document to his chief. Jacob had added the words 'Thank you – I refrain from comment'.[7]

It is easy to believe that John Flannery and his committee were constantly circulating stories about the impoverished conditions in which they were living, as the issue of their welfare continued to be raised in the Dail. During the final session in 1929 a backbencher named M. J. Hennessy asked Ernest Blythe once again to investigate the claims of the mutineers for compensation, as some of them were 'still suffering severe hardships'. Blythe replied patiently that he had reviewed the position on several occasions and had never found that the circumstances had altered at all since the Court of Inquiry had reported their findings. He said he would always be willing to examine any new considerations, but until they were presented to him he could see no advantage in re-opening the case.[8]

An attempt to force the issue was made in the Dail on 3 November, 1930, when Frank Fahy proposed a Private Member's motion to appoint a Select Committee 'to investigate and report as to the claim for compensation by way of pension or gratuity of certain members of the Connaught Rangers who mutinied in India in 1920'.[9] Fahy made a long speech, abounding in wild and inaccurate statements about the mutiny, but including certain disclosures relating to James Daly which, if they were true, would suggest that he had participated in a much wider mutinous conspiracy even prior to the outbreak at Solon. According to Fahy, Irish regiments in the British Army were seething with discontent in the early months of 1920, and were in continual contact with one another 'with a view to united action'. The military authorities knew about this and, in order to minimize the chances of trouble, they had posted all the Irish regiments overseas and had separated them as much as possible. After the 1st Connaught Rangers had arrived in India James Daly had been 'in communication with men in other units, and was looking forward to united action'. Mr Fahy went on to stress the remarkable valour of the Connaught Rangers mutineers:

In India they were surrounded by British regiments and they had undoubtedly memories of or had known of other mutinies which took place in India on two previous occasions when the mutineers were blown from the cannon's mouth. These men took the chance of a similar fate befalling them. The fact that they took action far away from Ireland and surrounded by thousands of British troops makes their action all the more meritorious from the Irish point of view.

Fahy gave a vivid description of the attack on the armoury at Solon by a band of patriots 'headed by Daly and armed with bayonets'.

However, their courage was to no avail as an extra guard had been mounted beforehand, and 'the mutineers were dispersed by rifle fire'. He made no direct complaints about the conduct of the courts martial, but he forcibly condemned the treatment accorded to the convicted men during their imprisonment for its harshness and inhumanity. Private Miranda died in Dagshai after being overcome by the excessive heat there. Private Shallow died four weeks after his release from the rigours of his confinement at Maidstone, and the health of nearly all the others had been affected by what they had endured. When they were freed from prison there had been a general belief among them 'that the Free State Government would make provision for themselves and their relatives, or give some compensation for what they had lost in the matter of pensions or gratuities. They were disappointed. Nothing was done for them and their claims were gradually lost sight of.'

It became apparent in the course of Frank Fahy's speech that he had been in touch with John Flannery's group, as he went on to relate how 'An agitation was carried on by a few men who lived in Dublin and neighbourhood and a committee was formed'. Without mentioning Flannery by name, he summarized his letters to the President and the Minister for Finance urging that the mutineers should be compensated in the same way as ex-members of the R.I.C. But his pleas had no effect. 'The dice were loaded against these men from the outset. They started without resources or organization, and had very little chance of proving their claims.'

Fahy concluded by asserting that most of the surviving ex-Connaught Rangers mutineers were living in dire poverty and were destined 'to end their days in the workhouse'. He said he had details of two of them who had already been buried in paupers' graves. One was Michael Kearns who had died the previous summer from the effects of his 'rigorous imprisonment'. The other was described by Fahy, with his natural flair for inaccuracy, as Patrick Kelly, a sergeant-major who had been sentenced to imprisonment for life. In fact, Patrick Kelly was a corporal and had received a sentence of seventeen years' penal servitude.

The next speaker was Ernest Blythe, who elaborated at some length on his earlier replies to questions regarding the compensation of the mutineers. He reiterated the reasons why the ex-Connaught Rangers could not be likened to ex-members of the R.I.C. and he again reminded the House that there were many civilians in the country who had received no compensation, even though they had run great risks during the recent troubles. Turning to the punishment inflicted on the men he said:

> There has been much talk of bad treatment in prison. Of course, there are people whose health suffers in prison, but I would not be inclined, without a good deal of evidence, to pay much attention to the allegation of ill-treatment. In the old days, some people in the prison I was in were very much inclined to write home about bad treatment when such did not exist, and because of that, I have a disposition to doubt the allegation of ill-treatment. [10]

The Minister for Finance then revealed that out of the sixty-one mutineers who had been released from prison (the number was actually sixty) thirty-one had been given Government employment, mostly for short periods.

After several other speakers had supported Frank Fahy's Motion the debate was adjourned. It was resumed on 10 December when Fahy again addressed the Dail at some length, concentrating on the destitute circumstances in which most of the mutineers were then living. He mentioned six examples including John Flannery who, though unemployed, was maintaining an invalid mother and a widowed sister. Others were without work because they were broken down in health or had been unable to find suitable employment. Most of them were looking after elderly parents, and one had a wife and three children who were 'practically starving'. 'I am convinced,' said Fahy, 'that history will judge us very harshly if we do not come to the rescue of the survivors of the mutineers of the Connaught Rangers.'[11]

There were 125 Members present when the Dail divided at the end of the debate. The voting was 57 in favour of the Motion and 68 against, so Frank Fahy had failed to secure his Select Committee by 11 votes. This was a comparatively close result considering that it had been a non-party proposal to which the Government had never concealed their opposition. The Division Lists showed that De Valera and all his close associates had backed the Motion, whereas Cosgrave and his Ministerial colleagues had voted solidly to reject it.[12]

After a decade in office the Cosgrave Administration had lost the confidence of the majority of the Irish electorate. Apart from purely national issues, its task was not being simplified by the world-wide depression of the early 1930s with its resultant commercial stagnation and mass unemployment. At a General Election in February, 1932, Fianna Fail won sufficient seats, with the support of the Labour Party, to form a new Government headed by Eamon De Valera. The effect on Anglo-Irish relations was immediate. De Valera abolished the oath of allegiance to the Crown and discontinued the payment of interest by the Irish Free State on the capital sum advanced by Britain under the Land Purchase Acts of the late 19th and the early 20th centuries. Britain retaliated by imposing tariffs on Irish exports, and very soon the two nations were engaged in an economic war. The Irish people showed their approval of De Valera's policies by returning him to power at another General Election in January, 1933, this time with an absolute majority.

The mood of the Dail was now more favourable than it had ever been for the proponents of compensation for the Connaught Rangers mutineers. Not only had De Valera voted in favour of Frank Fahy's motion in 1930, but it had also been supported by Sean MacEntee, who was now the Minister for Finance, and Frank Aiken, the new Minister for Defence. It was not long before the matter was raised again. On 28 February, 1934, in reply to a question in the Dail, a Government Minister announced, 'It is proposed to set up a Committee of Inquiry at an early date to consider the claims of ex-members of the Connaught Rangers arising out of the mutiny in India'.[13]

The Committee of Inquiry, consisting of three members, was appointed on 10 July, 1934. Their terms of reference were to examine the claims for compensation made by any mutineers who had been wounded or injured during the mutiny, or had suffered financial loss through taking part in it, or had contracted illnesses attributable to prison sentences served in connection with it. They had also to consider claims put forward by widows and children of deceased mutineers, who had died of wounds received during the mutiny or been executed as a result of it, or who had died of a disease attributable to imprisonment served in connection with it. The Committee presented its Report to the Defence and Finance Ministers on 29 June, 1935.[14]

At the start of their proceedings the Committee had advertised widely for claimants in Irish national and local newspapers. They had found out that twelve of the mutineers who had served prison sentences were now dead, and the whereabouts of six others was unknown, although they were believed to be still alive. Since a total of sixty mutineers, including Egan, the only man to be wounded, had been sentenced to terms of imprisonment, and of these eighteen had either died or disappeared, it meant that there should be no more than forty-two possible claimants from among the survivors. However, the Committee reported that no less than 183 ex-Connaught Rangers had claimed compensation, as well as eight dependents of men whose deaths were said to have resulted from causes 'arising out of the mutiny'. They explained this discrepancy in numbers:

> It appears that the position existing after the mutiny was that while the mutineers were in prison, pending the setting up of a court martial, and for some time after, all the personnel of the Connaught Rangers were placed in internment by the Military Authorities as a measure of precaution. After the mutineers had been removed to prison the men who remained were induced to return to duty, and the Battalion was reorganized. Strict discipline then prevailed, with the result, as reported to the Committee by the Mutineers' Association, that petty misdemeanours, which were ordinarily regarded as normal incidents of Battalion life, were treated with more than usual severity.[15]

The Committee did not elaborate as to how the spell of harsher discipline had undermined the health of certain claimants, but went on to say that they had found it impossible to bring these cases within their terms of reference, and they had decided to exclude them. That left the claims of the forty-five mutineers who had been convicted for taking part in the mutiny and had been sentenced to imprisonment. Seven of these men had been serving in the British Army on long-term engagements, that is twelve years or more, and the Committee recommended that they should be paid the same pensions as they would have received if they had completed their service in the normal way. The remaining thirty-eight had been on short-term engagements of less than twelve years. In their case, the Committee's recommendation was that they should each receive a gratuity 'not exceeding £120', the actual amount to be agreed between the Minister for Defence and the Minister for Finance.

The Report stated that two claims had been received from 'widows or children' of deceased mutineers, whose deaths were said to be 'due to causes arising out of the mutiny'. The Committee recommended that a flat-rate weekly pension should be awarded to each of them. In addition, there had been six claimants who were outside the Committee's terms of reference. One of these was the father of the executed James Daly (whose mother had died in 1930); another was the married sister of Private Smyth who had been killed in the raid on the armoury at Solon. The remaining four were described as being 'the unmarried next-of-kin of the dead men'.

A number of ex-mutineers had claimed to be suffering from disabilities 'arising out of the mutiny'. Some of them had contracted tropical diseases, such as malaria, and the Committee expressed the opinion that such ailments were 'to be associated with general service conditions in India – prior to the mutiny, rather than to the mutiny itself'. However, they were satisfied in the cases of twenty-two of the claimants that the disabilities of which they complained were genuinely related to the mutiny. They had ascertained, they said, that nineteen of the mutineers 'went on hunger-strike on two occasions in prison, with the result that they were placed in solitary confinement for a period of about three months'. An appendix to the Report set out the names of the men concerned and the resultant disabilities which some of them were experiencing. Joseph Hawes, now a hairdresser in his native Kilrush, was afflicted with 'Bronchitis and Nervous Disability'. Patrick Scally, who later emigrated to Canada where he worked as a stonemason, said his ordeal had caused him to develop tuberculosis. Two men apart from Hawes stated that they suffered with their nerves. Others complained of a variety of disorders, including sinus trouble, rheumatism and general debility. Patrick Mangan, a labourer in County Mayo, although he did not claim to have taken part in any hunger-strikes, said he had been in a delicate state of health ever since his release from prison, and Joseph Walsh, the author of 'The Ballad on the Mutiny', who was then working as a labourer in Dublin, set out his disability as 'loss of health', brought about by being kept in solitary confinement from the outset of his imprisonment until his eventual release. The Committee suggested that all these claims should be referred to a competent Medical Board and that if the Board was satisfied that the disability had 'arisen out of the mutiny or out of conditions associated with the mutiny' the claimant ought to receive a pension.

The Minister for Defence approved the Report of the Committee with the proviso that some items on the scale of compensation should be increased.[16] It was also endorsed by the Irish Cabinet at a meeting in August, 1935.[17]

The Connaught Rangers (Pensions) Bill was introduced in the Dail by the Minister for Defence on 29 April, 1936, and was approved without a division after only one Member, Frank MacDermott, had spoken in any way critically about the mutiny.[18] MacDermott, who sat as an Independent, had been educated at a Roman Catholic school in England and had served in the Irish Guards during the war. He had spent some time working for a firm of bankers in New York and was recognized to be a man of considerable intelligence. Politically he believed that the Irish Free State should remain as part of the British Commonwealth. He was not objecting to the Bill or opposing it, he said, but he did not want the public to get the view that what the mutineers did was entirely praiseworthy. In his view it had not been praiseworthy at all. He went on:

> They went into the British Army of their own free will, took the oath of allegiance of their own free will, took upon themselves the obligation of maintaining the splendid traditions of the Connaught Rangers, and yet in spite of that they mutinied while in the service of the Crown.

He did not consider that the exasperating conduct of the Black and Tans justified these men in going back on the oaths they had sworn, and in any case their protest had gone further. They had demanded that all the British forces should be withdrawn from Ireland and had flown the flag of the Republic. He could understand, Mr MacDermott continued, how 'even very moderate Nationalists' had been unwilling to join the British Army before the First World War. They had more reason for being unwilling to do so after the Easter Rising had taken place in 1916 and Sinn Fein had become the dominating influence in Irish politics,

> but if people were willing, after all these things, to go into the British Army, it does not seem praiseworthy that they should be so unstable as to turn completely round in a year or two. It is true that fearful brutalities were committed by the Black and Tans. It is equally true that fearful brutalities were committed by Sinn Fein, and moreover that Sinn Fein began it.

MacDermott went on to observe that the mutineers – he referred to them as 'these poor men' – took an action which he was sure they considered to be justified. However, there was a tendency for the Press to hold them up as being heroes and to suggest they were entitled to claim from the State even larger amounts of compensation than were provided in the present Bill. He could not accept that their conduct had been heroic. He ended:

> I am not going to oppose this Bill, but I thought it desirable to make these observations, because I think it is very easy for the moral sense of the community to be led astray by the sort of language that is used in connection with achievements of the kind that are rewarded by this Bill. What the State is doing for these men I regard as an act of grace. I do not regard these pensions as something they have a right to demand. The thing, however, that affects me most is that these men, in fact, have suffered for what they did and that many of them are in actual need.

Frank Aiken, the Minister for Defence, replying for the Government, said:

> Personally, I agree with Deputy MacDermott this far, that in ordinary circumstances, and even in extraordinary circumstances, if men have given a pledge of loyalty that they should withdraw from it without mutiny . . . But men sometimes find themselves in the position that they get orders which are against the laws of justice that they cannot obey. A number of these Connaught Rangers had joined up at John Redmond's request to fight for small nations. After the war they were given inducements to stay on in the British Army and were transferred to India. When they were serving in India they found that the British Empire, which had asked them to fight for small nations, had started to crush their own small nation . . . My opinion is that in the circumstances the Connaught Rangers were altogether praiseworthy in doing what they did. The British, who had originally invited a number of Irishmen to fight for small nations, at the end of the war, when it suited their purpose, started to crush this small nation, and used methods that even the Germans did not use against the Belgians.

Aiken did not specify the proportion of the mutineers who were to benefit from the Bill who had, in fact, joined the British Army during the early stages of the war in response to John Redmond's appeal. A Memorandum prepared for the Cabinet by the Minister for Finance a few weeks later was more specific. There were, he said, forty-four possible claimants who had served for less than ten years at the time of the mutiny. Of these thirty-three, exactly three-quarters, had enlisted within three years of the outbreak of the mutiny. The figures, which had been supplied to him by the Department of Defence, were:

> Service of one year or under.......15
> Service of two years or under........13
> Service of three years or under ....5[19]

All these men had volunteered for the Army after the Easter Rising of 1916; indeed fifteen of them had done so after the Republican Dail Eireann had been set up in Dublin on 21 January, 1919, and had declared that a state of war existed between Ireland and England.

In general, the Dail debate on the compensation of the Connaught Rangers mutineers was reported objectively and with comment by the English Press. Two weeks later the Londoner's Diary in the *Evening Standard* referred to what was described as 'an interesting sequel' to the

Irish Government's proposals. 'The men themselves have added a touch of Irish comedy to the Bill,' wrote the diarist. 'They have held a meeting and have decided not to accept the pensions and gratuities on the ground that they are inadequate.'[20]

Several amendments were made in the Connaught Rangers (Pensions) Bill while it was passing through the committee stage. A special clause was added to provide a weekly allowance for James Daly's father. In a Memorandum prepared by the Department of Defence it had been stated that the reason for this amendment was that 'the part played by Private Daly deserves some recognition by the State, and that the best manner of doing so is to provide for his aged father, who it is understood is now in necessitous circumstances'.[21] Another amendment granted permanent pensions, instead of one-off gratuity payments, to all the mutineers who had been serving for short-time engagements of less than twelve years provided that they had enlisted before 18 April, 1918, just over two years before the mutiny.[22]

In spite of the fact that the only mutineer who had been wounded either at Jullundur or Solon was Private Egan, and that he was complaining of no more serious after-effects than rheumatism, a comprehensive schedule was appended to the Bill setting out the various types of disablement which would qualify for a pension. Included in the list were 'loss of two or more limbs', 'total loss of sight', 'loss of both feet' and 'wounds, injuries, or results of them, resulting in a disabled man being permanently bedridden'. From the physical conditions which were enumerated, the Bill might well have been concerned with the aftermath of a hard-fought campaign, though it is true to say that it did not relate solely to the skirmish at Solon, but also to diseases 'attributable to the mutiny' or arising directly from it. It is still difficult to envisage how a sentence of imprisonment served in a British or a British-administered gaol would have caused, say, the 'loss of a leg and one eye'.

The Pensions Act was finally passed into law in July, 1936, without further modification. All claims under its provisions were dealt with from then on by the Ministry for Defence. In February, 1937, it was revealed in the Dail that there had so far been 105 applications under the Act, of which three had been granted and 102 were still under consideration.[23] In reply to a parliamentary question during the following June, Frank Aiken stated that out of the 106 [sic] claims received by his department thirty-seven had been successful, eleven were being considered and the remainder had been refused.[24]

The Ministry of Defence in Dublin was clearly encountering a certain amount of difficulty in checking the personal details of the applicants under the new Act and in weeding out the spurious claims. It was therefore decided to enlist the assistance of the British Government. On 12 November, 1936, the Irish Free State High Commission in London wrote to the Dominions Office, enclosing a list of sixty of the mutineers, and asking if it could 'obtain by favour of the War Office' particulars of the men's army service, confirmation that they had been involved in the mutiny and particulars of their sentence. In addition, they enquired about the circumstances of Private Daly's execution and the shooting of Private Sears and Private Smyth.[25] After consultations had taken place between the War Office and the Dominions Office, a Memorandum was prepared by the Permanent Under-Secretary in the War Office for the Secretary of State and the Adjutant-General. In it he wrote,

> I told Mr Stephenson (Dominions Office) when he came to see me that the War Office could not be expected to supply information for the purposes of enabling mutineers to be rewarded for their 'national motives', unless it was decided by Ministers as a matter of policy that we should do so.

The Permanent Under-Secretary went on to say that he had been informed that Malcolm MacDonald, the Dominions Secretary in the Government, 'while he does not like it', was in favour of giving the information to the Irish Free State High Commission.[26]

The Adjutant-General added his own comments to the War Office file on the subject:

> It is quite unreasonable for the Government of any Dominion to expect the War Office to give information in order that men who, while serving in the British Army, committed the offence of mutiny under the Army Act, should be rewarded. If the Irish Free State Government wish to reward these men, they should rely on their own sources of information.[27]

This opinion was endorsed by Duff Cooper, who had very recently been appointed Secretary of State for War. He returned the file to the Permanent Under-Secretary with a brief directive:

> I really do not think that the War Office can be expected to assist the Irish Free Government in this matter, and I should like to see their request refused. But I observe that Mr Malcolm MacDonald is in favour of giving the information. As a refusal might cause him embarrassment, you will probably wish to ascertain the reason why he has adopted this line before giving a decision.[28]

Malcolm MacDonald raised no objections to the refusal, and in December, 1936, the Irish Free State High Commission was told that the information they required was not available for the purpose of determining claims under the Connaught Rangers (Pensions) Act.[29]

During the spring of 1937 the Irish Government tried again to obtain information from the British authorities with regard to a claim under the Connaught Rangers (Pensions) Act, but this time they approached the matter from a different angle. On 19 March the High Commission wrote to the Dominions Office saying that the widow of Corporal Patrick Kelly was claiming that her husband's death was attributable to the mutiny. The letter requested a report 'giving particulars of the medical history of the deceased while serving in the British Army'.[30] Kelly, a Solon mutineer, had been sentenced to ten years' penal servitude, mitigated to seven years on promulgation, as well as being reduced to the ranks and discharged with ignominy. The Dominions Office referred the letter to the War Office with a query as to whether previous decisions not to furnish the Irish Government with the particulars of service of the Connaught Rangers mutineers applied to their medical records as well. The War Office took the view that the information was required 'in connexion with an Act passed to reward disloyalty to the Crown' and that application should be refused.[31] The Irish Free State High Commission was informed that 'particulars of the nature desired regarding to Kelly are not available'.[32]

The Irish Government made a final attempt to unearth part of the records of the mutineers in July, 1937, by attempting to bypass the War Office and to obtain the information they needed from the Home Office. The Irish Free State High Commission sent two letters on 2 July, 1937, making identical requests, in respect of Francis Moran and James Devers for reports giving particulars of these men's medical history during their imprisonment, as they had both applied for pensions under the 1936 Act.[33] Moran had been sentenced to ten years' penal servitude for his part in the mutiny at Solon, and this term had not been reduced by the confirming authority. Devers, another Solon mutineer, had originally received a sentence of life imprisonment but this had been commuted to penal servitude for ten years. Like all the other mutineers they had been discharged with ignominy, which meant they had ceased to be in the Army when they were serving their sentences in English prisons, and came under the jurisdiction of the Home Office rather than the War Office.

In view of the two earlier refusals the matter was referred to the War Office for their opinion before a final decision was taken. After giving the matter careful consideration the Permanent Under-Secretary wrote a Minute for Duff Cooper on 30 July. He said that the position was made more difficult by the attitude both they and the Home Office had adopted in the past when the Irish Government had made similar requests under the Irish Free State Pensions Act of 1932. This enactment provided pensions for persons who had been in various anti-British organizations, such as the I.R.A., and who had served sentences for their activities in English prisons. No objection had ever been raised by either the Home Office or the War Office to the disclosure of information relating to their medical history during their imprisonment. If objections were going to be taken in the present instance, he continued,

> our argument should be based on the possible effect on the discipline of the Army today if it were known that the British Government was, through any Department of State, assisting the administration of the Connaught Rangers (Pensions) Act 1936. We think a distinction can clearly be drawn between seditious activities by persons who at the time were free to exercise 'private judgement', and mutiny by men who were at the time serving in the Army under oath, and we could argue that an apparent condonation of the latter would have a more unfortunate effect. You will no doubt wish to consult [the Adjutant-General] on the matter.[34]

In fact, the Adjutant-General agreed completely with the views the Permanent Under-Secretary had expressed. In a separate Minute he wrote:

> It would have a deplorable effect in the Army if it were known that any Government Department gave information which would assist disloyal and mutinous ex-soldiers to obtain reward for their disgraceful conduct.[35]

In due course the Irish Free State High Commission was notified that their latest request for information could not be granted. As far as is known they made no further applications of a similar nature from then on.

Chapter 15

THE ULTIMATE ACCLAIM

In August, 1926, the inaugural meeting was held in Dublin of a new, voluntary organization called the National Graves and Monuments Association, a name which was subsequently altered to the National Graves Association. The initial aims of this group were to compile a complete list of all 'patriot graves' in the Dublin area, to renovate them when necessary and to preserve them in good condition. After a few years the Association widened its scope to include patriot graves in the whole of Ireland, and also to the erection of suitable memorials to deceased national heroes. Their first memorial headstone was put up in Glasnevin cemetery on the northern side of Dublin City, to sixteen Volunteers killed during the 1916 Rising. The unveiling ceremony took place on Easter Sunday in March, 1929, and was performed by the then Commanding Officer of the Dublin Brigade of the I.R.A. The inscription carved in the headstone read,

> To perpetuate the memory of members of the Irish Volunteers and Irish Citizen Army who fell fighting for the freedom of Ireland, Easter 1916, whose remains are interred in this Plot.[1]

In succeeding years a number of other memorials were constructed to commemorate leading figures and events in Ireland's struggle for independence.

The Day to Day feature in the *Irish Press* on 20 January, 1949, devoted almost its entirety to the Connaught Rangers' mutiny. After describing the events at Jullundur and Solon, the writer said:

> On June 28, 1949, a long-due tribute will be paid to these fearless Irishmen who risked death in support of an ideal. For the last eleven

years there has been lying in a sculptor's yard in Dublin a cenotaph made in honour of the mutineers who laid down their lives. It was paid for by surviving mutineers, each of whom donated a share of his service pension to this end; it has since remained in the sculptor's yard until a place worthy of it could be found. Now a site has been put aside in the National Circle in Glasnevin Cemetery where the cenotaph is to be erected.[2]

Readers were told that many of the original mutineers were still 'alive and flourishing', including John Flannery who had been a civil servant in Dublin for eighteen years. Flannery, who was described as the man who had been in charge of the mutiny, wrote to the *Irish Press* two weeks later to say that a full story setting out his own part in the mutiny would be published in the near future.[3]

The Connaught Rangers' cenotaph in Glasnevin was unveiled on 27 June, 1949. After Requiem Mass had been celebrated in the Franciscan Church on Merchant's Quay the congregation marched to the cemetery led by the Dublin Brigade of the I.R.A., a firing party composed of veterans of the Volunteers who had taken part in the 1916 Rising, members of the Citizen Army Association, a guard of honour, representatives of the National Graves Association and two girls' pipe bands. Press reports stated that Joseph Hawes, 'the originator of the movement', Stephen Lally and Patrick Gogarty, all survivors of the mutiny, were in the guard of honour. No mention was made of John Flannery. The unveiling ceremony was carried out by Francis Kearney, the mutineer who had organized the occasion. In his speech Kearney said that he and his comrades had decided not to serve in the Army any longer in protest against the atrocities the British were carrying out in their homeland; they had torn down the Union Jack, the symbol of imperialism, and had raised the tricolour of the Republic in its place. The heroic men who had died in the mutiny, he went on, deserved commemoration among the long line of those who had given their lives for Ireland. The firing party then fired a salvo from their rifles, the Last Post was sounded and the girl pipers played a Reveille. Before the laying-on of wreaths Hawes spoke a few words. He said he was glad that he had lived to see the day on which the memorial was erected. The headstone recorded that James Daly had been executed for his part in the mutiny, Peter Sears and Patrick Smyth had been shot while it was taking place, and John Miranda had subsequently died in a prison hospital. It also listed the names of all the other mutineers.[4]

Until the War Office File Number 141/90 was opened to public inspection very recently, it was generally unknown that in September, 1922, during the Civil War in Ireland, twenty-seven of the imprisoned mutineers had petitioned the Home Secretary for their immediate release so that they could fight for the Provisional Government of the Irish Free State against the Republican rebels. From the statements they made to newspapers immediately after their liberation in January, 1923, the majority of mutineers had continued to support the pro-Treaty Government. Nevertheless, the Republicans in Ireland had always been to the fore in their adulation of the mutiny. In the early months of 1949 the Offaly-Westmeath Old I.R.A. Memorial Committee requested the Minister for External Affairs to use his influence to have 'the remains of James Daly (Connaught Rangers) who was executed in India exhumed for re-interment in Tyrrellspass, his native place'.[5] It might not have been a coincidence that the Offaly-Westmeath I.R.A. Committee were at the time making arrangements for a memorial of their own to be erected in the main street of Tyrrellspass.[6] The I.R.A. had played a prominent part in the unveiling ceremony of the Connaught Rangers' Cenotaph at Glasnevin. A notice appeared in the *Dublin Evening Mail*, a paper in which the Old I.R.A. often listed activities, on 18 June, 1949:

United Conference of Old I.R.A. – The United Conference requests that all the Old I.R.A. and kindred bodies participate in the ceremony arranged by the Connaught Rangers' Mutiny Memorial Committee on tomorrow week; parade will assemble at 41 Parnell Square at 11.15 a.m. and move off at 12 noon to Glasnevin Cemetery.[7]

A week later the Dublin *Evening Mail* published detailed instructions for the I.R.A. units which were taking part in the unveiling ceremony, with another request that members should make an effort to attend this tribute 'to the Connaught Rangers who gave their lives for Ireland in the mutiny in 1920'.[8]

The State pensions paid to the mutineers under the 1936 Act had been increased in June, 1948, to accord with the improved pension conditions applicable to the National Army. There was a great deal of resentment among the ex-Connaught Rangers whose applications for pensions under the Act had been refused. A statement by a Government Minister at Question Time in the Dail on 1 December, 1949, seemed to indicate that a far more indulgent attitude than formerly was being adopted in the consideration of such claims. Mr Brendan Corish, the Parliamentary Secretary to the Minister for Defence, had been asked if he would introduce legislation to enable unsuccessful claimants for pensions to have their cases re-examined. The Minister replied that it was not proposed to take such a course. He went on:

> I should like to say that there is ample opportunity, and it is a comparatively easy task to establish a claim for a pension under these Acts. The qualifications are comparatively simple. To qualify for such a pension it is necessary for the applicant to have been a member of the 1st Battalion of the Connaught Rangers, to have joined in the mutiny and to have been sentenced by the General Court Martial to death or to a sentence of imprisonment for any period not less than twelve months. Every applicant has ample opportunity to apply and it is a comparatively simple thing to establish a claim.[9]

The qualifications enumerated by the Minister were considerably less restrictive than those prescribed by the Connaught Rangers (Pensions) Act, 1936. For instance, it appeared from what he said that it was no longer necessary for the claimant to show that he had forfeited his entitlement to a pension or gratuity through having taken part in the mutiny, or that he suffered illness or disablement as a result of it. Even so, Mr Corish's statement did not satisfy the Member who had raised the matter that day. In a supplementary question he asked the Minister to agree that any mutineers who had been sentenced to terms of imprisonment less than twelve months in duration, and later had been 'unemployed and in distress', were entitled to have 'some consideration' given to them as well.[10]

One Member in the Dail wanted the principle governing the payment of pensions to the ex-Connaught Rangers' mutineers to be extended to another category of Irish patriot. He asked the Minister of Defence if it would be possible to amend the provisions of the Connaught Rangers (Pensions) Acts so as to make them applicable, in addition, to the Irish prisoners-of-war in the British Army who had volunteered for service with the Germans in Sir Roger Casement's Brigade. The Minister replied that, although these men could not be included in the present Act, he would consider the suggestion which had been made.[11]

During the penultimate year of the Second World War the Minister for Finance had been asked in the Dail if the Office of Public Works would provide a site for the erection of a memorial stone to the memory of James Daly. In reply he said that an application had already been made by the Connaught Rangers' Mutineers' Association for a site on which a memorial could be erected inscribed with the names of those who were killed or executed in connection with the mutiny, but they had been informed that the matter would have to be deferred until the present emergency was over.[12] Apparently nothing came of this scheme.

During the summer of 1953 the Westmeath County Council resolved to erect an I.R.A. memorial on the Green at Tyrrellspass, in commemoration of the men from the locality who had been killed fighting against the British during the Troubles and against the Free State Army in the Civil War. It was intended that the name of James Daly, the Connaught Rangers' mutineer, would also be included on the headstone. At that time the Green belonged to Lieutenant-Colonel Harold Boyd-Rochfort, a member of a wealthy Anglo-Irish family, who had an estate in the vicinity. The County Council approached Boyd-Rochfort stating that they wished to acquire the Green from him, but without telling him specifically why they wanted it. The Colonel replied by letter, in which he said:

> The Green is settled property and I am only tenant for life and, therefore, any decision in the matter affects others as well as myself. To my mind the village of Tyrrellspass is one of the prettiest in the country, and its main feature is the Green. This opinion of mine is, I know, the universal opinion of visitors and is the pride of the people who live there. My only desire is to see that the Green is kept as it has always been in the past and not built on or spoiled in any way, but remains for the use and enjoyment of the people . . . Perhaps you would be good enough to let me know for what purpose the County Council wish to acquire the Green. If the reason is purely to preserve the amenities, then it may be possible for me to arrange that it should be given to the Co. Council, subject to conditions ensuring that the present character shall be preserved and that no building or other structures should be placed thereon.[13]

At a meeting of the Westmeath County Council early in September one of the Councillors, M. J. Kennedy, who was also Parliamentary Secretary to the Minister for Social Welfare, said that Boyd-Rochfort was showing himself to be 'a rank anti-Irish bigot'; his objection, in reality, was to having an I.R.A. memorial on the Green, dedicated to the men who had given their lives for Irish independence. In Kennedy's opinion, if it was possible to take over the Green by force they should do so. When another Councillor pointed out that they had no legal powers of compulsory acquisition in the circumstances, Kennedy replied, 'Some fine morning a cross will go up and I defy them to pull it down'.[14] The threat was never carried out and the County Council plan for the memorial on the Green fell into abeyance. An alternative project, mooted in 1954, was the building of a memorial-porch at the village church in Tyrrellspass, dedicated to James Daly and five others 'who died in the fight for the freedom of Ireland'.[15] The idea was finally abandoned, probably because insufficient money could be raised to bring it to fruition.

As the mutiny of the Connaught Rangers became ever more firmly embedded among the foremost deeds of valour in the Irish struggle for independence, the feeling was growing in Ireland that the graves of the four soldiers whose deaths had resulted from the incident should no longer remain in a far-distant land. James Daly and John Miranda were still buried in the cemetery at Dagshai, and Patrick Smyth and Peter Sears, the victims of the raid on the armoury, in the cemetery at Solon.

In the autumn of 1954 Offaly County Council passed a resolution which stated:

> ... we the members of Offaly County Council assembled at Tullamore on the 16th August, 1954, request the Government to take steps to have the remains of the late James Daly and his Comrades of the Connaught Rangers who were executed for their part in the Mutiny in India, 1921, in protest against the Black and Tan atrocities in Ireland, returned to Irish soil for reinterment.[16]

This was sent to Dublin and the County Council were informed that it was being considered by the Minister for External Affairs.[17]

It appears that the Irish Government were in contact with the Government of India in the spring of 1957 regarding the possible exhumation of the remains of the four men and their transference to Ireland. In May, 1957, the Commonwealth War Graves Commission was asked for its views by the Indian High Commission in London, and replied with a request for full details of the arrangements which were to be made by the relatives of the dead men for the re-burial of the bodies when they arrived home. As the information was not forthcoming, the Commonwealth War Graves Commission was unable to assist in the matter.[18] On 3 August, 1957, the *Westmeath Examiner* reported that negotiations for the 'repatriation' of Daly's remains were taking place between the Department of External Affairs and the Indian Embassy, and were approaching their final stage. The paper stated in the same news item that a decision was soon to be taken whether or not to erect a memorial at Tyrrellspass to James Daly and the others from counties Offaly and Westmeath 'who fell in the War of Independence in Ireland'.[19]

Nothing had materialized from the talks between the Irish and Indian Governments by the autumn of 1957. On 25 October of that year the *Westmeath Examiner* published a letter from Stephen Lally, one of the four privates who had originated the protest at Jullundur. Lally had married James Daly's sister in December, 1923, soon after his release from prison, and later had moved to Eccles in Lancashire where he worked as a newspaper seller. In his letter, which he signed 'Stephen Lally (one of the Mutiny's leaders)', he said:

> Please publish, for me my few words of a great soldier, patriot and Irishman who offered his young life up on Liberty's Altar on November 2, 1920, by the action taken in that year by the Connaught Rangers for Ireland's freedom. This young soldier indeed must find a place in every Irish heart as he still rests in an Indian grave . . . like all our Irish patriots James Joseph Daly of Tyrrellspass, co. Westmeath, must live forever in our hearts and memories, and the request to have his remains returned to Ireland must never be given up. Those sacred remains of this young patriot and soldier with three more of his comrades must rest on Irish earth some day, please God soon.[20]

Stephen Lally was now playing a leading part in the agitation to get the bodies of the four dead men returned to Ireland. On 2 November, 1958, the anniversary of Daly's execution, Lally attended a service in his memory at Glasnevin Cemetery when veterans of the Dublin Brigade of the I.R.A. and survivors of the mutineers laid wreaths at the Connaught Rangers' monument. According to a report in the *Irish Press*:

> Speaking after the Last Post was sounded, Mr Stephen Lally, Manchester, a brother-in-law of James Daly, and himself one of the leaders of the Mutiny, said that thirty-eight years ago that day, Daly gave his life for Ireland. He and his comrades far away from their own dear land pledged themselves to the Irish Republic, and in pursuit of that risked their lives and suffered imprisonment. They would spare no effort to have the remains of Daly and the others reinterred here.[21]

Of sixty-five mutineers sentenced in India, said the *Irish Press*, less than a dozen remained alive.[22] However, there were still other ex-Connaught Rangers who considered that they should receive a financial reward from the Irish Government for the services they had rendered in India. During the previous summer all pensions payable under the Connaught Rangers (Pensions) Acts had been increased by fifteen per cent. While the measure was being discussed in the Dail, a Member had appealed for its provisions to be extended to the handful of people who were excluded, but who had lost their pension rights for their part in the mutiny, and had been sentenced to imprisonment or death. The country should give recognition to this small group, he said, because they were worthy of it. It was no credit to Ireland that some of these heroes had ended their days in the workhouse. When the Parliamentary Secretary to the Ministry of Defence asked him to identify the 'handful' of mutineers to whom he referred, the Member undertook to supply the full details later.[23] The matter cannot have been resolved, because, early in 1960, the subject of the Connaught Rangers (Pensions) Acts was raised again in the Dail and the same Member spoke once more of the 'forgotten heroes who were allowed to die in local workhouses'. On this occasion he proposed that the wives and families of ex-mutineers outside the scope of the Acts should be presented with a medal or a certificate in recognition of their services. The Minister for Defence undertook to look into the suggestion. In answer to another question he said that there were then thirty-seven recipients of pensions under the Connaught Rangers (Pensions) Acts.[24]

Further allegations of the unfair treatment of some of the ex-Connaught Rangers mutineers were made in the Dail on 9 March, 1961, when General MacEoin told Mr Kevin Boland, the Minister for Defence, that for the past few years he had been receiving complaints from people who said that they were entitled to pensions but had been refused them. Another Minister stated that he still thought the Connaught Rangers mutineers had been as brave as any of the men who had taken up arms in the Independence movement in Ireland and he was worried about the entitlement to a pension of the men who had become mentally ill 'as a result of having to endure the rigours of imprisonment in India'. Mr Boland informed the Dail that there were twenty-five mutineers still alive, and that he was completely satisfied that everyone who was entitled to a pension was in fact receiving one. The qualification was very simple to establish; a man only had to show that he had been court-martialled, convicted and sentenced for taking part in the mutiny.[25]

Negotiations were continuing between the Westmeath County Council and Lieutenant-Colonel Boyd-Rochfort about the erection of an I.R.A. memorial on the Green in Tyrrellspass. The Colonel still objected to any structure which might impair the beauty of the locality; he was also concerned that the proposed monument might have the effect of perpetuating the old antagonisms of bygone years.[26] Eventually a compromise was reached whereby Boyd–Rochfort would provide a site on the Green for a memorial to the men from the county who had given their lives for Irish independence. The statue, which would be a little over waist-high, would portray three young children walking optimistically towards the future. The utmost care was to be taken in its erection so that it would not detract from the picturesqueness of the Green. The memorial would be inscribed, 'To the memory of Westmeath and Offaly patriots who gave their lives for Ireland', but would commemorate in particular the deeds and valour of James Daly and five other local heroes. Three of these men had met their deaths in 1922 during the Civil War, two being executed at the order of the Irish Free State Government and one being killed in action fighting on the side of the rebels. Of the remaining two, one was shot dead in an I.R.A. attack on the police barracks before the Truce, and the last was said to have died in 1927 as a result of being tortured and beaten in earlier years.[27]

The I.R.A. Memorial Committee took over the arrangements for commissioning a sculptor and raising money for the project. A large donation was made by ex-I.R.A. men now living in the United States of America, and collections were made at I.R.A. Clubs in Westmeath and in all surrounding counties. After a service of blessing on Sunday, 30 August, 1970, the memorial was unveiled by Joseph Reddin, the former Adjutant of the Offaly Brigade of the I.R.A., before a crowd of about 2,000 people. At the outset of the ceremony 150 I.R.A. veterans marched through Tyrrellspass, led by a pipe band, and paraded in military formation on the Green. The oration was delivered by Thomas Malone, a local man and an old I.R.A. officer, who said he was proud of the fact that he was considered worthy to speak in praise of that gallant band who fought and died for Ireland. He commended especially the heroism of James Daly whom he described as the leader of the Connaught Rangers' mutiny. If the seeds sown by Daly and the others were to ripen in the hearts of young Irishmen and young Irishwomen, he declared, then they would not have died in vain. Joseph Reddin took the opportunity in his unveiling speech to make a bitter attack on the pro–Treaty politicians of the early 1920s, and referred to them as the 'junta' set up by Lloyd George. He reminded his audience that among the seventy-five prisoners executed by the junta during the Civil War were two of the men they were honouring that day. The anti–Treaty fighters, in his opinion, had been the cream of the country; they had passed the flag of freedom over to the next generation, untarnished and without dishonour.[28]

In June, 1969, the Irish Embassy in Delhi asked the Eastern Region of the Commonwealth War Graves Commission, whose offices were in the same City, if they would consent to the return of James Daly's body to Ireland. When India and Pakistan had become independent at the end of the Second World War, the British Government had decided that it could not continue to maintain the old cantonment cemeteries in either country, and in view of this the Commonwealth War Graves Commission considered that it would be unreasonable for them to refuse the Irish Embassy's request. The Indian Government were willing to grant their permission for the exhumation to take place. In April, 1970, the Irish Embassy in Delhi made similar applications for the return to Ireland of the bodies of Peter Sears, Patrick Smyth and John Miranda and again the Commonwealth War Graves Commission raised no objection. It appears that it was not possible to trace any of Miranda's relatives and this being so the exhumation of his body never took place.[29]

The negotiations between the Irish and Indian Governments and the Commonwealth War Graves Commission could not have been publicized in Ireland as on 26 February, 1970, Dr Hillery, Minister for External Affairs, was asked in the Dail if he would try to arrange the return from India of the remains of 'Corporal [sic] James Daly, late of the Connaught Rangers'. Dr Hillery replied that the Indian Government had already agreed to the repatriation of Daly's remains. He went on:

> Subject to the further wishes of the next–of–kin and in consultation with interested voluntary organizations, it was envisaged that the repatriation arrangements will be made through the Embassy in New Delhi.

Dr Conor Cruise O'Brien immediately informed Dr Hillery that Daly's relations wanted his body brought back by the National Graves Association and enquired whether this organization was going to be entrusted with the task. Two voluntary organizations would be involved, said Dr Hillery, the National Graves Association and the Federation of the Old I.R.A. Having elicited this information Dr O'Brien asked the Minister, 'Were the Connaught Rangers also in the I.R.A.?'. Without answering what seemed a very pertinent question, Dr Hillery replied:

> These people are interested but the main people who will be consulted are the next–of–kin and, if they wish, the cost would be borne by the State from India to Dublin.[30]

The bodies of James Daly, Peter Sears and Patrick Smyth were flown into Dublin Airport on the afternoon of Friday, 30 October, 1970. The party of about fifty who were waiting to receive them included representatives of the Irish President and Prime Minister, relations of the dead men and a survivor of the mutiny, William Coote, who was then 81 years old. Members of the National Graves Association, wearing black berets and purple armbands, formed a guard of honour. The flag-draped coffins of the three men were taken from the plane to a nearby church where a short service was conducted by a priest. They were then put into hearses which were driven to the Custom House in the centre of Dublin. This was to be an opportunity for Dubliners to pay their respects to the dead soldiers and to the memory of the Connaught Rangers mutiny. A procession formed up and marched from the Custom House to the Franciscan Church at Merchant's Quay, headed by the band of the Irish Transport and General Workers' Union and parties of pallbearers from the National Graves Association carrying the coffins. They were followed by members of Sinn Fein, detachments of the I.R.A., friends, relations and admirers. James Daly's coffin had been covered with the same tricolour flag which had lain over the coffin of Terence MacSwiney, the Lord Mayor of Cork, who had died at Brixton Prison in October, 1920, at the end of a two-and-a-half month hunger-strike.

Next morning the coffins of Smyth and Sears were taken for burial to Glasnevin Cemetery. In the afternoon a convoy headed by a hearse carrying Daly's body travelled to Tyrrellspass. Its arrival there was described by the *Westmeath Examiner* the following week:

> The gloomy clouds of an October evening scudded across a winter's sky as a small group awaited at St Patrick's Hall, Tyrrellspass on Saturday last. Then, the sun burst forth as a hearse followed by a large number of cars came into view. James Daly had come home. Over fifty years ago, as a lad in his 'teens, he had left Tyrrellspass to join the Connaught Rangers. These were the years when names like the Dardanelles, Ypres and the Somme were on everyone's lips; and James Daly left his native heath to soldier in climes far away. He paid the supreme sacrifice when, fifty years ago on Monday last, in his early twenties, he faced a firing squad in far-away India, having declined to give up his protest against the Black and Tan atrocities in Ireland.[31]

No ceremonies had been arranged for that day. The coffin was simply carried into the village church and placed before the High Altar to lie in state until the re-burial took place the following afternoon. Among the numerous people who came to pay their last personal respects were Daly's two sisters accompanied by their sons and daughters, who had returned to Tyrrellspass for the funeral. Others who visited the Church during the Saturday evening or the Sunday morning most probably included five of the surviving mutineers, Joseph Hawes, James Gorman, Eugene Egan, Patrick Hynes and William Coote. They were all elderly by then but they had chosen to be members of the guard-of-honour in the procession to the cemetery.

On the Sunday afternoon a crowd of about 5,000 had gathered in Tyrrellspass. The President, Eamon De Valera and the Prime Minister, Jack Lynch, were both represented by their A.D.C.s. Although a considerable force of gardai (police) had been drafted in for the occasion, the *Irish Press* reported that 'large numbers of Republican men in black berets marshalled the proceedings'.[32] At two o'clock a Requiem Mass was celebrated in the church for the repose of James Daly's soul, and his coffin was then placed in a hearse for the start of the public ceremony. The day was cold and a light rain was falling as the procession moved off. It was led by a colour party bearing the Irish National flag and the flags of the four Irish provinces. They were followed by pipers playing a lament and the brass band of the Irish Transport and General Workers' Union which had accompanied the cortège in Dublin the previous day. Then came the slow-moving, flower-bedecked hearse with the principal mourners close behind it. In the main body of marchers, said the *Westmeath Examiner*, were 'members of the Republican movement from many parts of Ireland including Belfast'.[33]

The procession passed through the village and then went round the Green where the new memorial had been erected. Finally it reached the cemetery on the outskirts of Tyrrellspass. Daly's coffin was removed from the hearse and carried shoulder-high by the pallbearers to the freshly dug grave next to the one where his mother was buried. As the coffin was lowered into the earth a bugler sounded the Last Post and the flags were dipped. Then prayers were recited, wreaths were laid and three speakers came forward to deliver their orations to the hushed throng.[34]

Seamus MacCiarnain, the Chairman of the National Graves Association, spoke first. He said that James Daly's relatives and friends, indeed the people of the whole of Ireland, had waited for a long time for his remains to be laid to rest in Tyrrellspass. They had waited with burning pride in their hearts for the little soldier boy who went out to fight for the liberty of small nations and who gave his life for the liberty of his own small nation. Tyrrellspass could be justly proud of her noted son, and Ireland justly could be rightly proud of all the Connaught Rangers, dead or alive. MacCiarnain finished by reading aloud Daly's last letter to his mother, written the night before his execution.

The Old I.R.A. officer, Thomas Malone, who had also made a speech at the unveiling ceremony of the memorial on the Green, recalled that his own mother had taught Daly at the village school in Tyrrellspass. He said that this was the proudest moment of his whole life, to be considered worthy to speak in praise of the noblest of the martyrs, who had given his life for Ireland in faraway India.[35]

The 77-year-old Joseph Hawes, making perhaps the last public pronouncement on the Connaught Rangers' mutiny, said he was thankful to God for having been spared to see this glorious event when his dead comrade was brought home for burial in his native soil. He went on:

> He was as brave a man as ever stood before a firing party. We have had many brave men, down through the years, in this country; but none of them was braver than James Daly.[36]

That evening, just after the official ceremony was over and the crowds had departed, a volley of shots was heard from the cemetery. Later the Westmeath branch of the Irish Republican Publicity Bureau put out a statement:

> A firing party from the local unit of the I.R.A. rendered military honours at the grave of James Daly in Tyrrellspass, at 20.00 hours, in the presence of the relatives of the deceased.[37]

National Legends which are founded on historical events are prone, in every country, to misconception, embellishment and distortion. The authentic facts, however, must be accepted in their entirety. They are immutable and absolute. Their interpretation will always depend on the person who assesses them.

SOURCE NOTES

CHAPTER 1 (pp 1–8)

1. T. P. Kilfeather, *The Connaught Rangers* (Anvil Books, 1969), p. 119.
2. Ibid, p. 112.
3. S. Pollock, *Mutiny For the Cause* (Leo Cooper, 1969), p. 34.
4. H. F. N. Jourdain & E. Fraser, *The Regimental History of the Connaught Rangers*, vol. 1 (RUSI, 1924), p. 570.
5. *Manual of Military Law* (War Office, 1914) Rules of Procedure, Rule 98(a), p. 627.
6. Ibid, Rule 4 (c), (d) & (e), p. 572.
7. *Roscommon Herald*, 18 February–11 March, 1922.
8. *Longford Leader*, 20 January–10 March, 1923.
9. J. Hawes unpub. Ms.: *The Connaught Rangers' Mutiny In India* (Kilrush, 1949). IWM: K.45546, pp. 1–2.
10. Kilfeather, op. cit. p. 130.
11. S. Pollock, Script: *In Search Of A Mutiny*, BBC Home Service, 1963. NAM: 6312–219.
12. C. Townshend, *The British Campaign In Ireland* (OUP, 1975) p. 27.
13. Pollock, Script, op. cit. The reference to Hawes' brother being an IRA volunteer was edited from the BBC Home Service programme broadcast on 12 December, 1963.
14. 'Exhibit C', *Roscommon Herald*, 4 March, 1922.
15. Hawes Ms, p. 2.
16. Letter: Hawes to Editor, *Irish Press*, 20 February, 1949.
17. Hawes Ms, p. 2.
18. *Irish Press*, 20 February, 1949.
19. Statement: L/Cpl. O'Brien, *Roscommon Herald*, 11 March, 1922.
20. Interview: L/Cpl. O'Brien, *In Search of A Mutiny*, BBC Home Service, 12 December, 1963.
21. Ibid.
22. Statement: Sgt. J. Shaw, *Roscommon Herald*, 11 March, 1922.
23. 'The Connaught Rangers Mutiny By One Who Knows', *Sunday Independent*, 13 February, 1925.
24. Statement: C.S.M. J. Cahill, *Roscommon Herald*, 11 March, 1922.
25. Statement: C.S.M. E. Tame, *Roscommon Herald*, 4 March, 1922.
26. Statement: Lt. W. D. Robertson, ibid.
27. Statement: Maj. R. L. Payne, *Roscommon Herald*, 23 February, 1922.
28. Hawes Ms, p. 3.
29. Ibid.
30. Ibid, p. 4.

31. Statement: Sgt. J. Shaw, *Roscommon Herald*, 11 March, 1922.
32. Ibid.
33. Hawes Ms, p. 4.
34. Enclosure: General Despatch No. 105 (Army), para. 14, 9 December, 1920. L/MIL/7/13314.
35. Ibid.
36. Statement: Sgt. J. Shaw, *Roscommon Herald*, 11 March, 1922.
37. Statement: Col. H. R. G. Deacon, *Roscommon Herald*, 18 February, 1922.
38. '... One Who Knows', op. cit. 22 February, 1925.
39. Hawes Ms, pp. 5–6.
40. Statement: Cpl. Murphy, *Roscommon Herald*, 4 March, 1922.
41. Statement: Lt. L. Leader, *Roscommon Herald*, 18 February, 1922.
42. Statement: Lt. I. Kelly, *Roscommon Herald*, 18 February, 1922.
43. Hawes Ms, p. 7.
44. Ibid, p. 7.
45. Ibid, see also Statement: T/Cpl. Murphy, *Roscommon Herald*, 4 March, 1922.
46. '... One Who Knows', op. cit. 1 March, 1925.
47. General Despatch No. 105, op. cit.
48. Statement: C.S.M. E. Tame, *Roscommon Herald*, 4 March, 1922.
49. Hawes Ms, p. 8.
50. '... One Who Knows', op. cit. 8 March, 1925.

CHAPTER 2

1. Exhibit 'A', *Roscommon Herald*, 18 February, 1922.
2. '... One Who Knows', *Sunday Independent*, 8 March, 1925.
3. Ibid.
4. Ibid.; also Kilfeather, op. cit. pp. 153–4.
5. '... One Who Knows', *Sunday Independent*, 8 March, 1925.
6. Ibid.
7. Ibid.
8. Hawes Ms, pp. 8–9.
9. Ibid.
10. Statement: Lt. L. W. L. Leader, *Roscommon Herald*, 18 February, 1922.
11. Hawes Ms, p. 9.
12. Telegram: No. 64, Viceroy to S/S, India, 9 July, 1920. Chelmsford Mss. Eur. E. 264/13.
13. Ibid.
14. Pollock, Script, op. cit.
15. 'Englishman Who Joined Irish Devils' Mutiny', *Observer*, 27 June, 1982.
16. Pollock, Script, op. cit. p. 15.
17. Statements: Ptes. McCormack & Salmon, *Roscommon Herald*, 4 March, 1922.
18. Ibid., Exhibit 'D'.
19. Statements: Sgt. Sheehan & Cpl. Murphy, *Roscommon Herald*, 23 February & 4 March, 1922.
20. Statement: C.Q.M.S. Moore, *Roscommon Herald*, 23 February, 1922.
21. Statement: Lt. W. Robertson, *Roscommon Herald*, 4 March, 1922.
22. Pollock, *Mutiny For the Cause*, pp. 50–1.
23. Kilfeather, op. cit. pp. 171–2; *Sunday Independent*, 22 March, 1925; Sgt. Edwards in Pollock, Script, pp. 18–19.
24. Pollock, Script, p. 17.
25. F. S. Keegan: 'James Daly–The One Who Was Shot', *Irish Press*, 31 October, 1970.
26. Interview with Charles Kerrigan by B. O'Floinn, Dept. of Folklore, U.C.D., 31 December, 1986.
27. Sgt. Edwards: Pollock, Script, pp. 18–9.
28. '... One Who Knows', *Sunday Independent*, 8 March, 1925.
29. Statement: Cpl. P. J. Kelly, *Longford Leader*, 10 March, 1923.
30. Enclosure: General Despatch No. 105, op. cit.

31. Interview with D. McWeeney by D. O'Dulaing: RTE Radio 'Mutiny At Solon', broadcast, 1 November, 1970. See also various witnesses' statements in *Longford Leader*, 3 February; 10 February; 10 March, 1923.

32. Interview with D. MacWeeney: RTE Radio, op. cit.

33. Interview with C. Kerrigan by B. O'Floinn, 31 December, 1987.

CHAPTER 3

1. 'Thrilling Melee In Connaught Rangers' Mutiny', *Irish Weekly Independent*, 14 March, 1925.
2. Ibid.
3. General Despatch No. 105, op. cit.
4. Statements: Lt. L. W. L. Leader; Lt. I. J. Kelly, *Roscommon Herald*, 18 February, 1922.
5. Statement: Lt. L. W. L. Leader, ibid.
6. 'One Who Knows . . .', *Irish Independent*, 14 March, 1925.
7. Hawes Ms, p. 10.
8. Enclosure, para. 14, General Despatch No. 105, op. cit.
9. Statement: Lt. L. W. L. Leader, op. cit.
10. Statement: Lt. Col. H. R. G. Deacon, *Roscommon Herald*, 18 February, 1922.
11. Interview with Mrs Carney by D. O'Dulaing, RTE, 1 November, 1970.
12. G. N. Molesworth, *Curfew on Olympus* (1965), p. 49.
13. Interview with D. MacWeeney by D. O'Dulaing, RTE, op. cit.
14. Statement: Maj. W. N. S. Alexander, *Longford Leader*, 27 January, 1923.
15. Interview with C. Kerrigan by B. O'Floinn, Department of Folklore, University College Dublin, 31 December, 1987.
16. Statement: Lt. D. MacWeeney, *Longford Leader*, 3 February, 1923.
17. Interview with Mrs V. Byrne by D. O'Dulaing, RTE, 1970.
18. Interview with J. Gorman by D. O'Dulaing, RTE, 1970.
19. Statement: Maj. W. N. S. Alexander, op. cit.
20. *The Ranger*, vol. VII, No. 28, May 1934, pp. 109–10.
21. Statement: L. Cpl. Franklin, *Longford Leader*, 10 March, 1923.
22. *Enniscorthy Echo*, 27 January, 1923.
23. Interview with P. Hynes by D. O'Dulaing, RTE, 1970.
24. Interview with J. Gorman, op. cit.
25. Statement: Lt. W. J. O'Brien, *Longford Leader*, 3 February, 1923.
26. Interview with C. Kerrigan by B. O'Floinn, op. cit.
27. Interview with J. Gorman, op. cit.
28. Statements: Lt. W. J. O'Brien; Lt. D. MacWeeney, *Longford Leader*, 3 February, 1923.
29. Interview with E. Egan by D. O'Dulaing, RTE, 1970.
30. Interview with D. MacWeeney, op. cit.
31. Kilfeather, p. 179.
32. Interview with C. Kerrigan, op. cit.
33. Ibid.
34. Kilfeather, op. cit. pp. 104–5.
35. Letter & Enclosure: MacWeeney to Lt. Col. F. W. S. Jourdain, 1 April, 1971, NAM 7609–35–12.
36. Interview with C. Kerrigan, op. cit.
37. Interview with E. Egan by D. O'Dulaing, RTE, 1970.
38. Interview with D. MacWeeney, op. cit.
39. Kilfeather, op. cit. p. 184.
40. Ibid.
41. Ibid.; Telegram: Viceroy to Secretary of State for India, 9 July,

1920. IORL, Chelmsford Ms. Eur.
E 264/13.
42. Interview with J. Gorman, op. cit.
43. Ibid.; Telegram: Viceroy to
Secretary of State for India, op. cit.
44. Interview with J. Gorman, op. cit.
45. Hawes Ms, pp. 10–12.
46. Interview with T. Tierney by D.
O'Dulaing, RTE, 1970.
47. Telegram: Viceroy to India Office,
15 June, 1916, L/MIL/7/18201.
48. Interview with Mrs Carney, op.
cit.
49. Brigadier-General C. I. Jerrard

quoted in Letter: H. Alleyne to A.
Y. McPeake, 15 December, 1974,
NAM 7609–35–12.
50. *Irish Weekly Independent*, 14 March,
1925.
51. Ibid.
52. Telegram: Viceroy to Secretary of
State for India, 9 July, 1920.
53. Statement: Maj. R. L. Payne,
Roscommon Herald, 23 February,
1923.
54. Hawes Ms, pp. 11–12; *Irish Weekly
Independent*, 14 March, 1925.
55. Ibid.

CHAPTER 4

1. Telegram No. 8433: Viceroy to
Secretary of State, 2 July, 1920.
Chelmsford Mss. Eur. E. 264/13.
2. Ibid, Telegram No. 8434.
3. General Despatch No. 105, op. cit.
L/MIL/7/13314.
4. Telegram No. 8484: Viceroy to
Secretary of State, 4 July, 1920.
Chelmsford Mss, op. cit.
5. *The Times*, 5 July, 1920.
6. Story based on Reuter's Report, 5
July, 1920, p. 118, L/MIL/7/13314.
7. *Freeman's Journal*, 5 July, 1920.
8. General Despatch No. 105, op. cit.
L/MIL/7/13314.
9. Telegram No. 8730: Viceroy to
Secretary of State, 21 July, 1920.
Chelmsford Mss, op. cit.
10. *The Times*, 13 July, 1920.
11. Telegram No. 9466: Viceroy to
Secretary of State, 21 July, 1920.
Chelmsford Mss, op. cit.
12. Hawes Ms, op. cit. pp. 13–14.
13. Ibid.; '. . . One Who Knows', op.
cit. 29 March, 1925.
14. '. . . One Who Knows', op. cit. 29
March, 1925.
15. Ibid.

16. Ibid.
17. Ibid.
18. *Irish Independent*, 1 January, 1965.
19. Hawes Ms, op. cit. p. 16.
20. Report on Military Prisons &
Detention Barracks in India, 1917.
L/MIL/17/5/1822.
21. Ibid, p. 16; Pollock, *Mutiny For
The Cause*, p. 75; '. . . One Who
Knows', op. cit. 5 April, 1925.
22. Hawes Ms, op. cit. p. 16.
23. '. . . One Who Knows', op. cit. 5
April, 1925.
24. Hawes Ms, op. cit. pp. 18–19.
25. *Longford Leader*, 20 January–10
March, 1923.
26. *Longford Leader*, 3 February, 1923.
27. Kilfeather, op. cit. p. 190; '. . . One
Who Knows', op. cit. 5 April,
1925.
28. *Manual Of Military Law*, 1914, op.
cit. Rule 18, p. 578.
29. Ibid, Rule 87, p. 622.
30. Pollock, *Mutiny For The Cause*, op.
cit. p. 82.
31. '. . . One Who Knows', op. cit. 5
April, 1925.

CHAPTER 5

1. Army of India: Northern Command Orders, 18 August, 1920. L/MIL/17/5/387.
2. *Manual of Military Law*, 1914, op. cit. Rules of Procedure, Rule 101, p. 629.
3. Ibid, p. 15.
4. Army Act, 1881, 44 & 45 Vict. C.58. sec. 7.
5. WO 141/90, 3 October, 1920.
6. Pollock, *Mutiny For The Cause*, op. cit. p. 82.
7. *Westmeath-Offaly Independent*, 13 January, 1923.
8. Hawes Ms, op. cit. p. 25.
9. 'One Who Knows', op. cit. 5 April, 1925.
10. Hawes Ms, op. cit. p. 26.
11. Ibid.: '... Song or Poem composed by '40' Walsh in Dagshai Prison about the Mutiny'.
12. General Despatch No. 105, op. cit. L/MIL/7/13314.
13. *Manual of Military Law*, 1914, op. cit. Rule 120, p. 639.
14. Army Act, s. 53 (8).
15. Ibid, s. 48 (8).
16. General Despatch No. 105, op. cit. L/MIL/7/13314.
17. ACI 570, 22 May, 1918.
18. The procedure was explored by Major C. W. Lowther MP during the committee stage of the Army & Air Force (Annual) Bill, 13 April, 1920.
19. Hawes Ms, op. cit. p. 27.
20. '... One Who Knows', op. cit. 5 April, 1925.
21. General Despatch No. 105, op. cit. L/MIL/7/13314.
22. Interview with C. Kerrigan by B. O'Floinn, op. cit.
23. Hawes Ms, op. cit. p. 28.
24. '... One Who Knows', op. cit. 5 April, 1925.
25. Ibid, 12 April, 1925.
26. General Despatch No. 105, op. cit. L/MIL/7/13314.
27. Letter (personal): Chelmsford to Montagu, 19 October, 1920. L/MIL/17/13314.
28. Telegram No. 162, Priority A: Viceroy to Secretary of State, 25 October, 1920. Op. cit. Chelmsford Mss.
29. Telegram No. 433-R: Viceroy to Secretary of State, 1 November, 1920. Op. cit. Chelmsford Mss.

CHAPTER 6

1. *Manual of Military Law*, 1914, op. cit. p. 38.
2. Army Act 1881, 44 & 45 Vict. C.58, sec. 54 (8).
3. General Despatch No. 105, op. cit. p. 74, L/MIL/7/13314.
4. Hawes Ms, op. cit. p. 28; '... One Who Knows', op. cit. 12 April, 1925.
5. Ibid, Hawes Ms, p. 28.
6. Ibid, '... One Who Knows', 12 April, 1925.
7. Kilfeather, op. cit. pp. 6–7.
8. '... One Who Knows', op. cit. 12 April, 1925.
9. Hawes Ms, op. cit. p. 28.
10. *Westmeath Examiner*, 11 December, 1929, pp. 3–4.
11. Kilfeather, op. cit. pp. 6–7.
12. P. Liddle, *The Soldier's War 1914–1918* (Blandford Press, 1988), p. 88.
13. Captain L. Gameson, RAMC, Ms Diary, 1914–1919, pp. 395–7. IWM No: P395/7.
14. Kilfeather, op. cit. pp. 6–7.
15. Hawes Ms, op. cit. p. 29.
16. *Cork Evening Echo*, 9 January, 1923.
17. *The Western People*, 13 January, 1923; *Roscommon Journal*, 27 January, 1923.

18. Interview with P. Hynes by D. O'Dulaing, RTE, op. cit.
19. Interview with C. Kerrigan by B. O'Floinn, op. cit.
20. Interview with J. Gorman by D. O'Dulaing, RTE, op. cit.
21. Hawes Ms, op. cit. pp. 29–30.
22. Kilfeather, op. cit. pp. 7–8.
23. Ibid, p. 8.
24. Death Certificate: James Joseph Daly. General Register Office, London, 30 February, 1990.
25. Hawes Ms, op. cit. p. 31.
26. Telegram No. 259: Viceroy to S/S, 4 November, 1920. Chelmsford Mss.
27. Telegram No. 5574: Viceroy, Army Dept, to Secretary of State, India Office, 12 November, 1920. L/MIL/7/13314.
28. Memorandum: Military Dept, 24 November, 1920. L/MIL/7/13314.
29. Letter: Montagu to Churchill, 22 November, 1920. L/MIL/7/13314.
30. Letter: Churchill to Montagu, 23 November, 1920. L/MIL/7/13314.
31. Parliamentary Notice, Session 1920: Mr Devlin MP to S/S, 24 November, 1920; Military Dept, India Office, L/MIL/7/13314.
32. Army Act, 1881, 44 & 45, Vict. C.58, sec. 131 (2).
33. W.O. Internal Memorandum: 6 December, 1920. WO 141/84.
34. Letter: W.O. to Under Secretary of State, India Office, 14 December, 1920. L/MIL/7/13314.
35. Hawes Ms, p. 31.
36. 'Mutiny At Solon', RTE Radio, broadcast, 1 November, 1970.
37. C. Townshend, *The British Campaign In Ireland 1919–1921* (O.U.P., 1975), p. 119; R. Bennett, *The Black And Tans* (Hulton, 1959), p. 53.
38. Interview with Mrs T. Maher by D. O'Dulaing, RTE, 1970.
39. Hawes Ms, p. 31.
40. Pollock, *Mutiny for the Cause*, p. 87.
41. Death Certificate: John Miranda, General Register Office, London, 30 February, 1990.

CHAPTER 7

1. *The Soldier*, December, 1957, p. 37.
2. F. Pakenham (Earl of Longford), *Peace By Ordeal* (Sidgwick & Jackson, 1972), p. 29.
3. Townshend, op. cit. p. 6.
4. Ibid, p. 9.
5. Ibid, p. 10.
6. C. Younger, *Ireland's Civil War* (Fontana, 1970), p. 88; A. J. P. Taylor, *English History, 1914–1945* (O.U.P., 1965), p. 12.
7. Townshend, op. cit. pp. 14–15; Younger, op. cit. pp. 85–8.
8. Townshend, op. cit. p. 16.
9. Ibid, p. 19.
10. Ibid, p. 19; Younger, op. cit. p. 20.
11. Townshend, op. cit. p. 20.
12. Younger, op. cit. p. 93.
13. Taylor, op. cit. p. 155.
14. Townshend, op. cit. p. 27.
15. Pakenham, op. cit. p. 38.
16. Younger, op. cit. p. 95.
17. Taylor, op. cit. p. 150.
18. Townshend, op. cit. pp. 50–7.
19. Ibid, p. 55.
20. Ibid, p. 65; Younger, op. cit., p. 49.
21. Townshend, op. cit. p. 65.
22. Ibid, p. 65.
23. Pakenham, op. cit. pp. 46–7.
24. Ibid, p. 45.
25. Ibid, p. 47.
26. Younger, op. cit. p. 109.
27. Bennett, op. cit. p. 30.
28. Younger, op. cit. p. 109.
29. Ibid, p. 100.
30. Townshend, op. cit. p. 83.
31. Younger op. cit. p. 108; Bennett, op. cit. pp. 57–8.
32. Townshend, op. cit. p. 42.
33. Ibid, pp. 46–7.

34. Bennett, op. cit. p. 36.
35. Ibid, p. 40.
36. Townshend, op. cit. p. 88.

37. Younger, op. cit. p. 109.
38. Townshend, op. cit. pp. 81–2; 97–8.

CHAPTER 8

1. Younger, op. cit. p. 105.
2. Townshend, op. cit. p. 56.
3. Ibid, p. 94.
4. Younger, op. cit. p. 105; Townshend, op. cit. p. 94.
5. Bennett, op. cit. p. 56.
6. Pakenham, op. cit. p. 42.
7. Younger, op. cit. p. 111.
8. *Leitrim Observer*, 13 March, 1920.
9. Interview with C. Kerrigan by B. O'Floinn, 1986.
10. Telegram P. (despatched from Army Dept.): Viceroy to Secretary of State, 4 July, 1920. Op. cit. Chelmsford Mss.
11. Ibid, 9 July, 1920.
12. Return Showing The Active Strength Of The Army & Royal Air Force In India, 1st Bn. Connaught Rangers. L/MIL/17/5/1242.
13. *Westmeath Independent*, 10 January, 1920.
14. *Westmeath Independent*, 24 January, 1920.
15. *Westmeath Independent*, 31 January, 1920.
16. Ibid.
17. *Westmeath Independent*, 3 April, 1920.
18. *Westmeath Independent*, 17 April, 1920.
19. *Westmeath Independent*, 24 April, 1920.
20. *Westmeath Independent*, 22 May, 1920.
21. Text cited in *Westmeath Independent*, 29 May, 1920.
22. *Westmeath Independent*, 5 June, 1920.
23. *Times Index*, January–March, 1920.
24. *Times* Index, April–June, 1920.
25. *Roscommon Herald*, 11 March, 1922.
26. *Roscommon Herald*, 18 February, 23; 4, 11 March, 1922.

27. G. N. Molesworth, *Curfew On Olympus* (1965), p. 49.
28. Telegram: General P. Radcliffe to C.I.G.S., 4 August, 1920: Note: H. W. to Curzon, 5 August, 1920. IWM, Henry Wilson Papers, 73/1/11, File 20B.
29. K. Jeffrey, *Military Correspondence of Field-Marshal Sir Henry Wilson, 1918–1922* (Army Records Society; London; 1985), pp. 298–9.
30. Bolsheviks & India / Special Bureau Reports : Special Bureau of Information Report No. 15, w/e 29 May, 1920. L/PS/10/887.
31. Ibid, SBI Weekly Report No. 23, w/e 24 July, 1920.
32. Ibid.
33. Letter: Lt.-Col. J. C. W. Francis to F. W. S. Jourdain, 21 November, 1970. NAM: 7609–35–12.
34. Pollock, op. cit. pp. 22–3.
35. Townshend, op. cit. pp. 110–11; Younger, op. cit. p. 111.
36. Letter: F. W. S. Jourdain to A. Y. McPeake, 17 December, 1963. NAM: 609–35–12.
37. Letter: F. W. S. Jourdain to Sir Gerald Templar, 20 May, 1971. IWM: Jourdain Papers.
38. Letter: F. W. S. Jourdain to *The Times*, 11 August, 1969. NAM: 7609–35–12.
39. Letter: W. G. Robertson to A. Y. McPeake, 3 January, 1971, NAM: 7609–35–12; Ibid.; Letter: MacWeeney to F. W. S. Jourdain, 1 April, 1970. NAM: 7609–37–12.
40. Brig.-Gen. C. I. Jerrard, cited in Letter: H. Alleyne to A. Y. McPeake, 15 December, 1974. NAM: 7609–35–12.
41. H. N. F. Jourdain, *Regimental*

History of the Connaught Rangers, Vol. 1, p. 570.

42. Pollock, op. cit. pp. 25–6.
43. C. I. Jerrard, op. cit.

44. Letter: MacWeeney to F. W. S. Jourdain, 1 April, 1971. NAM: 7609-35-12.

CHAPTER 9

1. Memorandum: Brig.-Gen. B. E. W. Childs to Adjutant-General, 16 January, 1921. WO 141/84.
2. Minute: Maj.-Gen. F. F. Ready to Adjutant-General, 31 March, 1921. Ibid.
3. W. O. Departmental Memo: Adjutant-General, 2 April, 1921. Ibid.
4. Letter: W.O. to Under-Secretary of State for India (USOS/IO), 6 April, 1921. L/MIL/7/13314.
5. Report: W.O. to D.P.S., 7 May, 1921. WO 141/84.
6. Memo: Ready to Adjutant-General, 6 May, 1921. WO 141/84.
7. Letter: W.O. to Under-Secretary of State for India, 21 May, 1921. L/MIL/7/13314.
8. '. . . One Who Knows', op. cit. 12 April, 1925.
9. Hawes Ms, op. cit. pp. 34–5.
10. Ibid, p. 39.
11. Interview with J. Gorman by D. O'Dulaing, RTE, 1970.
12. Interview with Charles Kerrigan by B. O'Floinn, op. cit.
13. Memo: L to M (i.e. Art O'Brien to Michael Collins), 13 December, 1920, re: Irish Prisoners in Gt. Britain 1920–1/ Maidstone. State Papers Office, National Archives, Ireland: DE2/453.
14. *Irish Bulletin*, Vol. 5, No. 18, 27 June, 1921.
15. *Irish Press*, 18 April, 1952.
16. *An Phoblacht*, November, 1970.
17. *An Phoblacht*, December, 1970.
18. *Westmeath Examiner*, 11 December, 1920.
19. *Westmeath Examiner*, 19 February, 1921.
20. *Midland Reporter & Westmeath Nationalist*, 6 April, 1922.
21. *Irish Weekly & Ulster Examiner*, 1 July, 1950.
22. *Westmeath Examiner*, 10 September, 1951.
23. *Irish Press*, 18 April, 1952.
24. Townshend, op. cit. p. 94.
25. Ibid, p. 112.
26. Bennett, op. cit. p. 176.
27. Pakenham, op. cit. p. 57.
28. Bennett, op. cit. p. 18.
29. Ibid, p. 164.
30. Ibid, p. 190.
31. Pakenham, op. cit. p. 45.
32. Bennett, op. cit. pp. 191–2.
33. *Irish Bulletin*, 21 May, 1920.
34. J. Leonard, 'The IRA and Ex-Servicemen' in *Revolution? Ireland 1917–23* (Trinity History Workshop, 1990), p. 118.
35. Ibid, p. 119.
36. Townshend, op. cit. pp. 129–30; Bennett, op. cit. p. 126.
37. Townshend, op. cit. p. 135.
38. Ibid, pp. 34–9; Taylor, op. cit. p. 156.
39. Townshend, op. cit. pp. 173–4; Younger, op. cit. p. 136.
40. Bennett, op. cit. pp. 43, 137.

CHAPTER 10

1. Pakenham, op. cit. p. 61.
2. Hopkinson, op. cit. p. 9.
3. Townshend, op. cit. p. 198.
4. Younger, op. cit. p. 159.
5. Ibid, p. 160.
6. Ibid, pp. 162–3.
7. Ibid, pp. 164–9.
8. Ibid, pp. 194–5.
9. Ibid, p. 195.
10. Ibid, p. 196–200.
11. Ibid, p. 196.
12. Ibid, p. 207.
13. Hopkinson, op. cit. p. 35.
14. Letter: E. J. Duggan to L. Curtis, 27 January, 1922. WO 141/89.
15. Ibid.
16. Extract from Cabinet Minutes, 30 January, 1922, ibid.
17. Note: 10, Downing Street to Secretary of State for War, 31 January, 1921, ibid.
18. Sentences of Men of the Connaught Rangers Convicted of Mutiny. Report by Secretary of State for War, ibid.
19. Extract from Cabinet Minutes, 21 February, 1922, ibid.
20. *Roscommon Herald*, 18 March, 1922.
21. Hopkinson, op. cit. p. 73.
22. Ibid, p. 71.
23. Ibid, p. 53.
24. Connaught Rangers in India, 1920, Mutiny. Some remarks by the Rev. Dr I. Collins O.S.F.C., WO 141/89.
25. Exchange of letters: Colonial Office / Secretary of State, War Office, 2 June, 1922, ibid.
26. *The Ranger*, vol. IV, No. 1, May, 1923, p. 6.
27. Ibid, p. 5.
28. Letter: D. J. Hannon to Winston Churchill, 21 July, 1922. WO 141/89.
29. Letter: Colonial Office to D. J. Hannon, 26 July, 1922, ibid.
30. Hopkinson, op. cit. pp. 134–5.

CHAPTER 11

1. M. Hopkinson, *Green Against Green* (Gill & Macmillan, Dublin, 1988), p. 181.
2. Ibid, p. 182.
3. W.O. Memorandum: Director of Personal Services to Adjutant General, 26 September, 1922. WO 141/90.
4. W.O. Minute by Judge Advocate General, 27 September, 1922, WO 141/90.
5. Petition of Pte. Joseph Hawes to the War Office, WO 141/90.
6. Petitions of Pte. Patrick Cherry & John Oliver, ibid.
7. Petition of Pte. Thomas Devine, ibid.
8. Petition of Pte. Michael Kearney, ibid.
9. Petition of L. Cpl. Hugh Hewson, ibid.
10. Petition of Michael Kearney, ibid.
11. Petition of Patrick Mannion, ibid.
12. Letter: S. Gwynn to A. Bonar Law, 31 October, 1922, ibid.
13. Letter: Lord Derby to A. Bonar Law, 12 December, 1922, ibid.
14. Letter: W.O. to S. Gwynn, 14 December, 1922, ibid.
15. *Freeman's Journal*, 9 October, 1922.
16. Ibid.
17. *Poblacht na h'Eireann*, 2 December, 1922.
18. Appeal to the British Military Authorities by General Bryan Mahon and Others, 21 December, 1922, WO 141/90.
19. Letter: W. Cosgrave to A. Bonar Law, ibid.
20. Letter: A. Bonar Law to W. Cosgrave, ibid.

21. W.O. Memorandum: Secretary of State to Adjutant-General, 18 December, 1922, ibid.
22. W.O. Memorandum: Adjutant-General to Secretary of State, ibid.
23. Extract from Cabinet Minutes, 19 December, 1922, ibid.
24. Letter: Derby to P.M., 20 December, 1922, ibid.
25. Extract from Cabinet Minutes, 20 December, 1922, ibid.
26. Telegram: Sir James Masterton-Smith to Secretary of State for Colonies, 3 January, 1923, ibid.
27. Letter: K. Lyon to Derby, 4 January, 1923. Derby Papers, P.R.O., Kew, WO 137/1.
28. Letter: Derby to Lyon 6 January, 1923, ibid.
29. Dail Eireann, Parliamentary Debates, Official Report, vol. 2, January 4, 1923.
30. Ibid.
31. Ibid.
32. Ibid.
33. Ibid.
34. *Poblacht na h'Eireann,* War News, No. 36, 16 January, 1923.

CHAPTER 12

1. '. . . One Who Knows', op. cit. 12 April, 1923.
2. Hawes Ms, p. 34.
3. *Irish Independent,* 5 January, 1923.
4. Hawes Ms, pp. 39–40.
5. *Catholic Herald,* 13 January, 1923; *Irish Independent,* 5 January, 1923; *Catholic News,* 13 January, 1923.
6. Interview: J. Gorman, 'Mutiny At Solon', RTE Radio, op. cit.
7. *Evening Herald,* 5 January, 1923.
8. *Irish Independent,* 6 January, 1923.
9. WO 141/90.
10. *Irish Independent,* 5 January, 1923.
11. *Evening Herald,* 5 January, 1923.
12. Interview: C. Kerrigan by B. O'Floinn, op. cit.
13. *Evening Herald,* 5 January, 1923.
14. Interview: J. Gorman by D. O'Dulaing, RTE, op. cit.
15. *Evening Herald,* 5 January, 1923.
16. *Evening Telegraph,* 5 January, 1923.
17. *Evening Herald,* 5 January, 1923.
18. *Freeman's Journal,* 6 January, 1923.
19. *Dublin Evening Mail,* 5 January, 1923.
20. *Freeman's Journal,* 6 January, 1923.
21. *Catholic Herald,* 13 January, 1923.
22. *Irish Independent,* 5 January, 1923.
23. *Evening Telegraph,* 5 January, 1923.
24. *Poblacht na h'Eireann* (Scottish edition), 13 January, 1923.
25. *The Nationalist,* 27 January, 1923.
26. Ibid.
27. Ibid.
28. Ibid.
29. *The Western People,* 13 January, 1923.
30. Ibid.
31. *Roscommon Journal,* 27 January, 1923.
32. Ibid.
33. *Western People,* 13 January, 1923.
34. Hopkinson, op. cit. p. 229.
35. Ibid. p. 256.
36. Ibid. pp. 257–8.
37. *Mayo News,* 7 July, 1923.
38. Dail Eireann Debates, vol. 7, 19 June, 1924.
39. Letter and Enclosure: Flannery to President, Irish Free State, 5 July, 1924. SPO File: S5374A.
40. Letter: Secretary to the Cabinet to Flannery, 10 July, 1924, ibid.
41. Letter: Flannery to Cosgrave, 19 July, 1924, ibid.
42. Letter: Flannery to Cosgrave, 22 July, 1924, ibid.

CHAPTER 13

1. Leaflet: Ex-Connaught Rangers' Committee, 28 August, 1924. SPO File: S5374A.
2. *Irish Independent*, 28 August, 1924.
3. Resolution passed at a meeting held on behalf of the ex-Connaught Rangers, Upper O'Connell Street, 27 August, 1924. SPO, File: S5374A.
4. Letter: A. Smyth to Flannery, 10 September, 1924. Ibid.
5. The Garda Siochana (Civic Guard) were the Irish Free State police force who replaced the R.I.C. in 1922.
6. Letter: Flannery to Irish Minister for Justice, 19 September, 1924. Ibid.
7. Letter: T. J. Coyne to Flannery, 20 September, 1924. Ibid.
8. Letter: Flannery to Irish Minister for Justice, 22 September, 1924. Ibid.
9. *Irish Independent*, 25 September, 1924; Precis: 'Deputation of Ex-Connaught Rangers' in Memorandum: Secretary to President's Office (S. Dolan) to Minister for Finance, 21 October, 1924. SPO File: S5374A.
10. *Irish Independent*, 27 September, 1924.
11. Letter: S. Dolan to Minister for Finance, 21 October, 1924, op. cit.
12. Letter: Ministry of Finance to Dolan, 5 November, 1924. SPO File: S5374A.
13. *Irish Independent*, 23 October, 1924.
14. Letter: Mary E. Larkin, Tenant's Association, to W. Cosgrave, 21 February, 1925. SPO File: S5374A.
15. Letter: Cosgrave to Blythe, 21 February, 1925. Ibid.
16. Letter: Mary E. Larkin to Cosgrave, 21 February, 1924. Ibid.
17. Letter: President's Office to Flannery, 23 February, 1925. Ibid.
18. *Sunday Independent*, 15 February, 1925.
19. Ibid.
20. Letter: Blythe to Cosgrave, 3 March, 1925. SPO File: S5374A.
21. Memorandum: President's Office to McCauley, Department of Finance, 5 March, 1925. Ibid.
22. Letter: Department of Finance to Banim, 2 April, 1925. Ibid.
23. Letter: Flannery to Cosgrave, 9 March, 1925. Ibid.
24. Dail Eireann Debates, vol. 10, 25 March, 1925.
25. Letter: Flannery to Cosgrave, 27 March, 1925. SPO File S5374A.
26. Dail Eireann Debates, vol. 11, 29 April, 1925.
27. Dail Eireann Debates, vol. 13, 12 November, 1925.
28. Dail Eireann Debates, vol. 17, 8 December, 1926.

CHAPTER 14

1. Dail Eireann Debates, vol. 21, 10 November, 1927.
2. Letter: M. J. Kearney to Irish Press, 10 October, 1970.
3. Townshend, op. cit. p. 115; Younger, op. cit. pp. 121–2.
4. Letter: Flannery to Cosgrave, 21 September, 1928. SPO File: S5374A.
5. Dail Eireann Debates, vol. 24, 14 November, 1928.
6. Note for Minister re: Parliamentary Question of Frank Kerlin for Tuesday, 13 November, 1928. Connaught Rangers Mutiny in India, SPO File: S5374A.
7. Minute: Military Department,

India Office, 20 April, 1929.
L/MIL/7/13314.
8. Dail Eireann Debates, vol. 32, 6
December, 1929.
9. Dail Eireann Debates, vol. 36, 3
November, 1930.
10. Ibid.
11. Ibid, 10 December, 1930.
12. Ibid.
13. Dail Eireann Debates, vol. 50, 28
February, 1934.
14. Report of the Connaught Rangers
Committee of Enquiry, 29 June,
1935. SPO File: S2733.
15. Ibid.
16. Letter: Department of Defence to
Executive Council, 24 August,
1935. SPO File: S2733.
17. Extract from Cabinet Minutes,
Cab. 7/255, 21 August, 1935. SPO
File: S2733.
18. Dail Eireann Debates, vol. 61, 29
April, 1936.
19. Memorandum For The Executive
Council Of The Views Of The
Minister Of Finance On The
Proposed Amendment Of The
Connaught Rangers (Pensions)
Bill, 1936, 7 July, 1936. SPO File:
S2733.
20. *Evening Standard*, 23 May, 1936.
21. Department of Defence
Memorandum: Connaught Rangers
(Pensions) Bill, 1936, 6 May, 1936.
SPO File: S2733.

22. Dail Eireann Debates, vol. 63, 21
July, 1936.
23. Dail Eireann Debates, vol. 65, 17
February, 1937.
24. Dail Eireann Debates, vol. 68, 8
June, 1937.
25. Letter: J. W. Dulanty to H.
Batterbee, 12 November, 1936.
PRO, WO 32/4236.
26. W.O. Minute: Widdows to
P.U.S., 24 November, 1936. Ibid.
27. W.O. Minute: A.G. to P.U.S., 27
November, 1937. Ibid.
28. W.O. Minute: W. to S. of S., 12
December, 1936. Ibid.
29. Letter: Widdows, W.O. to
Stephenson, Dominions Office, 8
December, 1936. Ibid.
30. Letter: O'Donovan, I.F.S. High
Commission to Under Secretary of
State, Dominions Office, 19
March, 1937. Ibid.
31. W.O. Minute: Edwards (for
A.U.S.) to P.U.S., 7 April, 1937.
Ibid.
32. Letter: Stephenson, Dominions
Office to I.F.S. High Commission,
21 April, 1937. Ibid.
33. Letter O'Donovan, I.F.S. High
Commission to Under Secretary of
State, Dominions Office, 30 July,
1937. PRO, WO 32/4235.
34. W.O. Minute: A.G. to P.U.S., 9
August, 1937. Ibid.
35. W.O. Minute: A.G. to P.U.S., 9
August, 1937. Ibid.

CHAPTER 15

1. *Tour of Glasnevin Cemetery*
(National Graves Association:
Dublin); *The Last Post* (National
Graves Association: Dublin: 1976).
2. *Irish Press*, 20 January, 1949.
3. Ibid. 3 February, 1949.
4. *Irish Independent*, 27 June, 1949:
Irish Press, 27 June, 1949.
5. *Offaly Independent*, 22 January,
1949.

6. Ibid. 15 January, 1949.
7. *Dublin Evening Mail*, 18 June, 1949.
8. Ibid. 25 June, 1949.
9. *Dail Eireann Debates*, vol. 118, 1
December, 1949.
10. Ibid.
11. Connaught Rangers' (Pensions)
Bill, 1948. Committee & Final
Stages. Ibid. vol. 111, 15 June,
1948.

12. Oral Answers. Ibid. vol. 92, 23 February, 1944.
13. *Westmeath Examiner*, 13 February; 5 September, 1953.
14. Ibid. 5 September, 1953.
15. Ibid. 27 February, 1954.
16. Letter: Secretary, Wicklow County Council to Secretary, Executive Council, Dublin, 25 October, 1954. SPO File: S5374.
17. Letter: Offaly County Council to Secretary, Wicklow County Council, 9 November, 1954. Ibid.
18. Letter: B. McGee, Information Officer, Commonwealth War Graves Commission to author, 4 October, 1990.
19. *Westmeath Examiner*, 3 August, 1957.
20. *Westmeath Examiner*, 25 October, 1957.
21. *Irish Press*, 3 November, 1958.
22. Ibid.
23. Connaught Rangers' (Pensions) Bill, 1957 – Second Stage. *Dail Eireann Debates*, vol. 163, 4 July, 1957.
24. Connaught Rangers' (Pensions) Bill, 1960. Ibid. vol. 179, 18 February, 1960.
25. Connaught Rangers' (Pensions) Bill, 1961 – Second and Final Stages. Ibid. vol. 187, 9 March, 1961.
26. *Irish Post*, 7 October, 1969.
27. *Westmeath Examiner*, 5 September, 1970.
28. *Westmeath Examiner*, 5 September, 1970; *Westmeath-Offaly Independent*, 4 September, 1970; *Midland Tribune*, 5 September, 1970.
29. Letter: McGee, C.W.G.C. to author, op. cit.
30. Oral Answers. *Dail Eirann Debates*, vol. 221, 26 February, 1970.
31. *Westmeath Examiner*, 7 November, 1970.
32. *Irish Press*, 2 November, 1970.
33. *Westmeath Examiner*, 7 November, 1970.
34. Ibid; *Midland Tribune*, 7 November, 1970.
35. Ibid.
36. Ibid.
37. *Irish Press*, 2 November, 1970; *Westmeath Examiner*, 7 November, 1970.

BIBLIOGRAPHY

UNPUBLISHED SOURCES

National Army Museum (NAM) – Jourdain Papers

Imperial War Museum (IWM) – Gameson Papers; Jourdain Papers; Hawes Ms., The Connaught Rangers' Mutiny in India (1949)

India Office Library and Records (IOR) – Nisbet Papers; Chelmsford Papers; War Diary, Army Headquarters, India 1919–1920; Connaught Rangers Mutiny, 1920, India Office Reports and Correspondence (L/MIL series); Indian Special Bureau Reports, 1919–20

Public Record Office (PRO), Kew – War Diary of the 1st Battalion, Connaught Rangers, 1914–1919 (WO 95); Derby Papers (WO 137); Register of Expirees & Sentence-Remitted Convicts (PCOM 6); Mutiny, Connaught Rangers 1920 (WO 32). Newly opened papers (W.O. 141/84 to 141/92).

National Library of Ireland: Maurice Moore Papers; Art O'Brien Papers; John Flannery Papers ('. . . One Who Knows')

State Paper Office (SPO), National Archives, Ireland – Connaught Rangers (Pensions) Bills and associated correspondence (S series); Michael Collins – Art O'Brien Correspondence (DE2 series)

PRIVATE RECORDS

Barr, S. – Ms. Article and Notes about Charles Kerrigan and the Connaught Rangers Mutiny

Duke, R. – Correspondence and Photographs

Fornara, A. – Badham Family Album

Garvey, Mrs – Ms. 'The Connaught Rangers' by Col. S. Garvey, 1978

Gill, D. – 'Unknown Army' Correspondence and Ms. Notes

Lally, S. – Family Papers

Power-Hynes, P. – Ms. Flyleaf Notes about the Mutiny and Daly's execution

RECORDED INTERVIEWS

O'Dulaing, D., Radio Telefis Eireann, Dublin with – Mrs V. Byrne; Mrs M. Carney; E. Egan; J. Gorman; J. Hawes; J. Hughes; P. Hynes; Mrs T. Maher

O'Floinn, B., Folklore Department, University College, Dublin with C. Kerrigan

RADIO AND TELEVISION PROGRAMMES

In Search of a Mutiny, 1969 BBC Home Service Radio Drama Documentary by S. Pollock

Mutiny At Solon, 1970 RTE Radio Documentary by D. O'Dulaing
Late, Late Show, RTE TV programme, 17 October, 1970
Seven Days, RTE TV programme, 3 November, 1970
Looking West, RTE Radio programme, 27 July, 1979

PUBLISHED SOURCES
Official Publications:
Dail Debates, Dail Eireann, 1919–1970
Hansard, Parliamentary Debates, House of Commons, 1919–1970
Distribution of the Army & Royal Air Force in India, 1919, 1920, 1921
Numbers Conveyed By Sea (U.K. – India), Bombay, 1919
Report on Military Prisons and Detention Barracks in India, 1911
War Office, Manual of Military Law

Journals and Magazines
Analecta Ordinis Minorum Cappucinorum
Capuchin Annual
Cathair na Mart, Journal of the Westport Historical Society
Catholic Directory of India
The Ranger

Pamphlets
Theatre Programme – The 88. The Old Vic, London, November 1979

Newspapers
Irish–Anglo-Celt – *An Long/War Sheet; An Phoblacht; An Stoc; An t'Oglac; Ballina Herald; Belfast Evening Telegraph; Belfast Weekly News; Bray & South Dublin Herald; Carlow Sentinel; Catholic Standard; Clare Champion; Colraine Chronicle; Connacht Sentinel; Connacht Tribune; Connaught Telegraph; Cork Constitution; Cork County Eagle & Advertiser; Cork Evening Echo; Cork Examiner; Cork Weekly Examiner & Herald; Cork Weekly News; Derry Standard; Derry Weekly News; Donegal People's Press; Drogheda Advertiser; Drogheda Argus; Drogheda Independent; Dublin Daily Press; Dublin Evening Herald; Dublin Evening Mail; Dublin Evening Telegraph; Dublin Saturday Post; Dublin Times Pictorial; Dundalk Argus; Dundalk Democrat & People's Journal; Dundalk Examiner & Advertiser; Dungarvan Leader; Dungarvan Observer; East Galway Democrat; Enniscorthy Echo; Enniscorthy Guardian; Farmers' Gazette; Fianna Fail Bulletin; Freeman's Journal; Galway Express; Galway Observer; Galway Sentinel; Kerryman; Kilkenny Journal & Leinster Advertiser; Galway Sentinel; Kerryman; Kilkenny Journal & Leinster Advertiser; Kilkenny Moderator; Kilkenny People; Kilrush Herald; Inniskilling Impartial Reporter; Ireland Over All; Irish Bulletin (Sinn Fein); Irish Catholic; Irish Field; Irish Freedom; Irish Independent; Irish Law Times; Irish Life; Irish People War Special; Irish Post; Irish Press; Irish Times; Irish Weekly Independent; Irish Weekly News & Ulster Examiner; Kerry News; Kerry People; Kerry Sentinel; Kildare Observer; Leader (Dublin); Leinster Express; Leinster Leader; Leinster Reporter; Leitrim Advertiser; Leitrim Observer; Limerick Chronicle; Limerick Leader; Limerick Weekly Echo; Longford Independent; Longford Journal; Longford Leader; Mayo News; Meath Chronicle; Midleand reporter; Munster Express; Munster News; Nationalist (Clonmel); Nenagh Guardian; Nenagh News; New Ireland; New Ross Standard; Northern Standard; Midland Reporter & Westmeath Nationalist; Midland Tribune; Nationalist & Leinster Times; Offaly Chronicle; Offaly Independent; Plain People; Poblacht na h'Eireann; Poor Law Journal; Roscommon Champion; Roscommon Herald; Roscommon Journal; Roscommon Messenger; RTE Guide; Saturday record & Clare*

Journal; Sligo Champion; Sligo Independent; Sligo Times; Southern Democrat; Southern Star; Sunday Independent; Sunday Press; The Free State; The Nation; Tipperary Star; Tuam Herald; Tuam People; United Irishman; Voice of Labour; Waterford Evening News; Waterford News & Star; Waterford Standard; Waterford Weekly News; Weekly Freeman; Weekly Irish Times; Weekly Summary; Western News; Western Nationalist; Western People; Westmeath Examiner; Westmeath Guardian & Longford Newsletter; Westmeath Independent; Westmeath & Offaly Independent; Wexford Free Press; Wexford People; Wicklow Newsletter; Wicklow People; Young Ireland.

British – Catholic News (Cumberland); Daily Express; Daily Graphic; Dover Chronicle; Dover Express; Dover Telegraph; Irish Catholic Herald; London Evening News; London Evening Standard; Manchester Guardian; News Chronicle; Observer; People; Poblacht na h'Eireann (Scots edition); Sunday Chronicle; The Times; Tenby Observer; Woking News & Mail.

Indian – Civil & Military Gazette; Hindustan Times; India & Foreign Review; Lucknow Pioneer; Sunday Pioneer; Sunday Statesman, Times of India; Tribune.

Books and Articles
Andrew, C. & Dilks, D., *The Missing Dimension*. Macmillan, London, 1984
Barr, S., Charles Kerrigan and the Mutiny of the Connaught Rangers at Solon, 1920; *Journal of the Westport Historical Society/Cathair na Mart*, vol. 10, No. 1, 1990
Behan, B., *Confessions of an Irish Rebel*. Arrow, London, 1967
Bennett, R., *The Black and Tans*, New English Library, London, 1970; Hulton, 1959.
Capuchin Order, *Le Missionori Dei Minori Cappuccini*, Rome, 1935
Coogan, T. P., *Michael Collins*, Hutchinson, London, 1990
Draper, A., *Amritsar*, Cassell, London, 1981
Drew, R. (ed.) *Medical Officers of the British Army, 1660–1960*, Vol. 2. Wellcome Library, London, 1968
Dwyer, T. Ryle, *Eamon De Valera*, Gill & Macmillan, Dublin 1980
Dwyer, T. Ryle, *Michael Collins and the Treaty*, Mercier Press, Dublin, 1981
Gilbert, M., *Winston Churchill, Vol. IV, 1917–1922*, Heinemann, London, 1975
Griffiths, K. & O'Grady, T. E., *Curious Journey*, Hutchinson, London, 1982
Hinchy, R. A., The Connaught Rangers' Mutiny; *An Cosantoir, Vol. XVIII*, No. 9, September, 1985
Hopkinson, M., *Green Against Green*, Gill & Macmillan, Dublin, 1988
Inglis, B., *Roger Casement*, Hodder & Stoughton, London, 1973
Jeffrey, K., *The Military Correspondence of Field-Marshal Sir Henry Wilson 1918–1922*, Army Records Society, London, 1985
Jourdain, H. F. N. & Fraser, E., *The Regimental History of the Connaught Rangers*, Vol. 1. R.U.S.I., London, 1924
Karsten, P., Irish Soldiers in the British Army 1792–1922; Suborned or Subordinate?; *Journal of Social History, No. xvii*, 1983
Kee, R., *The Green Flag*, Weidenfeld & Nicolson, London, 1972
Kilfeather, T. P., *The Connaught Rangers*, Anvil Books, Tralee, 1969
Leo, Fr., O.M. Cap, *The Capuchin Mission in the Punjab*, Suares, Bangalore, 1910
Leonard, J., *The IRA and Ex-Servicemen; Revolution?, Ireland 1917–23*. Trinity History Workshop, Dublin, 1990
Liddle, P., *The Soldier's War 1914–18*, Blandford Press, London, 1988
Lyons, F. S. L., *Ireland since the Famine*, Weidenfeld & Nicolson, 1971
Macardle, D., *The Irish Republic*, Gollancz, London, 1937; Irish Press, Dublin, 1951

MacEoin, U. (ed.) *Survivors*, Argenta, Dublin, 1980.

Mason, P., *A Matter of Honour*, Jonathan Cape, London, 1974

Meek, B. (ed.) *Songs of the Irish in America*

Molesworth, G. N., *Curfew on Olympus*, Asia Publishing House, Bombay, 1965

National Graves Association, *Tour of Glasnevin Cemetery*, Dublin, n.d.

National Graves Association, *The Last Post*, Dublin, 1971

Neeson, E., *The Civil War 1922–23*, Poolbeg Press, Dublin, 1989; Mercier Press, Cork, 1966

Nelson, J. E., Irish Soldiers in the Great War; *Irish Sword, Vol. XI, No. 44*, Summer, 1974

O'Callaghan M., *For Ireland and Freedom*, Roscommon Herald, Boyle, 1964

O'Donoghue, F., *No Other Law*, Anvil Books, Dublin, 1986; Irish Press, Dublin, 1954

O'Donnell, P. D., *Dun ui Mhaoiliosa; An Cosantoir*, June, 1974

O'Halpin, E., *British Intelligence In Ireland 1914–1921* in C. Andrews & D. Dilks, *The Missing Dimension*. Macmillan, 1984

Pakenham, F. (Lord Longford), *Peace By Ordeal*, Sidgwick & Jackson, London, 1972; Cape, London, 1935

Pollock, S., *Mutiny For the Cause*, Leo Cooper, London, 1969

Rumbold, A., *Watershed In India 1914–1922*, University of London, Athlone Press, London, 1979

Taylor, A. J. P., *English History 1914–1945*, Oxford University Press, 1965

Townshend, C., *The British Campaign In Ireland 1919–21*, Oxford University Press, 1975

Valuilis, M. G., The 'Army Mutiny' of 1924 and the assertion of civilian authority in an independent Ireland, *Irish Historical Studies, vol. XXIII, No. 92*, November, 1983

White & Co., *The Indian Guide & Directory*, Calcutta, 1920

Younger, C., *Ireland's Civil War*, Fontana, London, 1970; F. Muller, 1968

INDEX

Adjutant-General: Macdonogh, Lieutenant-General, Sir George, 119
Aiken, Frank: succeeds Lynch, 132; civil war ceasefire, 133; Minister for Defence,
   157; Pensions Act, 161, 162
Alexander, Major William: Solon mutiny, 21, 23; personality, activities, 27, 28;
   and Fr. Baker, 29
Allenstein, 85
Amnesty, for imprisoned mutineers: negotiations, 104, 105; campaign, 108–124;
   Act (Irish), 119, 120–124
Amritsar massacre, 12
Army (British) Act, 67; Army Council, on remission of sentences, 68, 120;
   Department, Government of India, telegrams India Office, 57, 58; withdraws
   from Southern Ireland, 120; Smyth's death, 139
Asquith, Herbert: and Irish Home Rule, 71, 72
Athlone; British troops action, 81
Auxiliaries (Auxiliary Division of RIC) (see Black & Tans)

Badham, Captain Leslie: career, 21; meets mutineers, 22; and attack on magazine,
   31, 32; arrests Solon mutineers, 35
Baker, Fr. Benjamin Thomas Edwin, OSFC: personality, assists Alexander,
   parleys with mutineers, 29; Solon magazine attack, 31–35; James Daly, 29, 32,
   59, 61, 62–65
Balbriggan: cited by James Daly, 68; Black & Tans destroy, 69
Barrow, Major-General Sir George: career, 15; investigates mutiny, 15; sends
   Jackson to Jullundur, 15; Northern Command orders, 49
Barry, Kevin: heroism, Memorial Hall, 151
Bennett, Richard: Black & Tans, 80
Black & Tans: organization, activities, 79; 80; 86, 100; imprisoned member
   assaulted, 93; reputation, 98, 160; atrocities, 176
"Bloody Sunday", 100
Blythe, Ernest: Cosgrave's letter, 143; Special Relief Fund, 144; ex-mutineers
   compensation, 146, 147, 150, 152, 153, 154, 155, 156
Boland, Kevin: Irish Defence Minister, 173
Bolshevism: duty of soldiers to oppose, 42
Boyd-Rochfort, Lieutenant-Colonel Harold: Tyrrellspass memorial, 170, 171; 173,
   174
Brixton Prison, 176

Buckley, Private John: Irish newspaper interview, 131
Burland, Private William, 135
Byrne, Alfred, TD: ex-mutineers' compensation, 147, 148

Cannes, 121
Cahill, Sergeant-Major: arrests mutineers, 7
Carney, Dr. Philip: Jullundur prison camp protest, 36
Carney, Mrs M.: politics, Jullundur mutineers arrest, 27; husband's anger, 36
Carrick-on-Shannon, 80
Carroll, Kitty: killed by IRA, 99
Carson, Sir Edward: opposes Irish Home Rule, 72
Casement, Sir Roger: activities, death, 73; Dowling, Irish Brigade, 121, 122, 133, 169
Cashel, Tipperary: Archbishop of, 82, 83, 105; honours Coman, 129–133
Censorship of mutiny, 25, 40; Irish units mail, 42
Chelmsford, Lord: response to mutiny, 14; offers free pardons, 44; communicates with Montagu, 57; James Daly's death, 59; prison sentence remissions, 66
Cherry, Private Patrick: Solon magazine raid, 54; loyal soldier, 115
Childers, Erskine: condemns military raids, 83, Truce negotiations, 103
Childs, Brigadier-General Wyndham, 40; remissions, 90; amnesty, 119, 120
Churchill, Winston: and Montagu, 66, 67; Commons statement, 67; Amnesty negotiations, 106, 110, 111; Secretary of State for Colonies, 109
Civil War, Irish: 109–110, 112, 114, 132, 168; ceasefire, 133
Clare, County: 1919 hurley match suppressed, 4
Climate: India, heat, 2, 35; causes injury, 36; provokes mutiny, 88, 89
Clonmel, 129
Collins, Michael: Easter Rising, 73; Minister of Finance, 74; IRA Director of Intelligence, on IRA tactics, 76, 77; told of imprisoned mutineers' treatment, 93; admits British undefeated, 102; 1922 Treaty negotiations, 103, 104; Chairman, Provisional Government, 108; civil war, 109; Irish Free State Commander in Chief, 112; death, 113, 115
Collins, Rev Dr: petitions Churchill, 110, 111
Colonial Office, 112, 121, 122
Coman, Private William, 129–131
Committee of Ex-Connaught Rangers: activities, 13, 137, 138; negotiations, 140–144
Committee of Inquiry: ex-mutineers' compensation, 157, 158, 159
Commonwealth War Graves Commission: reinterment enquiries, 171, 175
Connaught, Province: military enlistments, 1
Connaught Rangers, 1 Bn: pre-November 1919, 1; distribution of companies, 1920, 2; at Jutogh, 19; at Solon, 21; reinforcements, 80, 81, disbandment, 108, 111
Connaught Rangers, 2 Bn, 111
Connaught Rangers (1920 Mutiny) Committee, 147, 151
Connaught Rangers Mutineers Association, 151, 158
Connaught Rangers (Pensions) Act, 1936, 159–162, 164, 165; 1948, 168; 1949, 169; 1957, 172, 173
Cooper, Alfred Duff, British Secretary of State for War, 165
Coote, Private William, 176
Corish, Brendan: pensions statement, 168, 169
Cork, County, 120; city, 176
Correya, Father Antonio: Dagshai Chaplain, 38

Cosgrave, William: Easter Rising, 73; Local Government Minister, 74; Provisional
    Government Chairman and Dail President, 113, 133; death penalty, 114;
    Amnesty Act, 118, 120, 123, 124; ex-mutineers' compensation, 134, 135, 143,
    146, 147, 148, 150, 151, 152, 153, 155
Council of the Unemployed, 137
Counter-terror by Crown Forces, 77, 81, 82, 98; Irish Press condemns, 83; martial
    law in Ireland, 100, (see Black and Tans)
Court of Enquiry, 42; Flannery's testimony, 44
Court-martial of Connaught Rangers' mutineers: location, 45; Summaries of
    Evidence, 3, 45, 46; published accounts, 2, 3; character witnesses, 48;
    Evidence: inflammatory poster, 5; written threats, 14, 18; quoted testimonies:
    Robertson, 7; Flannery, 12; Stanton, Glenn, James Daly, 46, 47; mutineers'
    unrepresented, 47, 48; composition of court, 49; duration, 50; cross-
    examination, pleas, 50, 53; verdict, 51; Jullundur mutineers' sentences, 52;
    Solon mutineers' trial 53, 54, 55; sentences, 55, 56, 66, 68; War Office not
    involved, 56, 57
Curragh Mutiny, 72
Curtis, Lionel: draft Amnesty proclamation, 105, 106
Curzon, Lord: Wilson request for troop withdrawal, 185
Custom House, Dublin, 176

D'Abernon, Lord Edgar, 85
Dagshai Prison: description, 45; mutineers imprisonment, 45, 131, 47
Dail Eireann: founded, 74; suppressed, 76; at war, 99; Anglo-Irish Truce, 102, 103;
    Public Safety Act, 114; Amnesty Bill, 118, 119–124; ex-mutineers'
    compensation, 134, 145–148, 150–152, 153–162, 168–169, 173; James Daly's
    reinterment, 175
Daly, Private James Joseph: personal details, 19, 20, 23, 64, 69; Jullundur
    emissaries contact, 21; commands Solon mutineers, presents demands, orders
    march on Jutogh, 22, 23; insists on parleying location, 27; nullifies Alexander,
    Woolridge appeals, 28; demands gun rack keys, confronts MacWeeney, 29;
    Nolan's trial, 30; Fr. Baker, 29, 32, 59, 61–66; leads attack on magazine, 29–34
    arrested, 35; tells Hawes about Solon mutiny, 45, 46; trial, 46, 50, 53, 54, 55;
    awaits death, 59, 60; final letter, 60, 61; death, 61–66, 163; note to Hawes, 64;
    martyrdom, 93, 95, 96, 97; newspaper reports, 95, 96, 97; aftermath at
    Dagshai Prison, 131; Kevin Barry comparison, 151; mother dies, 158; aged
    father, 162; Glasnevin memorial, 167; reinterment campaign 168, 172;
    Tyrellspass memorial, 170, 171; exhumation agreed, 175; reinterment, 176–
    178
Daly, William – brother of James Joseph Daly, 4; joins Jullundur protest 19, 20;
    abandons protest, 6; trial, 54
Dardanelles, 176
Deacon, Colonel Henry: background, 8; addresses mutineers, 8; irresolution, 9;
    parleys with mutineers, 10; relieved of command, 11; gets letter from
    mutineers, 14; unpopular commander, 88
Death sentences, British Army procedure, 52
Defence, Irish Department of, 142, 159, 162
Delaney, Private Valentine: death sentence, 53; James Daly's death, 63, 64; Irish
    newspaper interviews, 131
Delhi, Irish Embassy, 175
Derby, Lord: Gwynn's appeal, 116; Amnesty Bill, 118, 119, 120, 121, 122, 123
De Valera, Eamon: activities, 73, 74; President of Irish Republic, 74; escapes from

Lincoln Jail, goes to USA, 75; Archbishop of Cashel supports, 82, 83; anti-British imperialism, 86; anti-Truce, 102; and 1922 Treaty negotiations, 103, 104; resigns Presidency, 105; civil war, 109, 112, 132, 133; mutineers condemn, 115, 117; contests 1923 Election, 133; arrested, 134; 1927 Election, 150; 1932 Election victory, ex-mutineers' compensation, 156; 1933 Election victory, 157; represented, James Daly's reinterment, 177

Devers, Private James, 164

Devine, Private Thomas: *Longford Leader* publishes Summary of Evidence, 46; Solon magazine raid, 54; assaults Black & Tan prisoner, 93; loyalty to Crown, 115; destitute, 135, 136

Dolan, Seamus: ex-mutineers' compensation, 140, 141, 142; chairs committee, 146, 148

Dominions Office, 163

Dover, Connaught Rangers' depot, 1

Dowling, Private Joseph, 121, 122–124, campaign to free, 133

Drink (alcoholic): at Solon, 23, 31, 32, 54; Payne and, 87

Drogheda, 135

Dublin: released prisoners welcomed, 128, 129; Tenants' Association, 137, 140, 143; Trades Council, 137, 140; reinterment ceremonies, 176

Duggan, Eamon: draft Amnesty proclamation, 105, 106

Duke of Wellington's (West Riding) Regiment, 151

Dun Laoghaire, 127

Dyer, General R. E. D.: Amritsar massacre, 12

Easter Rising, Dublin 1916, 73, 160, 166

Edwards, Sergeant: Jullundur emissaries arrested, 20

Egan, Private Eugene: shot at Solon, 32, 33, 162; James Daly, 34; visited in hospital by Fr. Baker, 35; trial, 53, 54; James Daly's reinterment, 177

Elections, General: British, 71, 72, 74, 116; Irish, 102, 110, 133, 150, 156

External Affairs, Irish Department of, 168, 171

Fahy, Frank, TD: ex-mutineers' compensation, 153–157

Fermoy: IRA raid, 75; IRA kidnapping, 78

Fianna Fail, 150

Figgis, Darrell, TD: Amnesty Bill debate, 123

Finance, Irish Department of, 138, 142, 169

Fitzpatrick, Colonel Ernest: mutiny communique, 40

Flannery, John, ("One Who Knows"): memoirs unreliable, 2, 26, 43; opposes mutiny, 6, 9; addresses meetings, 6, 15, 25; testimony unsupported, 6; appearance 9; joins mutiny, 9; elected spokesman, 10, 15; meets Deacon, 10; deters looting, 12, 21; on rumours, 13; opposes violence, 15, 16; parleys with Jackson, 15; exaggerates counterforce size, 26; omits reference to prison camp conditions, 36; blames Payne for prison camp skirmish, 37; rivalry with Hawes, 42; egotism, 43; and Court of Enquiry, 44; arraigned mutineers conduct own defence, 48; says mutineers plead "not guilty", 50; motives, according to Hawes, 51; segregation, 51, 53, 92, 125; death sentence, 53, 54; distrusts Indians, 86; imprisonment (England), 92; creates mutiny legend, 93, 94; release, 125, 126; non-enlistment in Free State Army, 129; Secretary, Committee of Ex-Connaught Rangers, 134, 150; poverty, 135, 140, 156; compensation campaign, 137, 138, 141, 142; duplicity, 142; lobbies Cosgrave, 143, 144, 146, 147, 151, 152; "One Who Knows" articles, 144, 145; Inquiry

Committee, 146, 147; civil servant, 167; Glasnevin commemoration absence, 167
Four Courts, Dublin: battle for, 109–111
Francis, Lieutenant-Colonel John Wolstan: causes of mutiny, 86, 87, 89
Franklin, Lance-Corporal: Nolan's trial, 30, 54, 55
French, Field-Marshal: orders Sinn Fein elimination, 78; advocates martial law, 100

Gaelic League, 137
Galway County Council: deplores IRA, 101
Gameson, Captain Lawrence, RAMC, 62
Gandhi, Mahatma: fosters Muslim–Hindu alliance, 11
Garda Siochana, 139, 177
Geraghty, William (see Keenan, Private William)
Gladstone, William Ewart: Irish Home Rule, 70, 71
Glasnevin Cemetary, Dublin: mutiny memorial, 166, 167; IRA parade, 168; 1958 commemoration, 172; Sears, Smyth reinterment, 176
Glenn, Company-Quartermaster-Sergeant: defies James Daly, 29; testimony, 47; mutineers attack, given protection, 51
Gogarty, Private Patrick: at Jullundur, 4, 6, 43; death sentence, 53; Flannery ignores, 141; Glasnevin commemoration, 167
Gorman, Private John: Solon magazine attack, 31; arrested, 35; death sentence, 53; trial, 54; James Daly's death, prison experiences, 91, 92; release, 126; James Daly's reinterment, 177
Griffith, Arthur: Treaty negotiations, 103, 104; President, 105, 108; death 113, 115
Grosvenor Hotel, Dublin, 129
Gwynn, Stephen, MP, 108; appeals to Bonar Law, 116

Hammon, Denis, 112
Hawes, Private Joseph: unreliable, untruthful 2, 16, 26, 63; origins of mutiny, 4, 5, 6, 89; background, 4; accounts of hurley match, 3, 4; Flannery, 6, 42, 43, 50, 51, 59; describes Jullundur Guardroom 7, 8; Deacon, 8; spokesman, 10, 15; insolence, 10; out-manoeuvres Nolan-Ferrall, 11; exaggerates counterforce size, 26; blames Payne for prison camp skirmish, 37; Irish priests 42; resistance useless, 43; Dagshai Jail, 45, 55; James Daly's death, 63, 64, 65; Daly's final note, 64, 68; Miranda's death, 69; Maidstone Prison, 93; creates mutiny legend, 93, 94; pro-Treaty, 115; release, 125, 126; Flannery ignores, 141; poor health, 159; Glasnevin memorial speech, 167; James Daly's reinterment, 177; last public pronouncement, 178
Hennessey, M. J., TD, 154
Hewson, Private James: trial, 54; condemns Irregulars, 115
Hillery, Dr Patrick, 175
Holyhead: released prisoners welcome, 125, 127
Home Office, British, 122, 123; witholds mutineers' prison records, 164, 165
Home Rule, Irish, 71; Bills, 70, 72, 76; League, 70
House of Commons: Questions, 41, 67
Hughes, Lance-Corporal: Jullundur mutineers intimidate, 19
Hunger strike: Sinn Fein prisoners, 85; imprisoned mutineers, 92, 93, 159; Terence MacSwiney, 176
Hynes, Patrick: Solon magazine attack, 30, 31; James Daly's death, reinterment, 63, 177

India Office (British): mutineers' trial reports, 57, 58; ex-mutineers' compensation, 153; Government of, 171, 175; Irish Embassy, 175

Irish Citizen Army, 166; Association, 167
Irish, Government: Free State, 108; mutineers support, 114–116; British
    withdrawal, Irregulars deaths, 120; British Commonwealth, 157, 159; High
    Commission, London, 163, 164; 1932 Pensions Act, 165; negotiates
    reinterment, 171, 175; (see also Departments listed by function)
Irish Guards, 85
Irish Republican Army: Hawes' brother a member, 4; War of Independence
    campaign, 74, 75, 76, 98, 99; Irish Nationalist Press supports, 84; and British
    ex-servicemen, 99, 100; casualties mount, 101; actions deplored, 101; sustain
    campaign, 102; civil war, 108, 109, 110, 112, 114, 120, 132, 133; brutalities,
    160; Glasnevin memorial, 167; James Daly's reinterment, 168, 169, 172, 174,
    175–178
Irish Republican Publicity Bureau, 178
Irish Self-Determination League: greets released prisoners, 127, 128
Irish Transport & General Workers Union, 176; brass band, 177
Irish Volunteers: proscribed, 4, 74; formed, 72; split, 73; 1916 Easter Rising, 73;
    Kevin Barry, 151; Glasnevin memorial, 166 (see Irish Republican Army)
Irregulars (see Irish Republican Army; Civil War)
Isle of Wight, 92

Jackson, Colonel, H.: addresses Jullundur mutineers, 15; parleys with Jullundur
    mutineers, 15, 16, 17; pays mutineers, 37; parleys with prisoners, 37
Jacob, General Sir Claud: no comment, 153
Jerrard, Brigadier-General Charles: Indian Army tentage, 36; causes of mutiny, 88;
    89
Jourdain, Colonel F. W. S.: on causes of mutiny, 86, 87
Judge Advocate General, 115
Jullundur: town and cantonment, 1; importance, 2; climate, 7; surrounded by loyal
    troops, 16; garrison units, 17; mutineers' prison camp, conditions, 35
Justice, Irish Department of, 139, 142
Jutogh hill station, 2; detachment remains loyal, 19, 41; James Daly orders Solon
    mutineers to march on, 23

Kasauli hill station, 20
Keenan (a.k.a. Geraghty), Lance-Corporal William: mutineers' emissary, 19;
    journeys to Solon, 20, arrested, 21; story disbelieved, returned to Jullundur,
    22, 25; release demanded, 25, 26; sentence, 52
Kalka railway terminus, 20
Kearney, Private Michael: petition, "renegade" De Valera, 115, 116; letter to
    mother, 117; organizes Glasnevin commemoration, 167
Kearns, Private Michael: death, 155
Kelly, Private Patrick: mutineers' emissary, 19; journeys to Solon, 20; arrested, 21;
    story disbelieved, returned to Jullundur, 22, 25; release demanded, 25, 26;
    trial, 52, 54
Kelly, Ignatius, Lieutenant: Hawes insolent, 10
Kelly, Corporal Patrick, J.: trial, 30, 155; service details witheld, 164
Kennedy, Councillor M. J., 170, 171
Kerlin, Frank, TD: ex-mutineers. compensation, 150, 152, 153
Kerrigan, Private Charles: personality, Solon events, James Daly's character, 23;
    attack on Solon magazine, 32; Smyth, 33; on Dagshai Prison, 55; James Daly's
    execution, 63, 65, 66; origins of mutiny, 80; contact with Indians, 86; English
    prison experiences, 93; release, 127

Khilafat movement, 11
Kilfeather, T. P., 89
Kilrush, 4

Lally, Private Stephen, 4; Jullundur mutineer, 6, 43; Daly's death, 63; Flannery
    ignores 141; Glasnevin commemoration, 167; James Daly's reinterment, 172
Land Purchase Act: abolition, 157
Larkin, Frank: Tenants' Association President, 140
Larkin, Mary: Tenants' Association, 143
Law, Andrew Bonar, British Prime Minister: Gwynn's appeal, 116; amnesty, 118,
    120
Lawford, Major-General Sir Sidney, 49
Leader, Lieutenant Leonard (Adjutant): encounters mutineers, 10; mutineers
    threaten to kill, 14; Jackson's parleying, 17; and jailed Jullundur emissaries, 25;
    arrests Jullundur mutineers, 26
Leeds, Lieutenant-Colonel Thomas: cautions Jullundur mutineers, 13
Leonard, Jane: Irish ex-servicemen, 99, 100
Lincoln Jail: De Valera escapes from, 75
Lindsay, Mrs: kidnapped, killed by IRA, 98, 99
Lievin, Fr. Laurence, OC: Jullundur chaplain, prison camp skirmish, 38
Limerick: Black & Tan actions, 79
Liverpool Jail, 126
Lloyd, Major Owen: courts-martial prosecutor, 49
Lloyd George, David: counter-terror, 98; 1922 Treaty, 103, 104; Amnesty
    negotiations, 106; resigns, 116
Loftus, Private John: trial, 54; acquitted, 55
Logue, Cardinal, 82
London, traversed by released prisoners, 127
Longford, Lord (Pakenham, Frank), 80
Lucknow Detention Barracks: holds Solon mutineers, 35, 131; prepared for
    Jullundur mutineers, 41
Lynch, Jack, 177
Lynch, Private John: claims mutineers ignore court, 50; undisciplined prisoner, 92,
    93
Lynch, Liam: death, 132
Lyon, Kenneth: Amnesty correspondence, 121, 122
Lyons, TD,: 148, 149

Machine Gun Corps, 17; 26; 95
MacCiarnain, Seamus, 177, 178
McConnell, Private Patrick: acquitted, 55
McCormack, Private: threatened by Jullundur mutineers, 18
MacCurtain, Tomas: death, 77
MacDermott, Frank, TD, 159, 160
MacDonald, Malcolm, 163, 164
MacEntee, Sean, 157
MacEoin, General Sean, TD, 173
McGowan, Lance-Corporal John: Jullundur committee member, 10; released, 125;
    destitute, 135; Army service, 136
McGrath, Lance-Corporal Patrick: trial, 54; release, 125
McNamara, Provost Sergeant, Solon: arrests Jullundur emissaries, 21; escorts
    emissaries to Jullundur, 22; arrests Solon mutineers, 35

Macready, General Sir Nevil: advocates counter-terror, 77
MacSweeney, Terence: death, 176
MacWeeney, Lieutenant Desmond: witnesses Solon events, 22; confronts Daly, 29; defends magazine, 31; Solon magazine attack, Daly's actions, 33, 34; criticizes Deacon, Hawes, Kilfeather, Pollock, 88, 89
Maher, Teresa (née Daly): recalls brother James, 69
Maidstone Jail, 92; conditions, 93; prisoners' petition, 114, 115; prisoners' release, 126, 127
Malone, Thomas, IRA Commander, East Limerick Flying Column, 174, 178
Manchester Prison, 126
Mangan, Private Patrick: health, 159
Mannion, Private Patrick: wife destitute, 116
Manual of Military Law: British Army courts-martial process, 3; Rules of Procedure, 47; definition of mutiny, 49
Merchant's Quay Franciscan Church, 167, 176
Military Service Act (Irish), 149
Miranda, Private John: death, 69, 92, 155; Glasnevin memorial, 167; remains unexhumed, 175
Molesworth, Major-General George: mutiny countermeasures, 27; on Sinn Fein influence, 85
Monarchs, British: King Edward VII, King George V, 72, 111, 120, 121
Montagu, Hon. Edwin: issues communiqué, 39; questioned in House of Commons, 41; and trials, 57; complains to Winston Churchill, 66
Moore, Colonel Maurice: free Dowling campaign, 133
Moorehouse, Private: remark, 22; Solon magazine attack, 30
Moran, Private Francis, 164
Moran, Private Thomas: insolent manner, 7; death sentence, 53
Mulcahy, General Richard, 102
Mullingar, 81; 95
Munro, General Sir Charles: response to mutiny, 14; mother from County Cork, 15; reduces sentences, 57; and death sentences, 59
Murphy, Corporal: ignores intimidation, 10; threatened by Regan, 18
Murphy, Lance-Corporal: detects Jullundur emissaries, 21
Murree, 15
Mutiny, in Connaught Rangers' 1 Bn: versions of, 2, 154–155. At Jullundur: causes, 3, 4, 5, 79 et seq; support for, 7, 8, 9; unreported incident, 9; official reports, 39; restrained, 119; mutineers: attitude to Indians, 85, 86; motives, 79; control, 11, 13; mutineers' elect committee, 10, 15; mutineers' demands, 10, 14; retain arms, 13; fears, 13; issue threats, 14, 18, 25; parley with Jackson, 15; to receive pay, 16; surrounded, 16; partially surrender arms, 17; numbers, activists a minority, 17, 18; intimidate, disarm loyalists, 18, 19, 26; send emissaries to Solon, Jutogh, 19; post sentries, 20; looting, 20; demand jailed emissaries' release, 25; arrested, 26; lodged in prison camp, 35, 36; numbers decline, 37, 41, 44; prison camp skirmish, 37; prisoners returned to Barracks, 38; ringleaders segregated, 43; resolve weakening, 44; imprisoned at Dagshai, 45. At Solon: actions, 21; Badham warns mutineers, 22; gesture of solidarity, 23; mutineers' morale, 24; Alexander, Fr. Baker meet mutineers, 28, 29; mutineers surrender arms, 29; threaten to recover arms, 30; tries Nolan, 30, 55; raid magazine, 30; drink, 31; attack magazine, 31–34; arrested, sent to Lucknow, 35; moved to Dagshai Prison, 45. Imprisonment: England, 90, 91; hunger strike, 92, 159; treatment in prison, 93, 131; heroic legend, 90 et seq; non-violence, 94; oath of allegiance stigma, 99; Devers, Moran, 164. Release: amnesty campaign, 105–124; prisoners' petition, 115; Gwynn's petition, 116;

Cosgrave, officers' petitions, 118; Bill debated, prisoners' release, 123, 124, 125, 126; public honours, 126–133; pro-Treaty views, 115, 129, 168. Ex-mutineers: poverty, compensation campaign, 134 et seq.; pensions, 159–162, 164, 165, 168, 169, 172, 173; unfairly treated, 173. Commemoration: Glasnevin and Tyrrellspass memorials 166, 167, 168–178; Republican adulation, 168
Mutiny for the Cause, 18

National Army, Irish Free State, 109, 141, 148
National Graves Association: aims, 166; reinterment campaign, 175–178
Newspapers – English: *Catholic Herald*, 128; *Evening Standard*, 161; *Observer*, 108; *Times*, 40, 41, 84 (Index), 87. Irish: *An Phoblacht*, 94; *An tOglach*, 75; *Cork Examiner*, 40; *Evening Herald*, 127; *Evening Mail*, 168; *Evening Telegraph*, 127, 129; *Freeman's Journal*, 41, 116, 117, 128; *Irish Bulletin*, 62, 94; *Irish Press*, 94, 177; *Irish Independent*, 125, 126, 128, 129, 141, 144; *Irish Press*, 166, 167; *Irish Statesman*, 83; *Irish Times*, 111; *Irish Weekly*, 96; *Leitrim Observer*, 80; *Longford Leader*, 3, 46; *Mayo News*, 133; *The Nationalist* (Clonmel), 129, 131; *Poblacht na h'Eireann*, 117, 129; *Roscommon Herald* 3; *Roscommon Journal*, 131; *Sunday Independent*, 2, 44; *Weekly Independent*, 43; *Western People*, 131; *Westmeath Examiner*, 95, 96, 97, 171, 172, 177; *Westmeath Independent*, 81, 82, 83; *Ulster Examiner*, 95; *United Irishman*, 71
New York, 159
Nolan, Lance-Corporal: slurs woman, tried by Solon mutineers' court, 30; Joseph Daly trial witness, 54, 55
Nolan-Ferrall, Major Henry: encounters mutineers, 10; Hawes out-manoeuvres, 11

Oath of Allegiance, 70, 99
'One Who Knows' – (see Flannery, John)
O'Brien, Art, 93
O'Brien, Dr Conor Cruise: James Daly's reinterment, 175
O'Brien, Lance-Corporal: political sympathies, 6
O'Brien, Lieutenant William: quizzes emissaries, 21; personality, career, 30; magazine attack, 31
O'Dwyer, Lieutenant-General Sir Michael: approves repression, 12
Offaly County Council, 171
Office of Public Works, 169
O'Higgins, Kevin: Amnesty Bill debate, 123
O'Laidhin, Sean, TD, 148
Oliver, Private John: loyal soldier, 115; destitute, 135; Army service, 136; no Army pension, 141
O'Shannon, Cathal, TD: Amnesty Bill debate, 123

Parkhurst Prison, Isle of Wight, 125
Parnell, Charles Stewart, 70
Partition, of Ireland, 100, 101; legislation, 102
Payne, Major Robert: addresses Jullundur protestors 7; temporary Commanding Officer, 11; seeks order to shoot prisoners, 37; addresses mutineers, 44; drunk, 87
Pensions, 153

Phillips, Francis, 130
Pollock, Sam: laudator of mutiny, 18; partisan, implausible, 19; mutineers' trial, 48; incorrect, 50; uncritical of Hawes, 69, 89; book poorly researched, 86; Jullundur mutiny causes, 88, 89
Poona: journal supports mutineers, 86; Jail assaults, 131
Portland Jail, 90; 92
Public Safety Act, Irish, 114
Punjab province, civil unrest, 1, 12

Ready, Major-General Felix: prison sentence remissions, 90, 91
Reddin, James, 174
Redmond, John: activities, 71; pro-British, 73
Regan, Private: utters threats, 18
Remission of sentences, 90, 91, 107, 1110, 115–124
Restoration of Order in Ireland Act, 98
Robertson, Lieutenant Walter: evidence about Jullundur events, 7; criticises Deacon, 88
Roman Catholic Church, Irish: condemns IRA, 77; Bishops, 82; Cardinal Logue, 82; Maidstone Jail chaplains, 126; Franciscans, 176
Roscommon: town honours Delaney, 131
Rowlatt Acts: generate strife, 12
Royal Army Temperance Association: Jullundur canteen, 6
Royal Dublin Fusiliers, 85
Royal Field Artillery, 17
Royal Fusiliers, 2 Bn: arrests Edwards, 20; executes James Daly, 61
Royal Irish Constabulary: IRA attacks, 75; ineffective, casualties, 76, 77; recruits threatened, 78; disbandment, 139; compensation, 143, 151, 155
Royal Irish Regiment, 1 Bn., 85; 95
Royal Munster Fusiliers, 95
Ryan, Rev. Dean, 130, 131
Rye, Private Frank: afraid of mutineers, 18

Salmon, Private: mutineers threaten, 18
Sarsfield, Lieutenant: attack on Solon magazine, 31
Scally, Private Patrick: health, 159
Seaforth Highlanders: counterforce, 17; 26; segregates militants, 43
Sears, Private Patrick: armed with bayonet, 34; death at Solon, 32, 163; Glasnevin memorial, 167; exhumation, 175; reinterment, 176
Sears, William, TD: Amnesty Bill debate, 124
Shallow, Private William: release from prison, 125; death, 155
Shaw, Sergeant: away from post, 6; 7
Sheehan, Sergeant: threatened by Regan, 18
Shrewsbury Jail, 125
Sinn-Fein: flags, rosettes, displayed by mutineers, 16, 27; Sinn Feiners, 6; fomented mutiny, allegations, 42; badges not worn by mutineers, 53; and De Valera 74; proscribed, electoral triumph, 74; Field-Marshal French attacks, 78; Mountjoy Jail hunger strike, 83; active in British Army, 85; Provisional, 94; jailed leaders released, 102; reinterment ceremonies, 176
Skibbereen, ballad of Old: significance, 5
Smyth, Annie: destitute, 138
Smyth, Lieutenant: announces death sentences, 51, 52, 55; Daly's death, 63

Smyth, Lieutenant-Colonel Bruce: urges RIC counter-terror, 77
Smyth, Private Peter: alleged drunkard, death at Solon, 33, 163; British Army
    liability, 139; family poverty, 135, 138, 140; sister, 158; Glasnevin memorial,
    167; exhumation, 175; reinterment, 176
Solon, cantonment, 2, 19; topography, 31; detachment at, 21; daily routine, 23;
    strategic importance, 27, (see Mutiny)
Somme, 176
Southampton, 92
South Wales Borderers, 2 Bn: counterforce, 17; 26; arrests Solon mutineers, 35;
    squad threatens to shoot prisoners, skirmish, 38, 39, 94
Special Relief Fund, Dail, 145; depleted, 146
Stanton, Regimental-Quartermaster-Sergeant: gives evidence against James Daly,
    46
Stephenson, John, Assistant Secretary, Dominions Office, 163
Stewart, Dermott, 140
Sweeney, Private Christopher: Jullundur protest 4; volunteers for guardroom, 6;
    43; disloyal, 51

Tame, Regimental Sergeant-Major E.: Hawes' activities, 13
Tenants' Association, 137, 140
Templer, Field-Marshal Sir Gerald: Jourdain letter, 87
Thurles, 82
Tierney, Private Thomas: Jullundur prison camp conditions, 36; consequences of
    free pardon offer, 44
Tipperary, County, 120
Townshend, Charles, Black & Tans, 98
Treaty, Anglo-Irish, 1922, 102 et seq, 120
Truce, Anglo-Irish, 101, 102; negotiations, 103
Truell, Major Edmund: appeals to A Company, 19
Tucker, Major Hugh: Judge Advocate court-martial, 49
Tudor, Major-General Sir Henry: advocates counter-terror, 78, 100
Tullamore, 171
Tyrrellspass, 46; James Daly's reinterment, 168, 172, 176–178; patriots memorial,
    170, 171, 173, 174

Ulster Volunteer Force, 72
Uniacke, Major-General Sir Herbert, 111

Walsh, Private Joseph: mutiny ballad 51; James Daly's death, 62; publicizes
    mutiny, 94; Flannery ignores, 141; commemorates James Daly's death, 142,
    143; health, 159
Walsh, Lieutenant Christopher, Solon guard commander, 29; defends magazine,
    31, 32
War Office: remission of sentences, 68; Amnesty Bill, 119; disclosure of
    information, 163, 164, 165; File number 141/90, 168
Wellington Barracks, Jullundur cantonment, 2; guardroom, 7, 8; mutineers
    control, 11; Jackson parleys at, 17; vacated by mutineers, 27; skirmish alleged,
    94; used as temporary prison block, 38; Irish priests visit, 42; ringleaders
    lodged in, 44; prisoners moved from, 45
Westmeath County Council: Irish prisoners' treatment, 81; IRA memorial, Boyd
    Rochfort, 170, 171, 173, 174

Westmeath-Offaly Old IRA Memorial Committee (see Tyrrellspass)
White, Sergeant-Major: Solon mutineers, 27, 28; arrests mutineers, 35
Willis, Colonel: commands firing-party, identity, 61
Willis, Lance-Corporal Patrick, 44
Wilson, Field-Marshal Sir Henry, 85
Windsor Castle, 111
Woking Jail, 90
Wood Edward, MP, Black & Tans, 98
Wood, Dr. George, RAMC: treats Solon casualties, 34
Woolridge, Colonel Herbert: addresses Solon mutineers, 28
Worthington-Evans, Sir Laming: opposes prisoners release, 106, 107

Younger, Calton, Black & Tans, 79; 80
Ypres, 176